Advanced
Boxing
Training, Skills and Techniques

Advanced Boxing

Training, Skills and Techniques

Rakesh Sondhi and Tommy Thompson

The Crowood Press

First published in 2011 by
The Crowood Press Ltd
Ramsbury, Marlborough
Wiltshire SN8 2HR

www.crowood.com

British Library Cataloguing-in-Publication Data
A catalogue record for this book is available from the British Library.

ISBN 978 1 84797 297 2

Typeset by Phoenix Typesetting, Auldgirth, Dumfriesshire

Printed and bound in Malaysia by Times Offset (M) Sdn Bhd

CONTENTS

PREFACE

The objective of this book is to present different ways of using the latest thinking in sports science to improve performance in boxing. The book is intended for boxers and combat sports athletes who possess the basic competencies and knowledge of boxing, and builds on our work in *tvp: Comprehensive Boxing Concepts* (BMC Global Services Publishing, 2005).

The Coaches

Rocky Sondhi began martial arts training in 1976 and has studied Pak Lai Hung kung fu and Shotokan karate. Since the mid-1990s he has also studied and coached boxing. He is presently concentrating on understanding coaching boxing and yoga. Rocky has opened the Elite Performance Academy in Nottingham, a state-of-the-art training academy designed for athletes wishing to improve performance based on the latest sports science-based methods. Rocky has designed a unique, accredited sports leadership programme based on boxing for sixteen- to eighteen-year-olds, which is being delivered to a number of colleges in the East Midlands.

Tommy Thompson began boxing in 1974, had sixty-nine contests and then retired through injury. His coaching career kicked off in 1981 and he has been Nottingham's only senior ABA coach since 1985. He has worked extensively with Brendan Ingle's stable in Sheffield. Boxers he has worked with include Johnny Nelson (WBO World Cruiserweight champion), Fidel Castro (ex-British Super Middleweight champion) and Prince Naseem Hamed. Since 2000 Tommy has been heavily involved with martial artists, teaching concepts of the arts through the principles of boxing. He has been working with the Winsper brothers, Jon Jepson and team, and Krishna Godhania. Tommy also works extensively with schools in the East Midlands, coaching boxing as part of the curriculum.

Rocky and Tommy have been inducted into the Combat Hall of Fame 2011

The Models

Sam Ray Smith. With a history of boxing in the family, Sam established a love for the sport and was always inspired by his grandad's example, although unfortunately he never met him. His boxing career started at Gilmore's Combat Sports Centre and since then he has been lucky enough to train and fight for numerous gyms, including Rocky and Tommy's Elite Performance Academy. Sam is a student at Leeds University, where he is reading Sports Science and also captains the Amateur Boxing Club. He presently

Rocky Sondhi and Tommy Thompson.

The authors reliving their good old days!

Nathan Sears, Arjun Rocky Sondhi and Sam Ray Smith.

competes in the 81kg division. To date he has won ten of his twelve amateur contests and hopes to compete at the Novice ABAs when he finishes university.

Nathan Sears began combat sports when he was initially introduced to Taekwondo between the ages of eight and ten. Nathan took up the Korean martial art of Tang Soo Do at thirteen and quickly accelerated through the ranks to 1st Dan black belt. At the age of seventeen, Nathan was selected to represent Team GB in the 2007 World Championships, where he was the youngest member to win double bronze medals. Nathan also won and successfully defended national titles in three different black belt categories. From this platform, Nathan began boxing in his second year at Leeds University and captained the university team in his third, in which he was introduced to Rocky and Tommy through multiple training courses that developed his technique and enabled him to win the English University BUCS at middleweight and best novice boxer of the tournament. Nathan continues to train and hopes to win an ABA title.

Arjun Rocky Sondhi began his martial arts career at the age of three with Shotokan karate, in which he trained till the age of 10. He then became interested in boxing and has maintained this interest ever since, finding boxing demanding, challenging and yet rewarding. Arjun has also played semi-professional football and competed for Nottinghamshire in athletics. He is presently concentrating on mixed martial arts and plans to compete at a high level in the future. Additionally, Arjun is studying for a BSc in

Raj Sharma.

Sport and Exercise Science at Leeds University with the ambition of working with elite athletes as a sports scientist after graduation.

The Photographer

Raj Sharma has ten years' experience in film, digital and digital creative imagery. Born in Nottinghamshire in 1978, he has a Computer Science degree from Loughboough University, and currently works as an Information Technology Consultant. His early interest in photography was mainly inspired by his father's collection of cameras and photographs. He has always had an eye for photographs, but his talent flourished when he captured imaginative and breathtaking images while travelling for eighteen months and he hasn't looked back since. His creative instincts have guided him to digital transformation of images, using IT and different framing techniques to put a unique slant on his photography, which has been displayed in City Art Fairs and local galleries. His current passions are travel and abstract photography, digital transformations – and his love for sport.

INTRODUCTION

Boxing is the ultimate challenge. There's nothing that can compare to testing yourself the way you do every time you step in the ring.
Sugar Ray Leonard

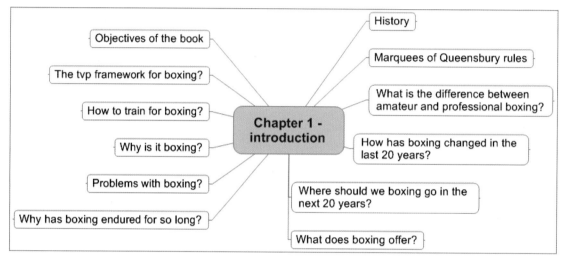

Mindmap overview of Chapter 1.

Early History

Boxing has a very strong history dating back many centuries, although this is rarely capitalized on when comparisons are made with the histories of Eastern martial arts, for example. Some martial arts are occasionally presented as possessing an exotic and mysterious past, whereas boxing can sometimes be perceived as brutal and lacking any real history. For this reason it may be useful to review the history of boxing and demonstrate its global and historic appeal.

Relief carvings depicting various fist-fighting events, found in Mesopotamia and later in Egypt, suggest that boxing has been practised since at least the third millennium BC. The earliest evidence of fist fighting with gloves may date from Minoan Crete in the late second millennium BC. Boxing has had many forms, including an early variant that involved two seated men punching each

other. In its standing form, boxing, known to the Greeks as *pygme*, was introduced to the Olympic Games about 700 BC and boxing continued as one of the Romans' favourite sports. Due to its perceived barbaric nature, however, boxing was banned in some later cultures since it was considered as an insult to God due to the effect it had on the face. Such bans were frequently ignored, though, and boxing remained popular through the Middle Ages.

The seventeenth century saw the first documented bare-knuckle fights in England and towards the end of the century prizefighting became very popular. The first English bare-knuckle champion was James Figg in 1719. It was around this time that the term boxing was applied to the sport, although 'boxing' also included fencing.

To prevent the occurrence of deaths it was felt that rules had to be enforced. The first set was put forward in 1743 by the heavyweight Jack Broughton, who also introduced the use of padded gloves. Among Broughton's rules were:

* If a man went down and could not continue after a count of 30 seconds, the fight was over.
* Hitting a downed fighter and grasping below the waist were prohibited.
* Fighters could drop to one knee to begin a 30-second count at any time, although this was considered poor sportsmanship.

Broughton's rules were modified in 1838 to become the London Prize Ring rules, which stipulated:

* Fights occurred in a 24ft (7.3m) square ring surrounded by ropes.
* If a fighter was knocked down, he had to rise within 30 seconds under his own power to be allowed to continue.
* Biting, head-butting and hitting below the belt were declared fouls.

Marquess of Queensbury Rules

Further changes to the rules were introduced in 1867 with the Marquess of Queensberry Rules, which were drawn up by John Chambers and intended for both amateur and professional championships. The twelve-point code is given here, together with a few explanations:

1. To be a fair stand-up boxing match in a twenty-four foot ring or as near that size as practicable.
2. No wrestling or hugging allowed. [In general, boxers are prohibited from hitting below the belt, holding, tripping, pushing, biting, spitting or wrestling. The boxer's shorts are raised so the opponent is not allowed to hit to the groin area. They also are prohibited from kicking, head-butting or hitting with any part of the arm other than the knuckles of a closed fist (including hitting with the elbow, shoulder or forearm, as well as with open gloves, the wrist, the inside, back or side of the hand). They are prohibited as well from hitting the back, back of the neck or head (called a 'rabbit-punch') or the kidneys. They are prohibited from holding the ropes for support when punching, holding an opponent while punching, or ducking below the belt of their opponent (dropping below the waist of your opponent, no matter the distance between). If a 'clinch', a defensive move in which a boxer wraps his or her opponent's arms and holds on to create a pause, is broken by the referee, each fighter must take a full step back before punching again (alternatively, the referee may direct the fighters to 'punch out' of the clinch).]
3. The rounds to be of three minutes duration and one minute time between rounds. [A boxing match typically consists of a determined number of three-minute rounds, a total of up to twelve rounds (formerly fifteen). A minute is typically spent between each round with the fighters in their assigned corners receiving advice and attention from their coach and staff.]
4. If either man fall through weakness or otherwise, he must get up unassisted, ten seconds be allowed to do so, the other man meanwhile to return to his corner; and when the fallen man is on his legs the round is to be resumed and continued until the three minutes have expired. If one man fails to come to the scratch in the ten seconds allowed, it shall be in the power of the referee to give his award in favour of the other man.
5. A man hanging on the ropes in a helpless state, with his toes off the ground, shall be considered down. [When a boxer is knocked down, the other boxer must immediately cease fighting and move to the furthest neutral corner of the ring until the referee has either ruled a knockout or called for the fight to continue.]
6. No seconds or any other person to be allowed in the ring during the rounds.
7. Should the contest be stopped by any unavoidable interference, the referee [is] to name the time and place as soon as possible for finishing the contest, so that the match can be won and lost, unless the backers of the men agree to draw the stakes.
8. The gloves to be fair-sized boxing gloves of the best quality and new. [The introduction of gloves of 'fair-size' also changed the nature of the bouts. Gloves can be used to block an opponent's blows. Following their introduction, bouts became longer and more strategic with greater importance attached to defensive manoeuvres such as slipping, bobbing, countering and angling. Because less defensive emphasis was placed on the use of the forearms and more on the gloves, the classical stance of the bare-knuckle boxer, with forearms outwards and torso leaning back, was modified to a more modern stance in which the torso is tilted forward and the hands are held closer to the face.]
9. Should a glove burst, or come off, it must be replaced to the referee's satisfaction.
10. A man on one knee is considered down, and if struck is entitled to the stakes.
11. No shoes or boots with springs allowed.
12. The contest in all other respects to be governed by the revised rules of the London Prize Ring.

What is the Difference Between Amateur and Professional Boxing?

The simplest explanation of the difference between amateur and professional boxing is that one involves an exchange of money (professional) and the other does not (amateur). However, there are some other differences in the way the sport is undertaken.

Amateur Boxing

Amateur boxing is an Olympic sport with bouts typically limited to three or four rounds and scoring is computed by points based on the number of clean blows landed, regardless of impact. The boxers typically wear protective headgear, reducing the number of injuries, knockdowns and knockouts. Scoring blows in amateur boxing are subjectively counted by ringside judges. A referee monitors the fight to ensure that competitors use only legal blows. Referees will stop the bout if a boxer is seriously injured, if one boxer is significantly dominating the other or if the score is severely imbalanced.

Professional Boxing

Professional bouts are usually much longer than amateur bouts, typically ranging from ten to twelve rounds, though four-round fights are common for less experienced fighters or club fighters. Fifteen rounds was the internationally recognized number of rounds for championship fights until the early 1980s, when reaction to the death of Duk Koo Kim led to the typical number of rounds being reduced to twelve.

Headgear is not permitted in professional bouts and boxers are generally allowed to take much more punishment before a fight is stopped. The referee may stop the contest if he believes that one participant cannot defend himself due to injury: in that case, the other participant is awarded a technical knockout win. A technical knockout would also be awarded if a fighter lands a punch that opens a cut on the opponent, and the opponent is later deemed unfit to continue by a doctor because of the cut. For this reason, fighters often employ cutmen to treat cuts between rounds so that the boxer is able to continue despite his injuries.

The Changing Face of Boxing

Boxing has changed over the years due to a number of factors, including:

* ring conditions
* promoter demands
* coaching methods
* the influence of leading boxers

The beauty of boxing, in comparison to Eastern martial arts and combat sports, is that a boxer does not have to fit an exact psychological or physical profile.

The early eras of boxing were epitomised by the use of 1-2 combinations and a more erect stance that was carried over from the bare-knuckle days of boxing. There tended to be little lateral movement. There was some use of 3 and 4 punch combinations but they were a rarity. Punches tended to be straight, since bent arm punches were generally less effective. This may have been down to the lack of understanding of biomechanics.

In the early 1900s boxing tended to emphasise toughness and there was less stress on skill. Success was measured by your ability to remain standing after many rugged rounds (considerably more than today's twelve rounds). As the number of rounds reduced the focus on skill had to increase. In addition, more skill and movement was required and expected of the lighter fighters. Hand movement tended to be low, but the fighters managed their range very well. As fighters became more technically proficient there was an increase in the application of 3, 4 and 5 punch combinations. As fighters became more technically aware they increasingly relied on feints, slipping, ducking and other manoeuvres.

The early fighters tended to adopt a more crouched stance, which was very effective from a defensive point of view but rather limiting from an attacking perspective. Fighters such as Nigel Benn and Joe Calzaghe in modern times, however, have demonstrated that a more flexible approach combining the more erect and crouched stance can be very effective.

Over the last few decades greater importance has been placed on the development of movement and footwork. More creativity has been demanded due to the greater emphasis on 'thinking' in bouts. A better understanding of footwork patterns and the development of explosiveness has enhanced boxing beyond belief. The late 1960s, 1970s and 1980s were a golden era for boxing, and in particular heavyweight boxing. Legends such as Muhammed Ali, Joe Frazier and George Foreman took boxing to a new level, but then it seemed to stop. The last couple of decades, however, have seen a slowdown in boxing's progress and some cause for concern. Football and rugby have seen an increase in the speed of the game and teams of yesteryear would struggle against the teams of today. But can the same be said of boxing? Would today's fighters be that far ahead of the fighters of yesteryear? We do not think so. Why?

Coaching today has become very predictable. We see all fighters learning the same things and moving to the same patterns as control bodies and associations take the lead. Though this is very commendable, the problem is that this takes away the thinking and mental input demanded by top athletes and coaches in order to succeed and break new boundaries. It should not be common to walk in a gym and see fighters switching off while their coaches work with someone else.

Boxing needs to start incorporating the latest findings in sports science to develop the fighters' skills and abilities. We need to see boxers thinking about punches in terms of 'endless' combinations until the job is done, and not in terms of a finite number of punches. Boxers need to be able to throw punches from any angle and direction and still develop sufficient power to be effective. They need to be able to defend and counter intuitively. The modern day fighter needs to learn how to use every part of the ring and not get caught in a slugging match around the centre of the ring, as happens in many bouts. A few fighters in recent times have epitomised this way of thinking, such as Muhammed Ali, Sugar Ray Leonard, Prince Naseem and Joe Calzaghe, and it has been assumed that these fighters were naturally talented. This may be so, but we believe that with good coaching these attributes may be trained into fighters. This is the basis of our training method: T (Technique), V (Variety) and P (Predictability).

What Does Boxing Offer?

Boxing is an ideal combat sport that allows the most complete expression of one's fighting and athletic capabilities, embracing technique and variety in a way that other combat sports struggle to. The reason for this is the continuity of the fight, which encourages fighters to be adaptable and prepare for the unknown. Other martial arts tend to have a more stop-start nature, which removes much of the creativity that boxing demands. Good boxing also develops attributes such as footwork, power, speed and acceleration, which actually help enhance other combat sports. This is why boxing has become extremely popular among other martial artists. The boxing training method also demands a different style of development, if a fighter's potential is to be maximized. The traditional form of instruction used in other combat sports is inappropriate as it takes away much of the thinking that unpredictable situations require. A more proactive form of coaching is required to enable each fighter to isolate their own unique characteristics that can be called on by the fighter when needed.

Why Has Boxing Endured?

Boxing has endured for many reasons, but simply it is an athletic form that allows us to express our emotions in a positive, developmental manner. Anyone is capable of punching – well or badly. Boxing rules also happen to very simple and straightforward. Another reason for its popularity might be that there are no boxing gurus, founders or masters who claim to have superhuman powers or possess secret techniques that only they know. The only heroes in boxing are the boxers themselves.

Boxing is probably the best combat sport system in that it allows people to release their primal urge to express passion and athletic desire against a willing and able opponent. Yet it must be admitted that, in addition to its positive benefits and the considerable passion it inspires in its participants and viewers, boxing needs to face up to serious issues:

* Deaths and permanent injuries in the ring. These are rare, but do occur.
* Questionable decisions by fight judges.
* Promoters and/or networks controlling who fights who.
* Too many champions in each weight division.
* No current great, iconic heavyweight champion.

How to Train for Boxing

One of the challenges facing boxing is identifying ways by which a fighter's progress can be assessed. The reality is that not everyone studying boxing wants to fight in front of packed audiences, but they would still like to gauge their progress. This is where boxing could learn from other combat sports and martial arts. Within the tvp framework for coaching boxing, we have developed our own grading system, which assesses the development of attributes to become a better boxer. The grading system also assesses

---

Why 'Boxing'?
A question we are often asked is why boxing is called boxing. There are many reasons given, but our explanation relates to the way boxing should be practised. The punches that are a boxer's key tools are delivered within the confines of the human body in the shape of a box. Strictly speaking punches should not be delivered outside the frame of the body but only within the confines of an imaginary box bounded by the shoulders and elbows, when positioned by the hips. This ensures the most effective delivery of the technique.

The Boxer – The Athlete

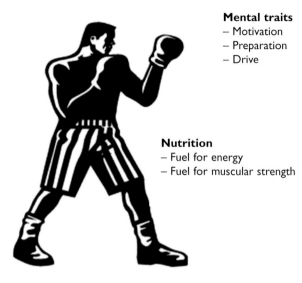

Physiological
– Fitness
– Strength
– Reaction times
– Power
– Speed
– Agility
– Quickness
– Recovery

Mental traits
– Motivation
– Preparation
– Drive

Attributes of an athlete.

Nutrition
– Fuel for energy
– Fuel for muscular strength

the boxer's ability to think for themselves in creative ways in a variety of situations. The tvp grading framework is designed to test the following:

* technique
* variety of technique
* a boxer's ability to produce the technique in unusual situations (level of predictability)
* physical fitness to compete
* ability to link different combinations of punches
* footwork
* a boxer's ability to express themselves in an effective way.

The tvp Framework for Boxing

This book has been written for boxers looking to advance their abilities and competencies in boxing. It is also designed for advanced fighters looking to become a champion. We have made certain assumptions about a boxer's ability, for example that readers have a fundamental understanding of the techniques of boxing and basics such as wrapping hands. We have, however, provided a short summary of these fundamentals, and for those wishing to look into the fundamentals in more detail we strongly recommend our earlier book *tvp: Comprehensive Boxing Concepts*, as this provides the drills and methods to develop the fundamentals to a very high level.

The objective here is to examine the various elements that create a better understanding of developing the boxing skills needed by a champion athlete. We have tried to provide a comprehensive training manual that adopts a creative approach by embracing the latest research and development methods in sports science, as well as our own research in boxing. There is also emphasis on the strategy and science of competitive boxing.

The Eastern martial arts are generally intended for those wanting to learn to defend themselves in a situation where the attacker and defender may have differing levels of fighting ability: here the principle of the first hit is vital. Boxing, on the other hand, is a combat sport in which both fighters in a contest will be equally matched: the primary differentiator will be their abilities and competencies as athletes. The elements that make up the attributes of the athlete are: mental, nutritional and physiological.

CHAPTER 2

THE ART AND SCIENCE OF COACHING

Don't judge each day by the harvest you reap, but by the seeds you plant.
Robert Louis Stevenson

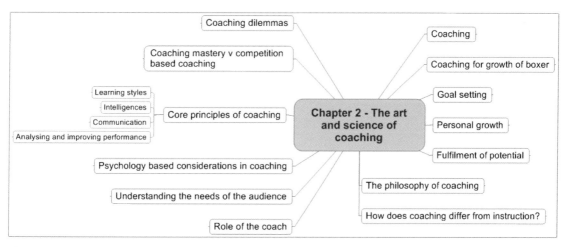

Mindmap overview of Chapter 2.

Coaching involves the development of boxers by creating a change, in a quantitative and qualitative way, that is structured and planned. The coach aims to improve the physical, mental, technical and strategic skills of the boxer.

Coaching is the creative adaptation, customization and application of scientific-based principles to a diverse range of boxers. Considerable science-based research is currently available from coaching, human performance and sports-related areas that takes away much of the subjectivity that has existed in the coaching of boxing in the UK, particularly at amateur level. Coaches need to be able to assess the research and find novel ways of applying this learning to boxers from a diverse range of backgrounds. The science provides an indication of the factors that contribute to success – nothing more. It would be foolish to assume that the results are totally conclusive, as they are based on statistics, but they do provide an indication and need to be adapted for specific situations to maximize the impact of the coach. Science can help design a training programme to help a boxer to fulfil their potential.

Coaching involves developing an understanding of the inner working of the individual being coached. A coach needs to be able to assess very rapidly the mental, emotional and physical states of the individual, and be prepared to adapt training schedules at short notice to maximize outcomes and minimize risk of deteriorating confidence and performance. It is essential for a coach to be adaptable and confident in diverting from set plans, based on changing circumstances.

A crucial part of coaching is building an individual's confidence and self-belief. At the higher levels of any sport there is a limited amount of technical knowledge that can be passed on to the individual by the coach, due to the level of knowledge that the boxer possesses. That is not to say there is nothing technical to be learned from the coach, but the technical credentials of the successful coach need to be based on innovation and detailed understanding of the various components of performance. This means that the coach must keep him or herself at the very forefront of technical knowledge in boxing and sport in general.

A major facet of coaching is the mental development of the boxer (see Chapter 3). The coach needs to have an innate understanding of the psychological make-up of their boxer and how this changes at different times and, more importantly, what drives these changes.

Coaching for Growth

The primary objective of good coaching is appropriate goal setting, personal growth, and mastery and fulfilment of the boxer's potential. A good coach should be able to stretch the boxer to his limits, and beyond, in a confident and safe manner.

Goal Setting

Goal setting has to be gauged and set to stretch the individual sufficiently to demonstrate progress, while not destroying confidence. Individuals usually set their goals either too high or low, depending on their ego or self-confidence, but the outcomes are still the same: failure. A coach with deep understanding and a close relationship with the individual can assist in setting the goal at an appropriate level.

Short-, medium- and long-term goals need to be determined and agreed with the individual: short-term goals in terms of boxing and sport cover one week to three months, medium term is three to twelve months and long term is twelve months and above. Sometimes the coach's planning needs to look much further ahead: preparing a boxer for the Olympics, for example, may require a development plan of up to four years.

The starting point to goal setting is to identify the long-term goals of the boxer and then to translate these into medium- and short-term goals. This ensures full alignment with the long-term objectives of the boxer. All goals should be SMART (specific, measureable, achievable, relevant and timebound) and need to be very specific and focused on the desired outcomes. Some people tend to make the goals very general and irrelevant to the desired outcomes. These goals need to be measurable. In reality everything is measurable, but sometimes you need to be quite creative in how the measurements are made. The key is to measure like for like, as this will give you feedback on progress. What is achievable is really dependent on the individual. The goals have to be specific and relevant to the individual's long-term objectives. A key element that is sometimes overlooked is making the goals timebound. This means we should stipulate the time frame within which the goals will be achieved. Coaches need to consider the development profile of the individual, as some develop more quickly than others, but also people tend to make

quick progress early on and then it begins to taper off.

An important aspect of goal setting is that the goals should be set against performance criteria and not outcome based. We need to ensure that the goals actually improve performance by doing the right things, for the longer term. Also make sure the goals are manageable in the short term.

There is no prescriptive way of looking at what is a realistic goal. This depends very much on the individual. Some embrace a challenge whereas others may get stressed by the challenge. The attitude and response towards the goals set will determine what is realistic and what is not. The coach needs to embrace the boxer's verbal expectations with their own understanding of the individual and make appropriate adjustments to those expectations.

Personal Growth

One of the primary objectives of the coach is to maximize the personal growth of the boxer. Clearly this involves, to a degree, consideration of the competition. However, the greatest improvement in the longer term comes from the boxer continuously improving, day on day, on his own personal performance. This should also be ingrained as a learning culture in the boxer, so that the growth is internally motivated and not externally driven. Progress each day, however small, is still representative of personal growth, which means the individual is always moving forward. At times personal growth needs to be the aim so that the individual does not feel pressured into always having to exceed expectations.

A key skill that the coach needs to possess to maximize personal growth is being able to understand how far the boxer may be stretched outside their comfort zones. The role of the coach is to take the individual to new limits without destroying self-confidence and self-belief. A good coach is able to manage the emotional strains of taking the boxer beyond their current limits and bring them back safely in order to embrace the learning experience.

Fulfilment of Potential

Coaching is usually geared towards two types of individuals. Firstly, coaching can benefit those seeking to sustain relationships with coaches for the benefit of personal security and building of self-confidence. Secondly, coaching is geared for results-driven and ambitious boxers who are seeking to win. These boxers are endeavouring to fulfil and stretch their own potential. As boxers get closer to fulfilling their potential, it does not stay static – it also increases, which means that successful boxers should never actually fulfil their potential because it continues to grow with the individual. This is why coaching is so important, since the

Rising potential.

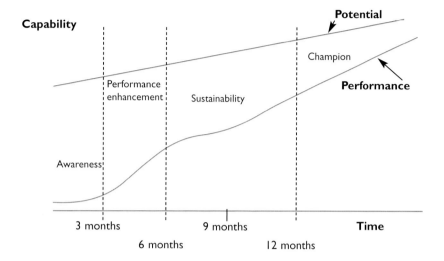

coach needs to understand how to stretch the individual and hence the potential.

The accompanying diagram shows how the development of an individual is likely to evolve and suggests that the style of coaching also needs to alter at different stages of a boxer's development. It also suggests that every boxer is capable of anything. This has to be the mindset of the coach, who must believe the protégé is capable of anything and needs to spend time thinking about the barriers to the boxer's performance.

The diagram also shows the different interventions that need to be used as the objectives of coaching develop over time. During the first three months the role of coaching is to build self-awareness. The boxer needs to understand why they behave the way they do in different situations and also be able to articulate their personal objectives. This first phase should involve a detailed assessment of personality and motivations.

The second phase is focused on performance enhancement. The coach needs to work closely with the boxer on personal outcomes to see a change in performance. Targets are quantified and actions are targeted to yield results.

The third phase reflects a natural tendency during a process of change where the performance gains start to slow down due to familiarization with the process and a slowdown in motivation due to the fact that the individual experiences a sense of satisfaction. The coach plays a key role at this stage in ensuring that the performance gains from the previous stage are sustained and ingrained in the boxer's make-up.

The fourth stage involves the boxer getting closer to their potential, while the potential increases. This is the champion stage when true winners are born.

The Philosophy of Coaching

A strong philosophy of coaching lies at the core of every great coach. It consists of principles and beliefs that guide actions and decision-making in dealing with boxers. A philosophy is not acquired from any one source, but rather from a compilation of experiences. These beliefs about life, coaching and sports guide and have an impact on us as we coach, teach and motivate the boxers, both in and out of the ring. It is difficult to discuss mental skills training effectively without a clear understanding of one's philosophy of coaching and how it impacts on implementation. We need to understand what drives us personally as a coach. In addition, we should be able to articulate our personal coaching brand through the values we portray.

Coaches must apply their philosophy of coaching within the context of three broad perspectives: coaching to help boxers develop physically, psychologically and socially; coaching to have fun; and coaching to win. These three converging perspectives are complex and unique to each person. In addressing these three areas, expert coaches integrate their knowledge with experience to bring out the best in their boxers.

How Does Coaching Differ from Instruction?

Coaching differs from instruction in that the instructor looks to show a technique to the boxer and feels that his job is done once he has demonstrated the technique. The instructor is more geared towards a group session in which one approach can be applied to all boxers. In our opinion, this approach is fine for a fitness session, but is inappropriate for the development of a champion boxer.

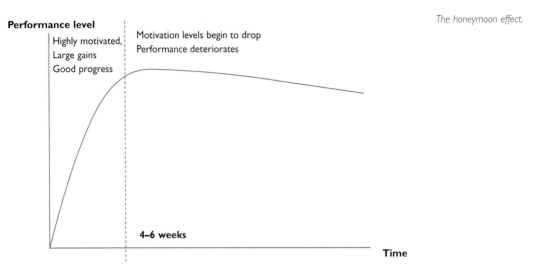

The honeymoon effect.

Role of the Coach

The coach is the person who will motivate, encourage and inspire their protégés to excel and stretch themselves beyond their normal levels of performance, so fulfilling their inherent potential. Many individuals will look at this and tell themselves that they do not need a coach, perhaps justifying this by their current levels of success. In some cases this may be true: the coach is rarely needed when things are going well. Many individuals will be successful due to a unique combination of attributes that gives them an advantage over other athletes. But this will

not last forever. There will always be someone who comes along and challenges the status quo, or there will be a change in the environment that demands a revisit of the training philosophy. This is where a coach is essential, to bring objectivity to situations where a change in direction is demanded. Progress, for whatever reason, will have stopped and changes, both physical and mental, need to be made to make the next leap in performance.

A coach will also help impose the internal motivation, through the creation of monitored stress, required to stretch the individual to performance levels with which the majority of individuals would struggle. The coach can also

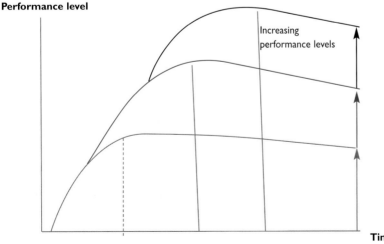

Coach-based interventions.

provide support to cope with the common fear of change and the introduction of change processes.

The reality is that the coach, through observation and communication, can monitor an individual's progress. As with any change programme, most people will experience the honeymoon effect, seeing a massive change initially, but then performance levels drop off due to familiarization and boredom. This is where motivation begins to drop, with overall performance following. The coach can then provide the motivation and redesign to ensure that progress levels are maintained.

The coach's role is to analyse the current performance level and the strengths and weaknesses of the boxer. This will help the coach define the specific needs of the boxer in the short, medium and long term. Based on this analysis the coach will design a programme that may mirror the champion's logbook (see Chapter 13).

Understanding the Needs of Audience

A key quality of a coach is being able to understand and define the needs of the boxer. This means that the coach should be looking to build a relationship with the boxer, both in and out of the gym. This will also allow the coach to understand the motivations, moods and drive of the boxer, allowing for increased customization of the programme.

To develop the boxer's potential, the coach needs to ensure that he customizes sessions against the following criteria:
* Objectives of the session in terms of physical and mental performance
* The needs of the individual boxer against the specific skills requirements for competition
* Stage of development of the individual against long-term development objectives of the individual

The message delivered to the audience needs to reflect the nuances of the audience. Everyone learns in different ways, but there is a common factor that people learn best based on learning preferences around their dominant senses: hearing, seeing, doing.

The coach also needs to understand the internal working of the athlete and the primary drivers of each individual. To help with understanding each individual, the coach should try to assess each against certain criteria. We suggest that you use the following leadership/personal development profile to assist in building the understanding of the boxer:

Spiritual values and beliefs: What are the boxer's personal priorities, values and beliefs? What are the foundations of those beliefs? Understanding the values and beliefs will provide the coach with an understanding of how far the boxer can be pushed and to what extent he will drive himself to his upper performance limits.

Emotional intelligence: An understanding of the emotional intelligence of the boxer will provide a useful insight into his ability to cope with the emotional challenges that he is likely to face during training and the time leading up to competition. In addition, this will provide the coach with essential information about the boxer to enable better handling of both winning and defeat situations after the competition. The key elements of the emotional intelligence that need to be understood by the coach are:
* Self-awareness: the ability of the boxer to recognize and understand their moods, emotions and drives.
* Self-regulation: the boxer's ability to control or redirect disruptive impulses and moods in an appropriate direction. Think before acting.
* Self confidence: the coach needs to understand the boxer's ability to portray self-belief and confidence, particularly when things are not going well.
* Motivation: where does the passion for boxing come from? This allows the coach to understand the boxer's ability to pursue goals with energy and persistence.

Social intelligence: This is the boxer's ability to interact with the coach, sparring partners and competitors. The key elements that need to be considered are:
* Empathy: the ability of the boxer to understand the emotional make-up of other people. Treat people according to emotional reactions. This is also a very powerful tool in being able to compete effectively.
* Social skills: proficiency in managing relationships and building networks. Ability to find common ground and build rapport with coaches and training partners. This allows the boxer to discuss, within his own network, how he can improve his level of performance.
* Attunement: the ability of the boxer to listen fully to the coach with genuine interest and full receptivity to ideas and areas for improvement.

Physical capability: The elements to be considered are aerobic, anaerobic and flexibility.

Mental thinking skills: This focuses on the IQ of the boxer, which is really assessing their ability to understand complex messages, so enabling the coach to make assumptions to the way in which the message will be communicated most effectively.

Psychology-Based Considerations in Coaching

There are a number of psychology-based factors that coaches need to understand in their protégés, especially in terms of stretching the boxer and assisting them to fulfil their potential. In addition, mood and motivation, need to be taken into account when designing training programmes and training sessions.

Moods

A mood is a long-lasting emotional state that may not be specific to a particular stimulus or event. Moods build up over a period of time, with some confusion as to what has actually started the mood, which is why they might provide the coach with a significant challenge. Generally, moods are a blend of a variety of challenges all coming together at the same time. As this state is quite long term in nature, it can have a huge impact on the training performance of an individual. Moods can impact on an individual's attitude and desire to train and perform.

Motivations

Motivation is the driver of goal-orientated behaviour and may be internally or externally driven. According to various psychology-based theories, motivation is based on the elementary need to minimize physical pain and maximize pleasure.

The main theory related to motivation is Maslow's hierarchy of needs, which states that human beings have wants and desires that influence their behaviour, but only unsatisfied needs influence behaviour – satisfied needs do not. Since there are many needs, they need to be arranged in order of importance, from the basic to the complex. The person advances to the next level of needs only after the lower level need is at least minimally satisfied.

As an individual moves up the hierarchy of needs, the coach will need to become more motivational and more creative in the design of training. Sometimes the coach will have to develop motivation by re-establishing the goals and ambitions of the boxer. Someone at the bottom of the pyramid is the most dangerous as he will be highly motivated to survive to satisfy his basic needs.

By understanding the motivations of an individual the coach will be aware of the boxer's limitations and how far he can be stretched outside his comfort zone.

The coach needs to understand the factors that will determine the level of motivation of his boxers. These include the boxer's background and upbringing, education, current level of achievement, personal ambition and self-perception.

Core Principles of Coaching

There are some key concepts that the coach will find useful in getting the best out of his boxer.

Learning Styles

Different people take in information and feedback in different ways. Coaches need to be aware of how their boxer learns in order to maximize the impact of their message. Sometimes coaches can pursue putting across a message in a format that just does not get through to the

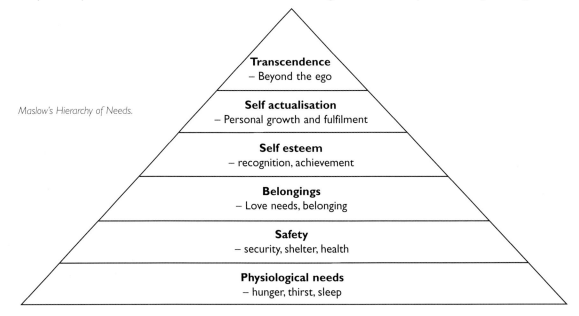

Maslow's Hierarchy of Needs.

Transcendence
– Beyond the ego

Self actualisation
– Personal growth and fulfilment

Self esteem
– recognition, achievement

Belongings
– Love needs, belonging

Safety
– security, shelter, health

Physiological needs
– hunger, thirst, sleep

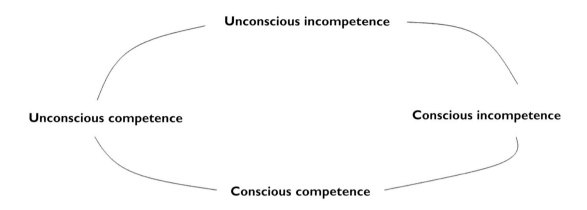

The Learning Cycle.

boxer. The different learning styles may be summarized as follows:

Feeling: this style relies on being able to relate to previous experience. The coach would relate the issues to previous experiences that the boxer might have.

Thinking: some prefer to take a concept and learn by discussing and debating this with the coach.

Doing: this is a very practical learning style where the coach demonstrates the key points by actually placing the boxer in a practical situation and reinforcing the points by doing.

Watching: some prefer to learn by reviewing their own physical activity or by watching someone else. Videotaping sessions is a very effective way of dealing with these people.

The thinking and feeling styles are interlinked and so are the doing and watching styles. In order to help understand how your boxer learns it may be useful to first complete a self-assessment learning styles test, such as that available at http://www.businessballs.com/vaklearningstylestest.htm.

Learning Cycle

There are four key stages to learning:

Unconscious incompetence: this is when you do not know you need to improve and are totally unaware of what needs to change. The coach needs to ensure that he makes you aware of what has to be changed.

Conscious incompetence: this stage is critical as it is really the start of the learning process. The boxer is aware of his weaknesses and what needs to improve.

Conscious competence: the boxer knows what he needs

to be done, but has to do it in a very premeditated way. This may involve doing it by numbers, for example.

Unconscious competence: at this stage the improvement has become intuitive and ingrained as a natural activity for the boxer.

Intelligences

An understanding of the key intelligences of the boxer will enable the boxer to maximize how the messages conveyed are put across in the most effective way. An effective way to assess your boxer's learning style is through applying Howard Gardner's multiple intelligence theories model, available at http://www.businessballs.com/howardgardnermultipleintelligences.htm#multiple%20intelligences%20tests.

Communication

Communication needs to be simple and clear. The most effective form of communication depends on the purpose of the message to be expressed. Some people respond to a more aggressive form of communication, while others respond to a more friendly form. This is why the coach needs to fully understand the individual and build a relationship where the individual does not feel threatened.

Analysing and Improving Performance

One of the most stressful activities for the coach is collecting data and analysing the performance of the boxer. There are many ways in which this may be done, but principally the coach needs to be clear about what he is measuring. For boxing, we have developed a method of

Key Intelligences (based on the work of Howard Gardner)

Intelligence	Features	What does this mean to the coach?
Linguistic	words and language	Talk more to your boxer
Logical-mathematical	logic and numbers	Quantify the benefits. Provide logical reasons as to why you are making your suggestions
Musical	music, sound, rhythm	Provide background music to support the way your message is conveyed
Bodily-kinesthetic	body movement control	Focus on doing
Spatial-visual	images and space	Use pictures and video to explain the message
Interpersonal (social)	other people's feelings	Identify to what extent you may use other boxers to help with the message
Intrapersonal (emotional)	self-awareness	Helping the boxer understand what his issues are

assessing the different characteristics needed for boxing (see Chapter 13). A regular logbook should be maintained of the outcomes of the assessment, so that progress may be quantified.

Coaching Mastery v. Competition-based Coaching

Coaches need to be clear of the objectives of the sessions, as this will impact on the style of the session. There are generally two types of coaching: coaching mastery and coaching for competition.

Coaching mastery focuses on learning technique and more time must be allowed to help the boxer understanding the technique. The mindset of this form of session is more relaxed and based on questioning: it is a major requirement that the boxer fully understands why he is learning a specific technique or strategy and what are the key success factors for this approach. The boxer should be allowed to intervene with questions to ensure maximum understanding of the concept. Coaching mastery differs from instruction in that the desired output is mastery of the concept, which means the boxer should be able to deliver the technique or concept in an intuitive way and does not have to think about it.

To develop mastery and intuition, the coach needs to follow a number of stages:
1. Develop an awareness of why the technique or concept is important.
2. Teach the basics of the technique with full understanding of why these elements are important.
3. Practise the technique on a step-by-step basis under the supervision of the coach in a structured and controlled situation.
4. Practise the technique in a random and chaotic environment at slow to fast speed. The coach may need to create a certain degree of control to ensure maximal learning

Competition based coaching is focused on preparing the boxer mentally and physically for the competition. This involves the coach creating an environment as close to the competition arena as possible. The boxer should be made to feel the pressure and stress, at both a physical and mental level, that will be experienced in competition. The primary objective of this form of coaching is to identify the responses of the boxer under pressure situations. This may involve physical activity, such as fitness-based exercises or boxing rounds, but may also involve more visualization-based techniques.

Coaching Dilemmas

Experience has shown that a key skill of the coach is the ability to recognize when the programme needs to change. To assist with this we have identified a number of coaching dilemmas that should enable the coach to keep an eye on the need for change when things appear to be going as predicted:

Positive reinforcement v. Providing a false sense of security: Providing your boxers with positive messages, especially in the public eye, is hugely beneficial, but there is a danger it can provide your boxers with a false sense of security. The coach needs to be careful that the positive messages are not actually lies and throwaway statements, and that they are balanced with the right messages.

Failure is one step closer to winning v. Winning is one step closer to failure: There is a mindset for maintaining motivation towards a goal by accepting failure as being a lesson that takes you one step closer to winning. However, the same can be true of winning when the boxer can become too satisfied, thus leading to losing. One of the factors that distinguish the very best coaches is the desire to keep winning and stay at the top.

Dependence through teaching v. Independence to create: The coach will take great pride in coaching a winner. The boxer will become more dependent on the coach as they realize the benefits of the coach's training programme. However, the champion athlete is renowned for being creative and therefore the coach needs to develop a level of independence to allow the boxer to take control of their development. The coach needs to ensure that the boxer fully understands the rationale for what they are doing and the benefits they provide.

Hunger to succeed v. Contentment to fail: This dilemma is connected to understanding the motivation level of your boxer. The more content your boxer becomes the more they are likely to fail. A degree of hunger has to be maintained.

We know it all v. Tell me: The coach needs to ensure that their protégés maintain a desire to learn, as this is an essential part of growth.

PSYCHOLOGY OF A CHAMPION

Champions aren't made in the gyms. Champions are made from something they have deep inside them – a desire, a dream, a vision.
Muhammad Ali

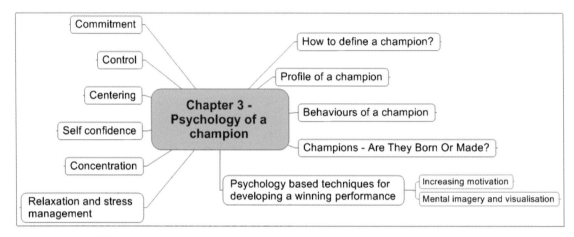

Mindmap overview of Chapter 3.

How to Define a Champion

Improving the level of performance of an individual requires an understanding of that individual and the characteristics of a winner/champion. This chapter will explain some of the features of a champion and how this affects the performance of the boxer in the ring.

A champion is constantly looking to learn and grow by setting themselves new boundaries that will stretch them outside their comfort zones. They face their weaknesses and issues head on. A key feature of champions is their attitude towards goals. Champions are always thinking in terms of goals and objectives, and also quantifying these objectives. The goals start off at a very high level in terms of their dreams and are then broken down into more manageable elements, and also into timeframes to tie in with the coaching model. Many people believe champions always win. However, our view of a champion is someone 'who gets knocked down six times, and gets up seven times!' Champions do not know when they are beaten. Champions see every loss as being one step closer to

winning. Champions see defeat as a key stage in the process of winning.

The Behaviour of a Champion

The US Olympic Committee recently asked past Olympians to complete a survey about numerous aspects of their development. One section, in which they were asked to list up to five factors that positively influenced their success and five obstacles that had to be overcome, was of particular relevance to this discussion. The percentages citing positive influences were:

Dedication and Persistence (58%): This related to the positive influence of the Olympian's inner drive, desire, persistence, and commitment to achieving their goals.

Family and Friends (52%): This support or influence included financial and emotional support, instilling confidence, providing an introduction to the sport, and the provision of stability.

Coaches (49%): Excellent coaches throughout their

development were identified as having a great influence on success.

Love of Sport (27%): Love of, and passion for, the sport greatly influenced success, often providing the necessary motivation to continue training in less than optimal conditions.

Training Programs and Facilities (22%): The opportunity to train with club, college, national level or resident teams and access to programmes and facilities was important.

Natural Talent (22%): A genetic predisposition or God-given talent played a role in the athlete's success.

Competitiveness (15%): A strong competitive nature and love of competition was identified as a factor influencing success.

Focus (13%): The ability to stay focused on goals and the task at hand, despite distractions, had a significant influence on success.

Work Ethic (12%): Hard work and a strong work ethic were factors that influenced success.

Financial Support (12%): The financial support from sources such as sponsorship, college scholarship, private donors, athlete grants and fundraising contributed to success.

Success in any aspect of life is all about preparation, which takes commitment and determination to succeed. We believe that anyone serious about long-term success in their sport, martial art or discipline needs to set aside twelve months of careful planning to drive them forward towards their goal. There are many who win occasionally, largely due to circumstances. We are referring to winning on a long-term, consistent basis and not a one-off. Additionally, these principles are not just relevant for competing athletes, but for anyone who wishes to be a success by achieving their pre-determined goals. Being a champion is not only about winning medals, but is, more importantly, about a winning mindset.

Being a Champion

Firstly, let's look at the makeup of a champion. Research published by Stephen R. Covey in *The 8th Habit: From Effectiveness to Greatness* (Free Press, 2004) claims that all humans possess four intelligences. An understanding of these can go a long way in determining the areas of focus to becoming a champion:

Mental intelligence: our rational and analytical intelligence. Mental intelligence goes a long way to explain the way we think – our logic. Mental intelligence in combat sports allows us to analyse why we perform the way we do and what needs to change, helping us to learn from our successes and failures. The very top champions always sound quite articulate and appear to be very good at analysing why they have won or lost fights.

Physical intelligence: the intelligence related to the body and its functions. To be more precise it is related to unconscious body performance. In combat sport it is the case of training the body to perform intuitively, without thought – doing the right things without thinking about it. Champions from many different sports always find it difficult to explain why and how they responded to a situation in the way they did, but they always end up doing the right thing. Just look at Prince Naseem at his peak. He did things that he probably would find difficult to explain, but they were almost instinctive for him.

Emotional intelligence: emotional intelligence is our self knowledge and self-awareness. Do we recognize our strengths and weaknesses from a mental, physical and emotional perspective, without being told by someone else? How many times have we seen champions lose because they were not emotionally ready? (For examples of this see the recent fights of Audley Harrison and the last few fights of Mike Tyson.)

Spiritual intelligence: this intelligence represents our vision and values: why do we live the way we do? It is our beliefs that basically shape our consciousness, which is our long-term commitment and motivation to achieving a goal. In recent years the martial arts magazines have been saturated with articles about the role and relevance of spirituality in martial arts.

Each of these intelligences contributes in different ways to our performance in our chosen art. Our mental intelligence enables us to analyse our strengths and weaknesses rationally, with no ego. Our physical

Definition of a champion.

Definition of a champion:
Someone who **learns** equally from the **failure** and **achievement** of **predetermined goals**, which are being constantly reviewed, so as to **stretch** the development of the **individual** to ensure fulfilment of the **potential** of the individual. Or
Someone who **Lives the Dream!!!**

intelligence breeds discipline to actually stick to the plans laid out. Making our body behave in an intuitive way demands repetition and focus: every champion has spent many hours doing the same old things. Discipline is essential to ensuring we put in the hard work when we least feel like it. Emotional intelligence creates passion, which will ensure our discipline is rewarded in a positive manner, reinforcing future growth and future targets. Spiritual intelligence provides us with long-term motivation through living our vision and values, as we fulfil our ambitions. Spiritual intelligence also creates personal humility and determination.

Observing champions such as Muhammad Ali and Bruce Lee demonstrates the importance that they both placed on all four intelligences, whether deliberately or by accident.

The creation of champions is the purpose of a comprehensive training programme followed by champion athletes all over the world. The focus of each session is divided into a number of critical components, outlined in the accompanying diagram, and the percentage of time that should be spent on each area is also given.

Generally, champions are defined as those who set big, hairy, audacious goals (BHAGs) and achieve them. However, this is only part of the story. The real attribute of the champion is that they never know when they are beaten. Champions have a mental nature that is always positive and a self-belief that they can achieve whatever they set their minds to. Champions also come from all walks of life and not just from a sporting context.

Champions are firstly champions to themselves. Champions do not need the external gratification that is sometimes associated with the egos that go with winners. True champions set their developmental goals and achieve these goals for personal growth and not external plaudits.

Are Champions Born or Made?

There is certainly a connection between the way an individual is brought up and the development of the qualities that make a champion. Many different schools of thought exist on whether a champion is born or made. Our view is that the answer is not straightforward. A certain upbringing can provide an inner drive that is irreplaceable. Unfortunately, you cannot state categorically that there is one way of bringing up a champion, although in some instances a tough upbringing creates an inner desire and motivation that provides a drive to succeed.

An inner drive can also be provided by ambition and a vision that the individual holds inside themselves, supplying a unique motivation that will push the individual beyond the normal realms of possibility.

How the Mainstream Defines Champions

Winning or losing an event does not necessarily define a champion. Nor does making it to the highest ranks of any given field necessarily indicate that someone rose

COMPONENT	ELEMENTS
Mental Training	Analysing personal and role model performance. Discussing strengths and weaknesses with coach.
Spiritual training	Meditation, visualisation
Emotional training	Yoga (mind/body awareness), breathing
Physical Training	Aerobic, anaerobic, nutritional; balance, core training
Combat Sport specific	SAQ (speed, agility and quickness), tvp (technique, variety and predictability)

The Champions Training Framework.

primarily due to inherent traits and not through external entities, such as networks, favouritism or alternative avenues that place social expectations above merit and talent.

Wannabes exist in all areas of life. It could be argued that the prominent position occupied by some has more to do with tradition than with their belonging to a special breed that possesses unique qualities. Thus, true champions should be defined less along mainstream ideals and more along esoteric themes that challenge ordinary lexicons.

Identifying a Winner

Whether it is athletics fitness or other endeavours, champions have certain qualities in common. Although not every common thread can be discussed here, champions possess some easily recognizable attributes that become immediately detectable to those honest enough to see with open eyes.

Champions don't make excuses. They take charge, lead by example and see through trends, distractions or gimmicks, regardless of the source. Champions uphold their convictions with or without outright approval, although they welcome opposing views.

As natural visionaries, champions often see possibilities before such things unfold. Life is not seen in separate parts, but rather as a synergistic whole with an interdependent nature perpetually straining for unison with the environment.

Champions tend to be inquisitive. They enjoy learning simply for the pleasure of becoming well-rounded. On the other hand, wannabes are often closed to alternative viewpoints, threatened by differences and instead vie to exist within collectives of like-minded individuals.

Champions aren't driven by egotism. They are unpretentious individuals who feel little ongoing need to prove their self-worth, which is a tendency associated with insecurity. Champions give their best efforts when required, but understand they cannot nor do they want to control all outcomes.

They acknowledge what they do not understand, can make mistakes and move on without feeling weak or overly apologetic, while wannabes rarely admit to shortcomings or ignorance. Champions realize they cannot satisfy everyone all the time and they have no compulsion to always be right or centre stage.

As realists, champions understand the world owes them nothing in terms of entitlement so they don't waste time waiting for good luck to happen. Because champions are an enlightened crowd, they make good things happen for themselves and those around them. And they have no

need to boast accomplishments – big or small – because their actions silently speak volumes. Wannabes campaign their presence.

Champions do not make excuses for failure, but see it as an opportunity to learn and make progress. Fear of failure is replaced by the pleasure of learning and growth. Champions also look no further than themselves for failure to deliver and achieve against preset goals. Champions take full responsibility and are always looking at addressing issues. They are emotionally detached from the outcome, but can accommodate other views and perspectives when considering their personal growth and are not resistant to change.

Mental Imagery and Visualization

Mental imagery, also called visualization and mental rehearsal, is a process of picturing in your mind a process to deliver a specific desired outcome. Whenever the boxer imagines themselves performing actions in their mind they are using imagery. To maximize the benefit of the exercise, the boxer needs to enter fully into the image with all their senses – sight, hearing, feeling, touching, smelling and performing – as this will create a closer link to reality.

The boxer needs to be in a fully relaxed state to maximize the benefit of the exercise. Mental and visual imagery increases and stimulates positive energy, which provides additional motivation towards delivering against goals. Mental imagery is likely to reduce performance anxiety and stress by allowing the boxer to play out different and challenging scenarios in the mind, thus providing an impetus to discover creative solutions to the challenges presented. An ideal tool to assist with the improvement of applying this technique is to watch old fights and analyse them (for examples see Chapter 12). This allows the boxer to explore what the greats might have done if they were in a similar situation. The mental playback is an ideal first

---

Key Techniques for Increasing Motivation

Goal setting: short-, medium- and long-term goals should be set, monitored and adjusted.

Rewards through providing positive feedback and information. This should not be materialistic or financial in nature.

Motivational music

Positive self-talk using the athlete's inner voice to provide motivation. A good example is Muhammad Ali's use of the statement 'I am the greatest': he claimed that if he said it enough everyone would believe it – which they did!

step to establishing appropriate winning techniques and tactics.

Boxing requires not only physical skills, but a strong mental game as well. Most coaches preach the line that sports are 90 per cent mental and only 10 per cent physical. Especially in sports where hundredths of a second or tenths of an inch separate the champion athletes from the mediocre, an extra edge can be crucial. Hence numerous athletes are turning towards mental imagery to take their game to the next level. Different uses of imagery in sport include: the mental practise of specific performance skills, improving confidence and positive thinking, problem solving, controlling arousal and anxiety, performance review and analysis, preparation for performance, and maintaining mental freshness during injury.

Mental imagery is left up to individual preferences and the circumstances. It can be done in or out of the ring, it can be of very short (within a few seconds or minutes) or long duration, sitting up, lying down, in complete silence or with a stereo, with eyes closed or open. Whatever state is chosen the boxer should be in a relaxed and receptive state in order for the image to go deeply into the mind. It is recommended to do visualization two or three times per week.

Mental imagery not only enhances competitive performance, but it can also enhance intrinsic motivation as well. The reason mental imagery works is that when a boxer imagines themselves performing to perfection and doing precisely what they want, they are in turn physiologically creating neural patterns in the brain, just as if they had performed the action. Hence, mental imagery is intended to train our minds and create the neural patterns to teach our muscles to do exactly what we want them to do.

Mental imagery may be used:
* To see success
* To motivate
* To perfect skills
* To familiarize
* To set the stage for performance
* To refocus

Mental imagery is applied by visualizing every detail, by engaging each of the senses and feeling the outcome like a professionally made film.

Step-by-Step Guide to Using Imagery

The first time you try imagery it's helpful to have a skilled facilitator or practitioner walk you through the process. This is referred to as guided imagery. You can also use CDs or MP3s, or record your own script to use as a guide. After you are comfortable with the technique, it's easy to practise these techniques on your own.

* Sit in a comfortable place where you won't be interrupted.
* Relax your body and take several long, slow breaths.
* Close your eyes and create a vivid and convincing image. This image can be one you've previously experienced, or one you simply desire.
* If you become distracted or find you are thinking about something else, simply acknowledge it and let it go.
* Focus on your breathing if you lose the image.
* Maintain a positive attitude.
* Imagine the sights, sounds, tastes, feelings and even smells of the experience.
* Take note of as much detail of the scene as possible. What are you wearing, who is there, what are you hearing, how do you feel?
* If your imagery session is not going the way you want it to, simply open your eyes and start over with your breathing.
* Always end an imagery session with a positive image.

Relaxation and Stress Management

The increased stress of competitions can cause athletes to react both physically and mentally in a manner that can negatively affect their performance abilities. They may become tense, their heart rates race, they may break into a cold sweat, worry about the outcome of the competition and find it hard to concentrate on the task in hand.

This has led coaches to take an increasing interest in the area of competitive anxiety and relaxation, focusing on techniques that athletes can use in competitive situations to maintain control and optimize their performance. Once learned, these techniques allow the athlete to relax and focus his/her attention in a positive manner on the task of preparing for and participating in competition. Psychology is another weapon in the athlete's armoury in gaining the winning edge.

Relaxation allows the boxer to embrace the situation and see the world from another perspective. Sometimes boxers become anxious and get too drawn into specific issues. Relaxation allows the creativity to come out. The key essence of relaxation is breathing. Deep breaths channelled through the abdomen are a very effective way of relaxing and managing competitive anxiety.

Concentration

Concentration is the ability to focus on something specific and maintain that focus over a relevant period of time. In the case of boxing, the relevant time will be the training session or the boxing competition. In many instances boxers focus on mistakes, which creates a negative mindset and takes them away from winning. In addition, this mindset reinforces the performance of mistakes. It encourages people to concentrate on mistakes, rather than shifting their thinking away from the mistakes. Our training methodology is based on focusing on the strengths of the boxer. Sometimes we can spend so much time working on things that are not natural to the boxer, that is in focusing on mistakes, that we forget to build on the strengths.

A key thing to remember is 'you only achieve what you believe'!

Self-Confidence

Self-confidence is an athlete's realistic expectations about achieving success. It should be stressed that self-confidence is not what athletes 'hope' to accomplish, but rather what they realistically may 'expect' to accomplish. Self-confidence is the sureness of feeling that you are up to the task in hand. Confidence can relate to a specific set of circumstances.

Overconfidence can also be a problem, leading to reduced effort and intensity that lower performance. When boxers feel confident, they are more readily able to turn sporting potential into superior winning performance. Conversely, when they feel unsure of themselves, the slightest setback can have a huge impact on performance.

Self confidence comes from a combination of the following elements:

Achievement: actually being successful is a great driver of confidence, but can also lead to self-confidence.

Being part of success: playing some role in someone else's success can rub off on people. Winning spreads to others associated with certain situations.

Verbal reinforcement: this is really the role of the coach and team to continually provide positive reinforcement to the boxer.

Visualization: playing 'winning' in your mind can start to become habit due to the mental association with winning.

Physiological states: the physiological states play a major role in developing the confidence of boxers and everyone else.

Emotional states: the emotional states provide the resilience to pursue dreams and goals, which in turn lead to the building of confidence.

Centring

Centring is a technique used to focus the boxer on the key goals and issues that will affect performance. Centring is achieved through breathing, thus allowing the boxer to find and maintain control in highly stressful situations. It is about the individual regaining control of his actions and his mental diversions, which can lead to a lack of performance. Under stress many people will allow their thoughts

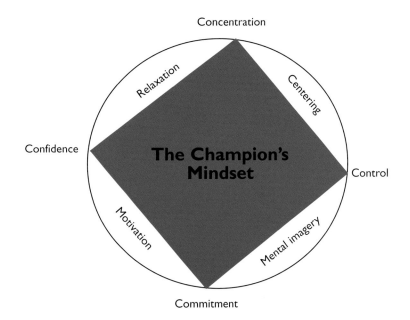

Training for Success.

to run away and basically make them take their eyes off the target. This is dangerous as mental energy is essential to finding focus in challenging situations.

Control

Through centring, control is retained with the individual. Control is a combination of mental and physical control. However, the key drivers to control are mental thoughts and processes, which in turn drive physical action. Many actions, both physical and mental, are based on momentum. This means that we have a tendency to do things because 'we have always done things this way'. The momentum of the situation, combined with our attitude of continuity, reinforces mistakes from the past. To create a winning mindset we need to identify our priorities and to what extent our current actions will actually deliver our desired goals. The decision-making process is thus a key part of control.

Commitment

Commitment is the energy that an individual is prepared to invest to achieve a preset goal. Commitment is also a function of energy, motivation and desire. How badly does the boxer want to win? This needs to be identified very early on in the process, so that the coaching can focus on the key areas of development.

NUTRITION AND DIET FOR THE CHAMPION FIGHTER

To eat is a necessity, but to eat intelligently is an art.
La Rochefoucauld

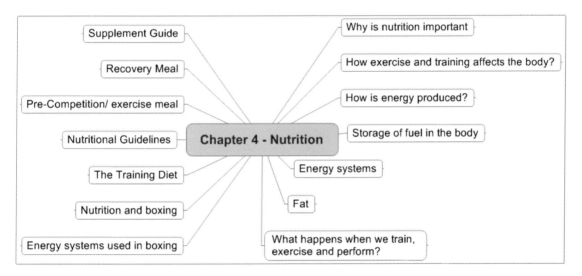

Mindmap overview of Chapter 4.

This chapter develops an understanding of the different nutrients and how they chemically interact with each other to deliver optimal performance. Through increasing our understanding of how the body responds to exercise and the impact this has on energy demands, boxers can significantly improve their performance. Nutrition is also vital for recovery processes and repair to take place.

More detail on meal plans and similar topics can be gained through specific books on dieting. The aim of this chapter is to explain in simple terms how our body's demands are met. An optimal diet supplies the required nutrients for tissue maintenance, repair and growth without excess energy intake.

Why is Nutrition Important?

Various sources suggest that an athlete's progress is 80 per cent due to nutrition and 20 per cent due to training methods. Nutrition provides the fuel for athletes to perform at their optimum level. An athlete is similar to a car: if you put the wrong fuel in a car then it will not run; if an athlete has the wrong nutrition then they will not be able to perform to the best of their ability. In order for athletes to have enough energy to exercise they must consume the correct amount of calories. It is important to realize that there is not a set amount that should be consumed by every athlete. The amount of calories consumed is dependent on those expended by the athlete and their goal, together with their weight, height and age. The correct fuel will help the athlete build quality muscle and prevent injury, as well as allow

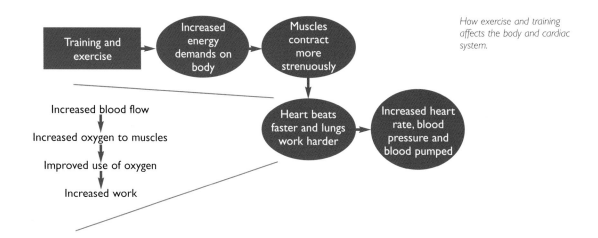

How exercise and training affects the body and cardiac system.

the athlete to sustain their performance in the ring.

Nutrition provides the fuel for physical development and more importantly for recovery. These are important considerations for both competing and training.

To gain maximum benefit from this section we need to understand how the body reacts to exercise and how the nutrients react chemically to deliver optimal performance.

blood stream. As we train more regularly, our capacity to perform increases, causing an improvement in our resting heart rate, which allows us exercise longer and harder than before. The next stage of development as a result of exercise is an increase in the amount of muscle in the body, which leads to more fat being burned since energy is needed to help fuel the body's increased metabolism.

How Does Exercise and Training Affect the Body?

Training increases the body's metabolism and also causes us to breathe faster and deeper, allowing an increase in oxygen supply to accommodate the increased metabolism. During exercise, the muscles use up the available oxygen to deliver mechanical energy. With strenuous exercise, our body's metabolism is greater than the oxygen supply, which causes it to use alternate biochemical processes in the body that do not require oxygen. These processes generate lactic acid, which start to enter the

How Is Energy Produced?

Energy is produced by adenosine triphosphate (ATP), which is itself produced by the body from a breakdown of the key nutrients (carbohydrate, fat, protein and alcohol), which are the four key fuels used by the body. Carbohydrate and alcohol are used for short-term energy, fats are used in the longer term and protein is used in the short term, when carbohydrates are in short supply.

To fully understand how energy is produced, it is important to understand, in simple terms, the chemical reactions that create energy. ATP is a small molecule

Storage of Fuel in the Body

Type of fuel	Where is it stored?	How does it work?
Carbohydrate	Stored as glycogen in muscles and liver	Limited supply in muscles. Liver glycogen maintains blood glucose levels in the body
Fat	Stored as fat tissue in all parts of the body	Used by the body as exercise is extended
Protein	Forms muscle and organ tissue	Builds muscles not as an energy source. Used as an energy source during latter stages of exercise or during a period of starvation
Alcohol	Used by liver	Broken down at a fixed speed. Cannot be speeded up by exercise

Energy Systems

Source	How does it work?	What is it used for?
ATP-PC (phosphagen) system	Uses ATP and phosphocreatine, which is stored in muscle cells. PC regenerates ATP rapidly by breaking down into creatine and a phosphate that attaches to ADP to create ATP	Generates energy for maximal bursts of strength and speed for up to 6 seconds. Used up very quickly
Lactic acid system or anaerobic glycolytic	Activated as soon as you begin exercise. Uses carbohydrate as muscle glycogen as fuel. Eventually broken down to form ATP and lactic acid	Used for exercises lasting up to 90 seconds
Aerobic system	Generates ATP from breakdown of carbohydrates and fat with oxygen	Produces larger amounts of ATP but not very rapidly

comprising an adenosine structure with three phosphate groups attached, hence triphosphate. Energy is released into the body when one of these phosphate groups split off from the adenosine structure, creating adenosine diphosphate (ADP, that is, two phosphate groups). This break off occurs as a result of the contraction of relevant muscles creating work. As the level of work increases, heat is given off, which then causes the ADP to convert back to ATP. This is a cyclical process.

The body is capable of storing enough ATP at one time to keep the body at rest. Exercise causes an increase in heart rate, which increases the demand for energy and as a result the ATP is used up very rapidly. This means that more fuel has to be broken down to continue the exercising.

At rest, muscle cells contain small amounts of ATP to satisfy basic needs. With strenuous exercise ATP needs to be regenerated from one of the systems given in the accompanying tables.

It should be noted that creatine is formed naturally in the body in the liver from different amino acids. After being broken down phospho creatine is recreated or forms creatinine (a byproduct of creatine phosphate in muscle), which is dispersed through the kidneys in the urine. The key sources of creatine are fish, beef and pork.

Lactic acid is a source of fuel that is converted to ATP with oxygen, which is why warm-downs are so important to increase the flow of oxygen, so that lactic acid goes through this conversion process. If increased oxygen is not present it will move to the liver where it will be converted back to glucose, and is cleared in the body after about 15 minutes.

The following are the key factors that affect the selection of the system to be used to supply energy:
* Intensity of exercise
* Duration of exercise
* Fitness level
* Pre-exercise diet

Keep fat intake to about 15–20 per cent of your total calories, depending on which part of the season you are in and what your body composition goals are. Fats should consist primarily of essential and monounsaturated fats. Essential fatty acids are a type of fat that the body cannot create from fish and walnuts. Monounsaturated fats, which are fats with one binding site, can come from olive or canola oils, seeds and/or avocados.

Energy Systems Used in Boxing

The key activities in boxing are:

Nature of activity	Main energy system	Main storage fuels used
Maximal short bursts of attack and defence lasting approximately 3–6 seconds	ATP-PC	ATP-PC
High intensity work and movement lasting up to 3 mins for each round	ATP-PC Anaerobic glycotic*	ATP and PC Muscle glycogen
Moderate–high intensity lasting 15–45 minutes	Aerobic	Muscle glycogen Fat

* Glycotic – an atp-producing metabolic process that converts glucose and sugars into energy.

Key lessons
* Ensure you carry out a dynamic warm-up to raise heart rate and energy demand at a manageable level
* Delay fatigue through:
  a. Increasing the glycogen store in muscles and liver
  b. Pacing yourself

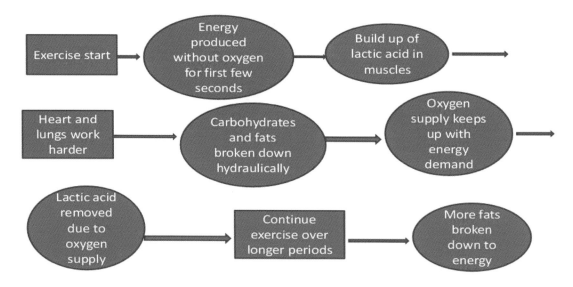

Impact of gentle exercise.

What Happens When We Train, Exercise and Perform?

A boxing training programme must focus on reactive power, power endurance, muscular endurance, anaerobic endurance and aerobic endurance to ensure optimal performance in the ring.

Nutrition and Boxing

Boxing involves a combination of intense short bursts of activity over an extended period of time. A boxer will fight for periods of 2–3 minutes over 3–12 rounds. The boxer will need to ensure that he has sufficient energy to manage the bursts of intense activity, which involves explosive movement using almost every muscle in the body. A high degree of strength endurance is required to be able to deliver powerful and quick punches, while moving with speed and agility.

To prepare for the fight night, boxers need to ensure that they possess sufficient energy to accommodate intense training, while ensuring they maintain an appropriate weight. Some boxers have to lose considerable weight to prepare for a fight, over a short period of time, causing dehydration. Dehydration results in a reduction in performance due to the body's inability to meet the exceptional needs of the training and fight situation.

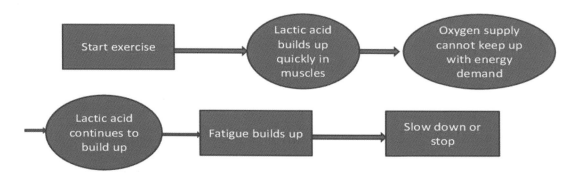

Impact of strenuous exercise.

The Training Diet

Season	Requirements	Protein	Carbs	Fats
In-season and pre-season	Energy for recovery and tissue repair, without adding body fat	30–40%	45–55%	15%
Off season	Add muscle	60%	20%	20%

Therefore, boxers need to maintain a nutrient-rich, low-fat diet to ensure optimal performance.

Key Considerations

* Boxers require a daily moderate- to high-carbohydrate (CHO) diet to fuel the ATP-PC system during practise, competition and weight training.
* Protein is essential for muscle repair and as an energy source. As the boxer reaches fatigue, due to strenuous exercise, the body may use its own muscle as an energy source. This may be undesirable as it is difficult to maintain and build the muscle mass.
* Crash diets can result in a loss of strength and muscle mass, rather than body fat.
* Boxers should aim to stay within 10 per cent of their competitive weight at all times, to limit the huge fluctuations in weight and the problems associated with this.

Nutritional Guidelines

The following are approaches in nutrition that ensure optimal performance:
* Eat fresh foods to ensure the body receives good quality calories.
* Eat approximately every 3-4 hours to maintain insulin levels and aid in physical and neural recovery.
* Eat complex carbohydrates, such as pasta, wheat bread, whole grain cereals, brown rice, potatoes, yams, sweet potatoes.
* Choose protein sources such as turkey, chicken, eggs, fish, lean cuts of beef, tofu, low fat cottage cheese.
* Choose healthy fat sources such as nuts, avocados and cold-water fish.
* Drink water or a sports drink to maintain hydration while training.
* Eat a diet that consists of a wide variety of foods by keeping in mind the basic food groups.
* Consume 25 to 35g of fibre per day via high fibre foods such as wholegrains, vegetables, fruit and cereals.
* Use meal replacement shakes, fruit smoothies or bars whenever necessary.
* Take a multi-vitamin or mineral supplement regularly.

Pre-Competition/Exercise Meal

The key objective of eating just prior to a period of strenuous exercise, whether training or competing, is to delay fatigue. The key factors that will determine the onset of fatigue and nutrient requirements are your level of conditioning and the duration of the activity.

Some basic rules in deciding what your meal should comprise are:
* Eat low-glycemic foods, such as wholegrain cereals, certain fruits, sandwiches made with wholewheat bread, etc., approximately two to three hours before a competition to maintain blood sugar levels over an extended period of time, which helps maintain mental focus.
* Avoid bulky foods, such as raw fruits and vegetables, dry beans, peas and popcorn, which can stimulate bowel movements.
* Avoid gas-forming foods, such as vegetables from the cabbage family and cooked dry beans.
* Drink 400–600ml (14–22 fl oz) of fluid two to three hours before exercise, depending on tolerance.

Recovery Meal

Following an intense session, your post-training diet can assist with your recovery and repair of the muscles used. High carbohydrate and low fibre foods should be consumed within 45 minutes after the session, and every two hours for four to six hours to replace glycogen stores. These foods should be combined with protein at a ratio of four to one, to speed the recovery process. Replacement drinks are an ideal source of carbohydrate and protein.

Supplement Guide

There are various supplements available for athletes to use. In a sport like boxing, where there are weight divisions, supplements are essential: boxers need to use supplements either to gain weight or to lose weight. It is vital that boxers have a broad knowledge of supplements and the strengths and limitations of all the different types. A boxer who needs to put weight on, for instance, would not take fat-burning supplements. Since many types of supplement are sold by a wide range of brands, before buying supplements an athlete must know their goal, be aware of the benefits of the supplement and read reviews on different brands of the supplement before making a decision on which to use. The supplements most commonly used in boxing are listed below.

Antioxidants

Antioxidants are substances that quench free radicals. They assist in reducing the symptoms and risks associated with high levels of free radicals generated during exercise. There are no toxic effects from large doses of antioxidant vitamins.

Creatine

Creatine has been shown to boost gains in lean muscle mass, strength and power. It increases the amount of ATP available as an energy source for muscle contractions. Having extra creatine in your body allows you to work your body to its maximum potential. Creatine promotes protein manufacture and causes water to be drawn into the cells, therefore resulting in an increase in lean body mass. Creatine is essential for boxers as it reduces muscle acidity, therefore allowing more lactic acid to be produced during a bout before fatigue sets in. During the loading period 5g of creatine should be taken four times a day for the first five days of consumption. During the maintenance phase the athlete should consume 5g of creatine twice a day.

Glutamine

Glutamine has been linked to protein synthesis and prevents muscles being catabolized. Glutamine helps increase growth hormone levels: recent studies have shown that 2g of L-Glutamine can increase growth hormone levels by more than 400 per cent. Another main function of Glutamine is that it protects the immune system from damage caused by intense sessions. Therefore it is essential for boxers to aid recovery after intense sessions and increase performance.

Whey Protein

Whey protein is the highest quality protein source and is used by the body to repair muscle damage. It is essential for boxers to repair the damage caused to their muscles as a result of intense training. During exercise whey protein helps to open up blood flow: an increase in blood flow will help increase performance as more blood is delivered to the active muscles, bringing more oxygen, while also removing more carbon dioxide from the active muscles. Lactic acid will then be removed from the muscles being used, so increasing the athlete's performance. Whey protein is very popular among athletes since it may be digested very quickly. There are a wide variety of protein shakes on the market. It is vital, however, when purchasing protein shakes, to read all the labels in order to understand the purpose for which the shake is intended. An athlete wishing to increase muscle mass, for example, will want a protein shake that is high in both carbohydrates and protein, whereas an athlete wishing to create a lean physique and lose weight should choose a protein shake that is high in protein, yet low in carbohydrates.

Multivitamins

Boxing is an intense sport that requires short intervals of speed and power. This results in your body burning minerals and vitamins. In order to stop your muscles from cramping up, it is essential to provide your muscles with the necessary vitamins and minerals. A multivitamin that is high in vitamin C, vitamin E, zinc and vitamin B is the ideal choice for a boxer in order to prevent muscle cramps. Vitamin B builds new muscle tissue and prevents muscle tissue loss as a result of intense training. Vitamins C and E protect the immune system and are both powerful anti-oxidants. Zinc is essential for the production of muscle-supporting hormones.

Ginseng

Ginseng boosts your cardiovascular, immune and nervous systems. It appears to build strength and endurance.

OVERVIEW OF THE TVP FRAMEWORK FOR BOXING

I hated every minute of training, but I said, 'Don't quit. Suffer now and live the rest of your life as a champion.'
Muhammad Ali

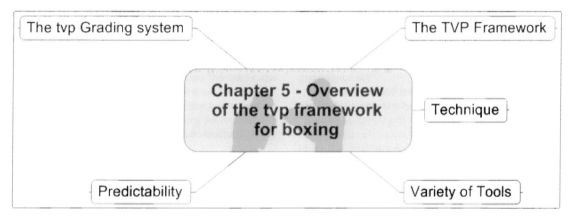

Mindmap overview of Chapter 5.

T	Technique
V	Variety
P	(Un)Predictability

One of the reasons why creative boxers and martial artists, or indeed any sportspeople, are not produced with regularity is that training sessions are too predictable and target the development of the average, rather than the outstanding. This may be in terms of pace, content or level of mental participation. Too many people expect a training session to be clearly road marked, with little emphasis on thinking and evaluation of impact of methods on outcomes. One of the most difficult things to do is to *create* your own session to develop the necessary attributes to be a winner. We have tried to design a framework that allows us to develop the most effective workouts. This chapter will look at a number of elements that make up the knowledge required for some to be accountable for the design of their workouts.

We will look at the tvp training framework, developed by the authors in *tvp: Comprehensive Boxing Concepts* (for

details see the Preface above), and all of the other factors to optimize your training.

Detailed research demonstrates that the characteristics of the greatest boxers can be captured in the tvp framework. Good boxers were epitomised by a certain quality of *technique*, a *variety* of technique and also the ability to be un*predictable*.

The top boxers possessed the ability to confuse their opponents by being unpredictable and technically very proficient. They also had certain attributes that enabled them to perform at the highest level. We have tried to study the attributes that should be devloped by the average boxer to make him the most effective boxer he can be.

The complete boxer needs to develop his technique to the highest level to ensure he has the ability to deliver effective and appropriate techniques in any situation. The complexity, in terms of variables, involved in ensuring that an appropriate technique and defence are used most effectively is huge. Thought processes involved need to be instinctive so that this is an automatic response. The boxer

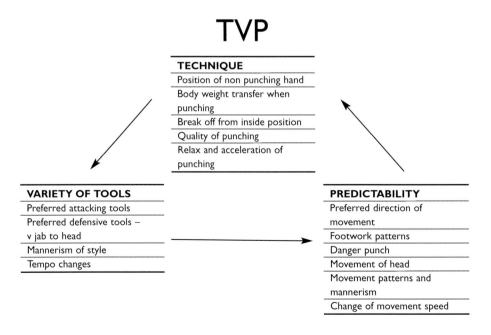

The tvp framework.

will find that the opponent will not necessarily behave the way he expects, so a certain degree of resilience and adaptability is required.

The complete boxer needs to ensure he possesses the best technique in terms of its effectiveness and explosiveness. This is achieved by employing the correct body mechanics in delivering the technique.

The good boxer also needs to ensure that he possesses a variety of techniques to cope with all the different styles of opponent he is likely to face. A variety of technique is needed to enable the boxer to tackle different situations.

In any sport, the performer that stands out is the one that does the unexpected. Boxing is no different. The greatest boxers had that ability to be unpredictable. In sport today too much coaching is focused on standardization, rather than encouraging creativity. This is why we consider the coaching of attributes to make the boxer unpredictable is vital.

The tvp framework encourages good training, either in groups or through personal training, to maximize the effectiveness of the competing boxer.

TVP

TECHNIQUE
Position of non punching hand
Body weight transfer when punching
Break off from inside position
Quality of punching
Relax and acceleration of punching

VARIETY OF TOOLS
Preferred attacking tools
Preferred defensive tools –
v jab to head
Mannerism of style
Tempo changes

PREDICTABILITY
Preferred direction of movement
Footwork patterns
Danger punch
Movement of head
Movement patterns and mannerism
Change of movement speed

The tvp framework elements.

Incorrect technique: elbow flaring.

Incorrect technique: non-punching hand too far forward.

Incorrect technique: non-punching hand too high.

Incorrect technique: non-punching hand too low.

Correct punching technique.

The tvp Framework

The tvp framework is based on the development of three core elements for the all-round fighter: Technique, Variety of tools and (un)Predictability. The ultimate aim of training in boxing is to be able to compete with confidence that you can win, irrespective of whether the opponent is experienced or a total novice.

The tvp framework is designed for boxers, irrespective of experience and standard, and is designed to develop the complete potential of the boxer. The aim is to get the boxer into The Zone – the area of training where he exhibits a broad range of excellently executed techniques in a creative way, unconsciously. The beauty of this framework is that there is no end point for the boxer. Improvement is possible irrespective of your standard.

In applying the tvp framework the boxer is also developing his strategic skills in being able to see specific weaknesses in opponents, as well as developing his own coaching abilities as he becomes aware of key characteristics in boxers.

Technique: What Makes a Good Punch?

A good punch should make contact with the desired target and return to its starting position as quickly as possible, ready for the delivery of the next technique. The technical requirements of good technique are:

Position of non-punching hand
The non-punching hand needs to protect the face and body, and be ready to deliver the next technique. By having the non-punching hand and the elbow in the appropriate position, the body is able to maximize the power generated and maximize the speed of delivery. The position of the non-punching hand is dependent on the distance between fighters. There are many instances where fighters become too rigid because they have both hands up, when they are clearly too far away to be attacked. The fighter needs to ensure that he fully understands and appreciates the role of distance: the further the boxer is from his/her opponent the lower his hands might be. The boxer has to find what is most comfortable and what will maximize his effectiveness. Prince Naseem and Muhammad Ali were masters at this ability to lower their defences when they were out of range, giving their opponent a false sense of security as they thought the lowered hands represented an opportunity to attack.

Bodyweight transfer when attacking and defending
Bodyweight transfer during the delivery of a technique is momentary. The power is transferred through the delivery of the punch and then restored to its original position instantaneously. This ensures the punch is delivered through maximum power and speed. As boxers become more competent the bodyweight transfer becomes internalized.

Quality of Technique Checklist
The quality of technique needs to explore the angle and line of delivery of the technique.:
* Line of delivery: need to be the shortest distance to the opponent or the most confusing line of delivery.
* Retraction: this can take many forms. The most basic is retraction to the starting point. However, retraction for more advanced boxers may actually mean getting into a position from where another creative attack may be delivered from an unusual angle.
* Use of hips, feet, elbows and shoulders: essential in delivering maximum power. However, the danger is that the boxer might try to isolate each of the body parts, thus giving less than maximal power. The key is appreciating that the whole body, operating in unison, is greater than the sum of the parts. Therefore, training needs to focus on engaging the whole body as one effective unit.
* Body lock off on opposite side to delivery: ensures accuracy of the punch.
* Position of head and chin during delivery and recovery.

Break off from the inside position
As boxers deliver a combination of techniques they leave themselves open to attack on completion of the combination. This is the point at which boxers will be at their most vulnerable. The coach needs to develop an automatic response comprising a break off after the last technique, from the inside position, of the combination. Boxers need to develop an ability to break off in different ways and directions.

Quality of punching and defences
Not surprisingly the mechanics of the delivery of the punch are crucial to ensuring an ability to deliver power, speed and variability in the punching.

Relaxation and acceleration of punching
The optimal technique is delivered by the boxer retaining a relaxed posture, allowing a pickup of speed as the technique is delivered from start to finish, when it arrives back at its starting position. Acceleration is defined as the rate of increase of speed, which means the speed of the punch, to deliver maximum force, needs to get faster as it makes contact and returns back to its start position. Achievement of this is ensured by engaging our fast twitch type IIa muscle fibres.

Variety of Tools

After the boxer has refined his technique, the principles of technique should be applied to a broader variety of technique to cope with different types of boxers. This also encourages boxers to investigate their potential from different perspectives. Good boxers will also read an opponent's strongest techniques, making it easier to counter. The elements that need to be specifically trained to develop a broad range of tools are:

Preferred attacking tools
Coaches need to understand the preferred techniques of their boxers, and look at developing a broader range of preferred techniques, making them more difficult to read. A tvp coached boxer should be able to deliver all techniques from a variety of positions with maximal force due to their ability to engage the whole body into the technique.

Preferred defensive tools
Similarly, the boxer needs to practise a broad range of defensive tools.

Mannerism of style
Boxers need to be aware of habits they employ as these can leave them open and predictable, if read by the opponent. The role of the partner or coach is to place the boxer under pressure so they do what they would do in a pressure situation and fall back on their habits or

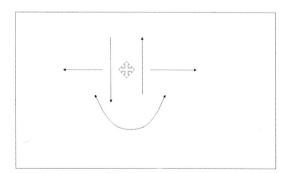

Direction options for movement.

mannerism of style. This effectively acts as a telegraph for the next range of techniques.

Tempo changes
A change in rhythm or tempo multiplies the possible combinations by a huge number. The boxer needs to be aware of any natural rhythms or tempo beats that he is delivering in his punching or movement, as his opponent will eventually read the situation and take appropriate action.

Predictability

Good techniques combined with a broad variety of techniques provide the boxer with a strong foundation for success. However, the champion boxer is able to use his foundation in unique and creative ways and so can be unpredictable. However, this ability has to be practised and isolated.

Head movement variations.

Predictability Checklist

In developing these attributes the boxer needs to:
* Identify weaknesses in their boxing make-up.
* Identify the benchmarks.
* Create training sessions around the isolated factors that need to be developed.
* Isolate specific areas and focus on these.

Preferred direction of movement

The fighter should be looking to be able to move in all different directions from any position with total ease. The first stage of the development is focused on awareness of any preferences in direction. Some people may prefer going left to right, for example. It is important to understand where your natural tendency to move lies. From this starting base you can explore how to develop the ability to move in all directions.

Footwork patterns

Footwork patterns adopted by the fighter are closely linked to preferred directions of movement. The boxer needs to be able to perform a complete range of footwork patterns and movements.

Danger punch

Boxers will try to set themselves up for the same technique that they feel most comfortable with. The boxer needs to be fully aware of their danger or favoured punch or technique.

Head movement

A boxer can make himself more unpredictable by continuously moving his head when delivering or receiving the technique. This also means that you are presenting a moving target, which is far more difficult to hit.

Movement patterns and mannerism

There are many different patterns of movement and style that can be incorporated in a fighting style. The universal pattern mentioned earlier demonstrates the different possibilities.

Change of movement speed

Boxers need to be able to change not only their direction, but also the speed of movement. The ability to change speed quickly, going from slow to fast or vice versa, is critical. These attributes do not suddenly appear – they have to be practised.

The tvp Grading System

One of the challenges that boxing faces is that not everyone actually wants to get into a ring and fight on a show night. There are many people training to improve their ability to fight and their physical attributes. An advantage of the martial arts and other sports is that these systems possess grading mechanisms that allow the athlete to assess the progress they are making over time. We have created a similar framework for boxing using the tvp coaching system. The tvp grading system is designed to test the development of physical attributes, rather than the athlete's ability to remember just a sequence of drills or combinations.

The tvp grading system comprises a number of elements:
* Movement and footwork patterns
* Techniques
* Forms: specially created progressive movements bringing together different combinations, footwork patterns, defences and counters
* Intuitive application of tvp in random situations
* Fitness: a key ability to be able to complete 3 × 3 minute rounds

The gradings are constantly being modified to ensure new developments are integrated immediately into an athlete's development programme.

The gradings are made up as follows (timescales are approximate and are based on three training sessions of 1 hour duration, as a minimum, per week):
* White belt – beginner (1–3 months)
* Red belt (4–6 months)
* Blue belt (7–9 months)
* Brown belt (10–12 months)
* Black belt (12–18 months)

The aim of anyone entering the grading system is to achieve Black belt status. The tvp Black belt will be expected to achieve the following:

Movement: Ability to carry out all footwork patterns in the tvp framework at varying speeds

Technique: Ability to delivery all techniques in creative ways through instinct

Form: 1–10

TVP: 3 × 3 mins – spar and hit the bag for 3 rounds of 3 minutes

Fitness: Target circuits of 2 × (6 × 30s) = 2 × 3 mins

THE ART OF BOXING

Attack is only one half of the art of boxing.
Georges Carpentier

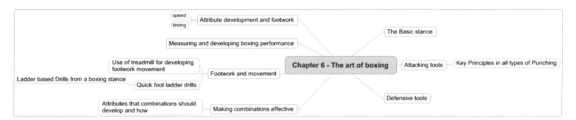

Mindmap overview of Chapter 6.

This chapter introduces you to the basics of the art of boxing, looking at the basic techniques needed to succeed. If you require more detail behind each of these elements and need drills to develop these techniques, please refer to *tvp: Comprehensive Boxing Concepts*.

The whole notion of developing the competence of boxing in individuals in this framework is based on three components. These are attacking tools, defensive tools and movement, including footwork.

Before we can start looking at the techniques needed in boxing, a strong foundation is a necessity. The basic stance is essential to ensure balance and optimization of power in the delivery of techniques.

The Basic Stance

A good basic stance is essential for the boxer to be able to move in a free and effective manner in all directions. A good and effective stance will allow the boxer to attack and defend himself without leaving himself vulnerable to

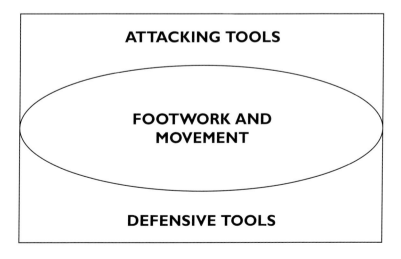

tvp core boxing components.

counterattack. Once the boxer has mastered the basic stance then he needs to be able to move in all directions without weakening his stance. In many instances, boxers have good stances that collapse with change. As people move the basic structure of their stance is destroyed. This occurs due to a loss of balance and redistribution of centre of gravity, leading to ineffective punches and defences while the boxer is moving. The stance needs to be maintained with minimal disruption during full and flexible movement.

A boxer should not be flatfooted but should feel the floor with the balls of the feet as though they were strong springs, ready to accelerate or slow his movements as necessary.

Potential Areas for Disruption Caused by Movement

Body part	Positioning notes	Vulnerabilities with movement
Head	Chin tucked into chest protecting throat area with forehead in a position allowing some degree of protection.	Head moves around uncontrollably and appears disconnected from rest of body. Sometimes caused by panic due to attack. Important to maintain focus through the eyes and head.
Right hand	By side of face. However, the hand should not be raised so high that it leaves the body exposed. This is achieved by lowering the head and achieving a tiger-like, curved stance.	Without training, the hand begins to drop and is then overcompensated by being raised too high. Movement takes the boxer's mind away from the hand to the feet. This holistic mindset needs to be trained.
Right elbow	Tucked in close to right hip providing full protection to the right side of body. The elbow should be placed on the right hip.	Elbow tends to float around in mid-air due to movement. By focusing the placing of the elbow on the hip, and then concentrating movement via the core of the body, and hence the hip, will ensure this position is maintained.
Left hand	Along centreline of body, approximately 2 fists away from centre of chest to minimize the degree of movement needed to attack and defend.	The left hand will sometimes drop and become disassociated from the rest of the movement. This may be caused by laziness or lack of feeling that the hand is dropping.
Left elbow	Tucked in close to the hip, allowing full projection from the hip when punching. The position of the elbow also ensures the correct body dynamics are used in the delivery of both defensive and attacking techniques.	The key danger with the left elbow is that a punch may be delivered with incorrect technique, by readjusting the elbow to compensate for the lack of input from the hip. However, we want to ensure we maximize the power with all techniques.
Chest	As with hip	
Hip	Positioned at around 45 degrees, with the ability to move either side by at least 45 degrees to maximize power	Generally, movement disengages the hip from the limbs due to incorrect mechanics of movement.
Knees	Slightly bent so as to be able to act as a shock absorber. Facing forward and slightly pushed outwards for improved balance and greater core stability.	Occasionally boxers straighten up too much, increasing the prospect of injury.
Heel	Lead heel: slightly off ground as it is easier to move a smaller area of the foot than a large area. Rear heel: off the ground due to reasons explained earlier.	There is a tendency for boxers to become flat-footed, which increases the prospect of injury due to increased resistance with the floor. This can also slow down movement.
Feet	Lead foot: slightly pointed inwards to facilitate rapid turning of waist for punching. Rear foot: Generally facing forwards to enable push for movement.	Key vulnerability due to movement is that the foot gets 'stuck' to the floor due to increased contact with the floor.

Starting position.

Fighting stance (side view): hands at height to protect face.

Fighting stance: shoulder width stance.

Fighting stance (side view): rear heel off ground, chin down, elbow tucked in.

Attacking Tools

The basic attacking tools in boxing are the:
* Lead hand jab
* Rear hand straight punch
* Uppercut
* Hook

These may be combined in many creative ways to increase the number of permutations possible. The core principles to delivering effective attacks are:

Explosion: delivering the technique with no telegraphing and minimizing the start time for the technique

Broken rhythm: breaking any rhythm in the delivery of a set of techniques

Body shifting: transferring body weight to maximize delivery power of the technique

Tempo changes: break patterns and tempo of attack with total body control

Relaxation and acceleration on punching: maximizing power in combinations through minimal effort

Key Principles in All Types of Punching

* All of the punches are driven from the feet upwards. The boxer should train to get the feet moving first in response to any trigger.
* Body should be totally relaxed to maximize power.
* Use the opposite side of the body as a lever for maximizing power.
* Make sure all punches are whipped out, meaning that they keep gathering pace until they return to their start position.

* Punch through your target to maximize power and impact.
* The power of the punch depends on the distance it travels.
* Bring the punch back along the same line to which it was thrown.
* Make sure there is no tension in the process of delivering your punch.
* Punch with your feet.
* Ensure your feet are in range before throwing your punch.
* Power comes from a drive off the feet, followed by the trunk and shoulder turning around an imaginary axis.
* The arms are the transmitters of force, which comes from the rest of the body. The arms should be relaxed until the last few inches of impact.
* Ensure the opposite side is kept firm to maximize leverage for maximum power.
* Arms out at 50mph – back at 100mph.

The Traditional Punches

This section will look at the technique involved in all of the basic single punches. The punches we will be covering are:

Jab
> Lead hand jab to the head
> Up jab
> Speed jab
> Short arm jab
> Blinding jab
> Jab to the body

Power jab
Attacking jab
Hook
Lead hand hook
Rear hand hook
Rear hand straight punch
Uppercut
Lead hand uppercut
Rear hand uppercut
Arm shots

In addition all punches can be delivered in a number of different ways:
Combinations
Feinting/non-contact hitting
Diversionary/drawing
Non-direct hitting
Countering
Counterattacking
Counterpunching

The Jab

Lead hand jab to the head
This is the primary and most used punch in boxing. The lead hand is the most instinctive punch used and also the most versatile, as the jab has the shortest distance to travel to the target. The lead jab is driven by the elbow directly from the hips and feet. The key to the mechanics of the punch is that the elbow follows a straight line as long as possible, as this represents the shortest distance between the start and end points of the punch. The punch is turned just before the point of contact. If the fist is turned too early the elbow will stick out and reduce the effectiveness of the punch, so timing of the rotation is critical. The turning of the fist will create a rotation of the elbow, which reduces the more extended

Up jab.

the arm. An important factor is that the punch finishes when it is returned to the starting point, not when it hits the target.

Up jab
The line of delivery of the up jab is suddenly changed by turning the fist upwards, and coming inside the opponent's defence.

The up jab is thrown out as a normal jab, but is turned at the very end as it makes contact with the target. This causes the punch to come inside the opponent's defence. The timing of the turning of the fist is crucial because if the fist is turned too early it becomes an uppercut and needs to be dealt with in a different way. The primary muscle engaged in the delivery of the up jab is the bicep.

Speed jab
The speed jab is a continuous firing of jabs, not giving the opponent time to recover, with the objective of confusing the opponent. This is ideal for getting close to a tall opponent or to gain the inside position against the opponent. This is mainly an arm-driven punch.

The speed jab is a series of short jabs that hardly come off the target. The idea is to redirect the opponent's

Lead hand jab to the head.

Speed jab.

Blinding jab.

attention away from his own actions and attacks. The speed jab may be mistaken for a number of continuous complete jabs.

Short arm jab

The short arm jab is a stopping technique used to stop an ongoing attack. As the opponent closes ground, a short jab is delivered to stop the opponent in his tracks. A key feature of the short arm jab is that the arm is not actually fully extended, with the punch being delivered before the opponent's attack has reached its maximum effectiveness.

Blinding jab

The blinding jab plays a number of vital roles as a:
* Range finder: helping the boxer gauge the distance to the target prior to an attack.
* Diversionary punch: diverting the opponent's attention and causing confusion.
* Impairing vision: to restrict the view just prior to landing a punch.

Power jab

The power jab relies primarily on power. This involves the boxer getting all of his body weight and power behind the punch.

Jab to the body

The body represents the biggest target area and is less mobile than any other part of the anatomy. The punch begins with the boxer squatting so that his hands are at the appropriate height without dropping his hands.

Attacking jab

This involves dropping the rear leg to get in line, push off the back foot with the front foot leading and attack with the jab.

The Hook

Lead hand hook

The lead hand hook to the head is probably the most effective punch in the boxer's repertoire. There are many variations of the lead hand hook in terms of angle and distance, but the basic principles remain the same. These can be visualized by picturing the sides of a clock and delivering punches along the different angles.

The key advantages of the lead hand hook are:
* It places the boxer closest to the opponent.
* The punch is not clearly visible.
* It travels a short distance to the target area.
* It is very difficult to defend.

The most common faults with the hook are:
* Pulling back prior to making contact.
* Winding up the punches prior to delivery.
* Punching past the centreline.

Lead jab to the body.

4 punch combination: hook.

4 punch combination: lead hand hook.

4 punch combination: rear hand punch.

4 punch combination: rear hand uppercut.

Right hook.

Right hook: close in.

Rear hand hook
The dynamics of the rear hand hook is similar to the lead hand hook. The effectiveness of the delivery might be enhanced by switching stance as the hook is delivered. This also provides additional power. A disadvantage of the rear

hand hook is that it is probably the easiest to anticipate from the opponent's perspective.

Rear Hand Straight Punch

The rear hand punch, more than any other, begins with the feet. The most common errors in delivering the rear hand punch are that the punch is left extended too long or the hand is brought back along a different line. Many boxers tend to leave the rear hand out too long. The hip plays a major role in ensuring the punch comes back along the same line and twice as fast as it when out.

The rear hand can suffer from an over-rotation of the hip, but this is less obvious than other punches due to the limited range of movement in delivering the rear hand. This means that the boxer has to ensure that one side of the body is locked as the punch is delivered.

Uppercut

Lead hand uppercut
The power for this punch comes very much from the ground, feet and hip. The boxer needs to ensure that the hand does not drop, leaving his face exposed. The boxer

Double rear hand.

Lead uppercut (1).   *Lead uppercut (2): slight dip.*   *Lead uppercut (3).*

needs to bend the knees to allow an appropriate starting point for the punch, while ensuring the hands are protecting the head. The distance travelled by the arm towards the target should be minimal, with the elbow being driven from the hip, by the feet.

A key aspect of the biomechanics of this punch is that the whip from the waist is more upwards than horizontal. In delivering the punch the boxer needs to ensure that he does not go past the target causing him to be im-balanced.

Rear hand uppercut
The rear hand uppercut has similar dynamics to the lead hand uppercut, but the challenges are similar to the rear hand hook.

Arm Shots

This involves the punch being delivered from the shoulder as a pivot point, rather than the hip, with the power being limited. This is a very good punch for creating a sudden shock and distracting the opponent.

Punch Deliveries

The basic punches mentioned above can be delivered in many different ways depending on the role and objective trying to be achieved. The different ways of delivering the punches are:

Right uppercut: starting position.   *Right uppercut: slight dip.*   *Right uppercut: follow through.*

Combinations

All of the principles with regard to punching, balance and alignment of the body have to be observed in delivering combinations. On many occasions, however, boxers try delivering combinations with their bodies in inappropriate positions for the follow-on punches. (For fuller details see below.)

Feinting/Non-contact Hitting

The boxer needs to maintain a mindset that he is actually

Non-contact hitting series: starting position.

Non-contact hitting series: lead hand to the body.

Punch to the body.

Non-contact hitting 1: rear hand to head.

Non-contact hitting 1: feint to body.

Non-contact hitting 2: lead hook to head.

Non-contact hitting 2: to body, rear hand block by target.

Non-contact hitting 3: lead hand to body, target drops both hands.

Non-contact hitting 3: rear hand to head.

Non-contact hitting 4: rear hand to head.

Non-contact hitting 4: target responds with left elbow.

Non-contact hitting 5: target responds with rear elbow.

Non-contact hitting 5: left hand hook to head.

Non-contact hitting 6: target responds with dropping left hand.

going to throw the punch fully. Rather than thinking he is throwing a feint, the boxer should think as if he is throwing a contact punch. This ensures that the correct body mechanics are maintained and that a response is achieved. This is why referring to this as a non-contact punch rather than a feint is more appropriate. Referring to this as a feint leads to the boxer totally changing the dynamics of the punch.

Jab, Hook and Uppercut as Non-contact Punches

The mechanics for these techniques are identical to delivering the actual techniques themselves, except there is no contact with the target due to the punch being pulled back just before contact.

The key to delivery is to move forward by sliding the front foot towards the opponent (by extending the stance, not stepping forward) while at the same time the rear hand is pulled slightly backwards so that it gives the impression of coming towards the target.

Non-contact hitting 7: target responds with dropping rear hand.

Non-contact hitting 7: left hook.

Non-contact hitting 8: rear hand to hand.

Non-contact hitting 8: attack with lead hand to head.

Non-contact hitting 9: lead hand to head causing target to raise arms.

Non-contact hitting 9: sink to attack to body.

Non-contact hitting 9: lead hand to body.

Feinting with feet 1: steps wide with lead leg.

Feinting with feet 1: follow with lead hook.

Front foot feint 2: starting position.

Front foot feint 2: feint with front foot.

Drawing 1.

Drawing 1: start position.

Drawing 1: drop rear hand to expose face.

Drawing 1: target responds with lead hook to face.

Drawing 1: layback to avoid hook.

Drawing 1: respond with rear hand.

Diversionary Jab/Drawing

The diversionary jab involves diverting the attention of the opponent for a split second, opening up a gap to land a jab. The objective is to get the opponent to take his eye off the jab that will be coming towards him. Ways in which this diversion can be achieved are:

* Drop the lead hand towards the knee and bounce it off explosively towards the target as a jab. The key is to drop the hand just as the boxer begins to move. If the hand is dropped much later than this he will be leaving himself open for an attack. It is also vital that the hand is dropped in an explosive manner from start to completion of the jab.
* Move the lead towards the left or right (for orthodox stance) and then explosively move the left hand towards the target with the jab. The main danger is that the boxer moves the hand too far out leaving an opening for a counter. As a rule of thumb, it is advised that the lead hand should not move outside of the box of the body.
* Move the lead hand towards the sky and then explosively jab towards the target.

Drawing 2: start position.

Drawing 2: attacker drops lead hand.

Drawing 2: target responds with rear hand, attacker cuts in with lead uppercut.

Drawing 3: starting position.

Drawing 3: draw lead hook to body by raising rear elbow.

Drawing 3: respond with rear uppercut.

Drawing 4: start position.

Drawing 4: raise lead elbow to draw rear hook to body.

Drawing 4: respond with lead uppercut to head.

Drawing attack to the body 5: start position.

Drawing attack to the body 5: raise both elbows to expose body.

Drawing attack to the body 5: target drops to attack body, attacker responds with lead, rear, lead hand combination.

Drawing attack to the body 5: with combination (a).

Drawing attack to the body 5: with combination (b).

Drawing attack to the body 5: with combination (c).

A diversion may also be used with the rear hand. The rear hand can be moved in similar directions to the lead hand.

Non-direct attacking principles

Non-direct attacking is a very advanced form of punch and involves the boxer changing the line of direction as the punch is being delivered. This will involve changing the punch completely. For example, the punch may have been sent out as a jab, but is changed mid-flight to a hook or uppercut.

Non-direct punching should not be premeditated as the first punch will not get the desired response from the opponent and render it useless. The boxer should be alert and flexible enough to be able to see the response as his first punch is being delivered. The point at which the punch will change direction is dependent on when the opponent responds.

Countering

There are two forms of countering: the counterattack and counterpunch.

Counterattack

This is the delivery of an attack just after your opponent has launched an attack, but lands before his attack has reached you. The initial movement is towards attacking as opposed to defending. The key success factor is the boxer's ability to read the intentions of the opponent and to possess the reflexes to deliver something quickly before he is attacked himself. The boxer does not allow the opponent to complete his technique.

In practising counterattacking it is vital that the boxer ensures that practise is focused on using visual stimulus to launch the attack. There is a tendency for people to use

Attacking Tools and Key Success Factors for Delivery

Punches	Basic	Counterpunch	Feinting or non-contact punching	Drawing	Counterattacking
Lead hand jab	Punch along the centreline from the hip	As basic, but retaining an attacking mindset while defending	Throw a basic punch but with the control to stop it at a critical moment	Expose your face to attack by dropping your guard, intentionally	Build your reactions to respond to opponent's attack
Rear hand	Explosion	Attacking mindset	Broken rhythm	Confidence	Speed
Hook	Minimal radius of action	Ability to anticipate	Demonstrating intent of initial movement	Exposing centreline and confidence to respond	Ability and confidence to avoid attack
Uppercut	Minimal exposure of face when delivering attack	Ability to anticipate	Ability to sell the delivery without exposing yourself too much	Exposing centreline	Ability and confidence to avoid attack

Counterattack 1: (1).

Counterattack 1: (2).

Counterattack 2: (1).

Counterattack 2: (1) different angle.

Counterattack 2: (2).

Counterattack 2: (2) different angle.

aural stimulus, which is not appropriate for the skills required.

Counterpunch
The counterpunch differs from the counterattack in that the counter is preceded by a defence of some description, such as a slip, parry or duck. This suggests that the counterpunch is easier to deliver as it works off a more physical stimulus, that is a defence, than the counterattack. The boxer allows the opponent to complete his technique so that he is able to carry out a defence.

Attacking Tools Summary

Attacking tool	Essential features	Critical skill
Traditional jab	Alignment. Use of hip. Turning of fist at end of technique	Explosion
Up jab	Turning of fist as the arm extends to its maximum	Timing
Short arm jab	Generating power through body	Timing
Speed jab	Ensuring contact with opponent is maintained for as long as possible	Speed
Power jab	Put all of the body behind the punch	Power
Blinding jab	Blocking the opponent's vision	Range
Arm shots	Punches delivered using the arms only	Timing
Feinting or non -contact hitting	Visualizing the complete punch and finishing it at around 90% of the technique	Selling the punch
Non-direct attack	Changing the direction and line of the punch after about 75% of the technique	Confidence
Counterattacking	Punch in anticipation of the opponent completing his technique	Timing
Counterpunching	Punch immediately after the opponent's attack	Timing

Defensive Tools

As with the attacking tools, there are core principles of defending that all boxers should fully understand:

Retraction: the ability to recover when attacking. The boxer is at his most vulnerable at the point of attacking, so needs to maximize his ability to recover from an attacking position.
Meeting the attack: the confidence to attack an attack. Attacking could be the most effective way of defending.
Breaking off: the ability to move away from danger after an attack, so as to reduce the risk of attack from your opponent.

We will look at a number of ways by which the boxer is able to defend, including:

* Footwork movements: using footwork movements to stay clear of the opponent
* Body defences: using different parts of the body to defend
* Hand defences: using hand-based techniques to defend

Attacking Tools Applications

	Combinations	Feinting/ non-contact hitting	Diversionary/ drawing	Non-direct hitting	Counter-attacking	Counter-punching
Lead hand jab	X	X	X	X	X	X
Up jab	X		X		X	X
Speed jab	X				X	X
Short arm jab		X				X
Blinding jab		X				
Jab to body	X	X	X	X	X	X
Power jab		X	X	X	X	X
Attacking jab	X	X			X	X
Lead hand hook	X	X	X	X	X	X
Rear hand hook	X	X	X	X	X	X
Rear hand straight	X	X	X	X	X	X
Lead hand uppercut	X				X	X
Rear hand uppercut	X				X	X

Double jab: first punch.

Double jab: second punch.

Double jab: withdraw punch.

*   Covering up: using limbs of the body to protect against attack

Defensive Tools In-Depth

The key to successful defence is to defend with an attacking mindset. This will enable the boxer to quickly turn defence to attack. It also removes a survival mentality and substitutes an attacking mentality. The boxer needs to ensure they are not relying on host indeterminable factors to decide at the last minute which technique will be most effective. Instead, the boxer needs to present himself in a way that minimizes the risk of an attack being effective.

All defences need to comprise minimal movement from the extended limbs such as the arms. Instead the body needs to be engaged as fully as possible, as early as possible. The defender should ensure there is no energy transfer to your opponent, which may leave you vulnerable to a counter.

All boxers should be comfortable with a good variety of defences, against every punch available. This will avoid being predictable and increase the pressure on the opponent to be more creative, thus pushing them to their limits. An increased number of defences in your portfolio will allow the boxer to cope with many different styles of boxer.

The mindset of the boxer in defence needs to force the opponent to commit the attack to as complete a position as possible. This is to avoid the opponent having time to react to the defence with a counter.

Defensive techniques and methods need to be continually practised in a variety of situations, against a variety of boxer types, until the defence has become intuitive and automatic, and can be delivered without a second thought.

The following are a series of defences to attacks to the head, either lead hand jab or rear hand punch to the head.

Defensive Tools Situations

	Moving towards attacker	Moving away from attacker
Footwork movement	Footwork involves pushing off the rear foot to increase the effectiveness of the defence	Footwork involves pushing off the front foot to maintain distance, and also the boxer should have his weight on the rear leg as he moves away from the attacker
Body defences	Involves moving off the straight line to avoid the attack.	Maintaining balance on both legs allows the boxer to shift his centre of gravity away from the attacker
Hand-based defences	Need to act sooner rather than later	Hand-based defences should be saved for the end of the technique
Covering up	Critical to success	Dependent on speed of attack
Moving with the attack	Less time to move with the attack	Very effective

Defence to lead hand to head: catching the punch.

Defence against rear hand to body: lead elbow (1).

Defence against rear hand to body: lead elbow (2).

*   Defender should not reach for the attack
*   Keep chin down, close to the sternum

Blocking

Blocking involves placing an obstacle in the line of attack. The obstacle may be an arm or hand.

The primary block involves maintaining the hand position by the face and turning the hand at the very last minute to catch the opponent's punch. However, the challenge is that the opponent will probably have all his bodyweight behind the punch and this will need to be countered by the defender reinforcing the catch with his own bodyweight. If the defender moves the hand too early to catch the attack, a good boxer will alter their line of attack, taking advantage of the defender's exposed area. A key to success is to visualize the defence being delivered by the defender's body and not just the hand. A certain degree of head movement is also required to ensure the block is successful.

A huge amount of confidence is needed with this defence to make it work. The only way to build this confidence is through practise and being comfortable with a strong line of attack to your face. Key success factors in delivering the defence are:
*   Strength behind the block
*   Block is delivered as late as possible

Push Away

The push away requires the front foot to initiate the movement, with the rear foot actually moving first. As the front foot initiates the movement, the rear foot will move, thus extending the stance, momentarily, as the front foot catches up to the original stance length.

Step Back

The step back involves the front foot moving through from being the front foot to the rear foot, thus changing the stance from orthodox to southpaw, or vice versa.

Parrying

Outside parry
The outside parry involves moving the head outside of the line of attack of the incoming punch, using the rear hand to shift the hand off the centreline. One of the dangers of this punch is that it can be left off-centreline too long, allowing the attacker to change his line of attack. Therefore, the parrying hand needs to return to the

Defence against rear hand: outside elbow (1).

Defence against rear hand: outside elbow (2).

Defence to lead hand to head using step back: start position.

Defence to lead hand to head using step back: completed position.

Defence to lead hand to head using outside parry: starting position.

Defence to lead hand to head using outside parry: move lead hand forward to create space for parry.

Defence to lead hand to head using outside parry: completing the parry.

Defence to lead hand to head using inside parry: start position.

Defence to lead hand to head using inside parry: intermediate position.

Defence to lead hand to head using inside parry: completed position emphasizing pushing away the attack.

centreline as soon as possible. Effectiveness of the parry is increased by committing more bodyweight to the front leg.

Inside parry

The inside parry involves moving the head inside of the attack, and moving the attacking limb from the inside to an outside position. Again, the contact time should be minimal, with the counter being delivered as soon as possible, to avoid providing an opportunity for the opponent to counter.

Parrying against the jab to the body

Parrying against a lead hand jab to the body involves deflecting the incoming punch away from the target, as with the previous parries. The hand needs to recover to the start position as quick as possible, so as to avoid being in a vulnerable position. Contact with the opponent's hand should be minimal. The use of the parry for punches to the body should be minimal as it might leave you heavily exposed.

The parry is ideally suited to a body attack where there is a full commitment from the attacker, making it difficult for him to alter his direction of attack.

Defence against rear hand to body: inside parry (1).

Defence against rear hand to body: inside parry (2).

Defence against rear hand to body: outside parry (1).

Defence against rear hand to body: outside parry (2).

Defence against lead hand to body: outside parry (1).

Defence against lead hand to body: outside parry (2).

Defence against lead hand: dipping technique.

Defence against rear hand to head: outside parry (1).

Defence against rear hand to head: outside parry (2).

Defence against rear hand to head: outside parry (2) close up.

Defence against rear hand to head: outside parry (3) close up (note the recovery to the original position).

counter to the body. Timing is also vital to ensure that the attacker cannot alter the direction of his attack.

Slipping

Slipping involves the movement of the head to either inside or outside the line of attack. Timing is critical to avoid allowing the attacker to change his line of attack. The degree of head movement is minimal and should be recovered to its original position as soon as possible. There is considerable surprise as to how little the head needs to move from centreline to avoid the attack.

Slipping inside
The slip inside has to be accompanied with the lead hand covering the attacker's rear hand, as the boxer will be exposed to the attacker's other punch.

Slipping outside
Slipping outside is a safer place to counter from as the boxer moves away from the opponent's strong right hand.

Dipping

Dipping involves moving the target (the head) below the line of attack. The key to success is to maintain a vertical spine, so that the dipping action does not move the face closer to the punch. The dipping action is driven by a squatting type movement. The eyes of the defender need to maintain eye contact with the opponent. As the boxer descends the hands should rise to maintain their relative position to the face. This also allows the delivery of a

Defence against lead hand: starting position.

Defence against lead hand: slipping inside.

Defence against lead hand: starting position (2).

Defence against lead hand: slipping outside.

Defence against lead hand: slipping outside (2).

Defence against rear hand to head: inside slip (1).

Defence against rear hand to head: inside slip (2).

Defence against rear hand to head: outside slip (1).

Defence against rear hand to head: outside slip (2).

Inside Wedge

The inside wedge, when executed correctly, can have a huge shock effect on the opponent, as he delivers his rear bent arm attack to the face. The lead arm moves inside the opponent's rear hand, wedging the forearm at the crook of the opponent's elbow. The opponent's arms stiffen, forcing the rear hand away from the target.

Layback

The layback involves a shift in the centre of gravity with no movement of the feet. The body is evenly positioned on the legs, and the centre of gravity is moved further away from the attacker, but allowing a quick recovery for a counter.

Defence against rear hand to head: inside wedge (1).

Defence against rear hand to head: inside wedge (1) close-up.

Defence against rear hand to head: inside wedge (2).

Defence against rear hand to head: inside wedge (2) close-up.

Defence against lead hand to body: inside wedge (1).

Defence against lead hand to body: inside wedge (2).

Defence against rear hand to body: inside wedge (1).

Defence against rear hand to body: inside wedge (2).

Defence to lead hand to head using layback 2 - start position.

Defence to lead hand to head using layback 2 - completed position.

Defence to lead hand to head using layback - completion of layback.

Defence to lead hand to head: rolling inside to out (1).

Defence to lead hand to head: inside to out (2).

Defence to lead hand to head: rolling outside to in (1).

Defence to lead hand to head: rolling outside to in (2).

Defence to lead hand to head: rolling outside to in (3).

Rolling

Rolling means dropping as in a dip and then moving to the inside or outside of the attacker. The key is to avoid bending forward at the hips as this will move you close to the attacker.

Defences Against Jab to the Body

Elbow block

The elbow block is a very effective block and embraces simple rotational movement around the spine, and using

Defence against lead hand to body: lead elbow (1).

Defence against lead hand to body: lead elbow (2).

Defence against lead hand to body: rear elbow (1).

Defence against lead hand to body: rear elbow (2).

the elbow to redirect the attacking jab. The elbow needs to be kept close to the body so as not to leave any aspect of the body open to an alternative attack. With the appropriate positioning of the elbow, readjustment is possible allowing the block to change to a parry, if necessary. As the jab nears the target area the body should be turned towards the jab, allowing the punch to be caught on the elbow or forearm. The elbow is kept close to the body, but not fully tucked in case the elbow is pushed back into the body by the force of the punch.

This is one of the safest blocks.

Shoulder blocking

Shoulder blocking involves deflecting the oncoming punch using the shoulder to redirect the path of the punch. The deflection is driven by the waist turn and needs to ensure that the shoulder is not moved too far away from the chin.

Generic Defending

Under this section we will look at some of the generic principles of defending. These essentially include covering up, footwork and head movement.

Covering Up

The three types of cover, which are appropriate for infighting as well as more distance-based sparring, are:
* Double arm cover
* Half cover
* Cross arm cover

Double arm cover

Both hands are kept in a high position, palms facing the defender, with shoulders rounded protecting the boxer against possible hooks. Elbows are kept into the sides, and should always present a moving target. There should be a very small gap between the gloves to watch the opponent, but not big enough for a punch to get through. Due to the position of the hands, the most natural type of follow-up punch will be straight punches.

Half cover

Many boxers have found this cover leaves them feeling open and vulnerable. For this cover to work the boxer will need to be on the ropes. This cover is ideal for a tall boxer where the ropes are relatively low.

Cross arm guard

From a crouching position the boxer will have the right arm protecting the head and chin. The left arm protects

Defence against rear hand to head: shoulder deflection (1).

Defence against rear hand to head: shoulder deflection (2).

Double arm cover (1).

Double arm cover (2).

Half arm cover (1).

Half arm cover (2).

Half arm cover (3).

the body with movement all the time. The boxer should be moving at all times. Covering should be treated as a last ditch effort.

Footwork and Movement

A key area of boxing that is often treated in a very insular way and separate from the rest of boxing is footwork development. We see footwork as the main foundation of boxing and the key differentiator between the champion and the also-ran. All boxing techniques are based on a strong foundation in the feet and the effectiveness of the technique is laid in the ability of the boxer to move economically. The foundation of the boxer is footwork.

The role of feet – front foot, rear foot
The role of feet in movement is based on the notion that you are trying to maintain the stance for as long as possible. A major factor in ensuring that balance and stability are maintained as the boxer delivers his punch is understanding how to make the feet work most effectively, while maintaining the structure of the stance. The key principle to movement is that the foot and leg furthest away from the target and desired direction will push the front leg to move first, followed by the rear leg. This movement suggests that the rear leg rebounds back to maintain the stance length and position, in the shortest possible time. This pattern of movement ensures maximum speed and power being generated from the floor through the body.

This skill of movement can be developed quite simply by getting the boxer to punch moving up and down and side to side, while punching focus pads.

Cross arm cover.

The key to succeeding with movement and footwork is to ensure that rear and front feet are slightly off the ground, so that the boxer is moving on the balls of his feet. The effectiveness of the movement is also maximized with a slight jump in the air for turning, to avoid injury. This method is used extensively in other sports. The athlete turns without the feet being in contact with the floor, thus avoiding friction and resistance, leading to injury.

Ability to move in all directions
The boxer needs to ensure that he is able to move in the following directions:
* Forward/backward
* Sideways to the left/sideways to the right
* Circular movement clockwise/circular movement anti-clockwise

Range of movement
The range of movement for each boxer is very much dependent on the individual's ability to maintain balance and stability, while covering different patterns across all areas of the ring. The primary requirement is to maintain the stance and ensure that this position is maintained as you move forward, backward and to the side. A broad variety of movement will allow the boxer to deliver a broad variety of punches from many different angles and positions. A boxer's ability to move will depend on the quality of the starting stance. This means good distribution of weight along the stance, with knees bent and an adequate push from the leg furthest away from the target. While moving the good boxer will maintain a good upper body balance and weight distribution, which allows him to utilize the full body behind the power of the attack.

A boxer's range of movement is enhanced by working on a mentality of beginning and ending in the same stance, as this will ensure the optimal delivery of the technique. However, this is only possible if the boxer stretches his movement during the interim phase of the delivery of the technique in the appropriate direction. The stretching movement also provides additional power in the delivery of the technique, so it plays a double role.

The key requirement for movement to ensure the

Varieties of Movement

Movement	Stance	Description
Forward	Orthodox or southpaw	Rear leg is bent and coiled to generate power, with rear foot off ground. Rear foot drives power through the right leg, extending the leg, causing the front foot to move first followed by the rear foot to maintain the stance length
Backwards	Orthodox or southpaw	Front foot is pushed into the ground causing the front leg to extend, pushing the rear leg away from the opponent. Once the rear leg has moved the front foot is recoiled to recover the original stance position
Moving sideways left/right	Orthodox/southpaw	The leg furthest away from the target is bent and extended to take the closest leg towards the desired direction, with the furthest leg recoiled to its original position
Moving in a circular direction	Orthodox and southpaw	The boxer turns on the ball of the rotating foot and ensures the stance length is maintained

boxer is delivering the most effective techniques is that the leg furthest away from the target is used to supplement the power of the punch. This is relatively straightforward for linear and lateral movement punches. However, the challenge is when you are punching with a circular movement. If you move using your front foot at the base of movement, the chances are that your end position will be misaligned with the target. This means that the front foot needs to move before you turn on the front foot. Therefore, the front foot needs to readjust itself so it is aligned with the opponent before producing the circular motion around the front foot.

Another key aspect of movement is the ability to maintain punching combinations as movement is achieved so that the momentum of movement is embraced in the punching power. We always encourage our boxers to continue punching as they move and also to keep moving as they punch. This ensures you are punching as one complete unit, thus maximizing power and speed.

Key footwork principles
* Use the foot and leg furthest away from the opponent to drive towards the target.
* In delivering punches use a pushing sensation rather than a pulling one.
* Ensure both feet are balanced on the balls of your feet, with heels slightly off the ground. The purpose is to reduce friction and hence increase speed, not over-stress the calves and ankles causing injuries.
* Make your movement a gliding motion, with minimal reduction of contact with the floor.
* The end position is the one most appropriate for delivering the technique, so you need to work back from that.
* Footwork should be from a stance that supplements the punching technique, not replaces the punching technique.

* Feet should never be too close or too far apart, except during the minimal transition stage from one position to another.
* Keep the upper body relaxed during movement.
* Maintain centre of gravity of body as you move to ensure you deliver maximum power.
* All movement involves the coordination of hands, feet and mind.
* Create your own rhythm in movement.
* Study the opponents' footwork and maximize the impact of any mistakes and errors made by him.
* The length of the step forward or backward should be aligned with the length of the step of the opponent.

Footwork Patterns

Variety of movement
One of the best ways to encourage free-moving patterns is to adopt the Universal Pattern of Movement, first touted by the famous American karate coach Ed Parker. Boxers need to be able to be flexible and mobile in multiple directions, due to the random nature of sparring. The pattern in the accompanying diagram suggests that there is no limit to the possibility of directions and footwork combinations. Boxers should examine and play around with the possibilities to become more creative and unpredictable.

As a training tool it is suggested that you draw the pattern and place your feet at any point and practise the different movements.

Good footwork will enable you to get out of challenging positions, such as on the ropes and in corners. Good footwork enables you to defend against any punch and attack in boxing. You are able to pull an opponent out of position with good footwork causing him imbalance.

You can defeat an opponent with feet, by pulling him

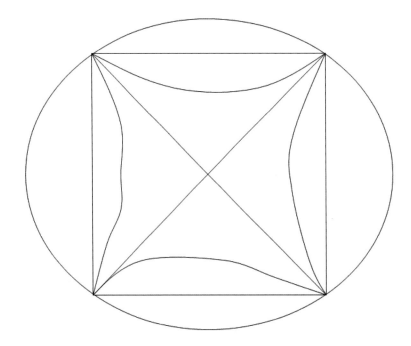

The Universal Pattern of Movement.

out of position. You can pressure an opponent with feet and can constantly change pace, thus confusing the opponent and keeping him guessing.

Also, bear in mind when using your feet for defensive purposes and attack, you leave both hands free to counter. As you can see movement, balance and footwork are all intrinsically linked.

Role of the front foot
The front foot in the stance essentially has two roles:
Range finder: the front foot needs to maintain distance, that is underneath or close to your opponent, while ensuring head is out of range.
Shock absorber: with the front knee bent, the front foot acts as a shock absorber when hit, allowing a timely response to the attack.

Role of the rear leg
The rear leg has the following roles:
Power Driver: the rear foot allows the hitter to transfer his body weight towards the target, with any punch.
Acceleration Enhancer: the rear foot allows explosion,

Footwork development: starting position.

Footwork development: push sideways.

Footwork development: push backwards.

Footwork development: push sideways to start position.

Foot stamping drill (1).

Foot stamping drill (2).

Foot stamping drill (3).

through the combination of elastic muscle and tendons in the leg.

Springback: the rear foot allows instant reaction to come back at an opponent.

Sidestep

The primary purpose of the sidestep is to change direction quickly in an explosive manner, maintaining balance and posture. This ensures the opponent is pulled out of position and needs to readjust his stance, thus providing an opportunity to gain advantage.

The sidestep is very effective against an opponent who is fully committed to his attack. The sidestep relies on the boxer's ability to push off from either the leading or rear leg in a split second:

* Make a slight pullback off your front foot
* At the same time, or possibly before, step off with your rear leg to the side, bringing your front foot back on guard to its original position in a short, balanced movement.

Sidestep (1).

Sidestep (2).

Sidestep (3).

Role of Feet in Body Movement

Footwork moves	Front foot (assuming orthodox stance)	Rear foot (assuming orthodox stance)
Moving forwards	Maintain balance	Pushing force
Moving backwards	Pushing force	Maintain balance
Moving to the left	Maintain balance	Side push force
Moving to the right	Side push force	Maintain balance
Circular movement to left	Pivot point	Push force
Circular movement to right (no change in stance)	Pivot point	Push force
Circular movement to right (with change in stance as boxer moves backwards)	Push force	Pivot point

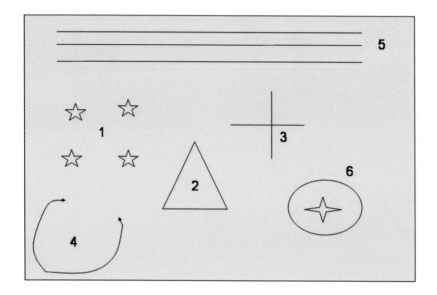

Movement patterns for warm-up.

Quick Foot Ladder Drills

A great tool for developing footwork and improving the boxer's ability to move is the quick foot ladder. The quick foot ladder has been designed for professional sports-people and athletes who need to develop speed, agility and quickness in their movement. We have devised a range of movements starting with developing the fast twitch fibres in the feet and leg muscles. These exercises are largely designed for developing quickness. However, our experience has shown that people are not really clear on how this changes and supplements their boxing style and technique. We have found that a key factor is to create quick foot ladder drills in the ring, with relevant boxing-based patterns. We have designed and identified a number of critical boxing-based footwork drills to enhance the style of the boxer.

Ladder-based drills from a boxing stance

The question we are always asked is, 'What is the relevance of the ladder when performing movement in a boxing stance?' The width of the ladder is excellent for

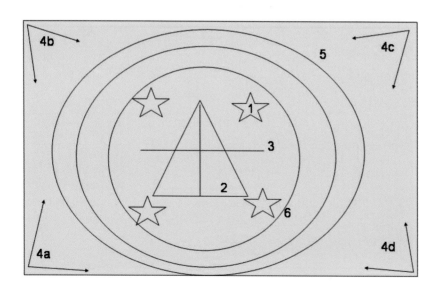

Movement patterns for circuit training.

Objectives of Quick Foot Ladder Training in Boxing

Objective	Drill	Output
Maintaining correct stance while moving	Using the ladder in stance while moving forward, backward and sideways, delivering punch combinations	Correct way of combining hand and feet movement
Transitioning from one stance to another	Delivering combinations from orthodox to southpaw, from linear to lateral and circular	Free-moving stances
Altering footwork pattern within a combination routine	Delivering combinations from one footwork pattern to another	Adaptability and unpredictability
Maintaining upper body balance while moving	Introducing variety of combinations while changing footwork patterns	Stability and power generation

ensuring that a relevant stance is maintained, with an appropriate width and weight distribution. The ladder also provides an ideal tool for maintaining an appropriate distance for movement. Eventually the boxer will be looking to move freely without having to look at the ladder, without losing the fundamental structure of the stance.

Another key benefit of using the ladder is to improve the boxer's ability to punch and move in all directions. One of the key aims of the coach is to ensure that the boxer is able to move forward, backward, left, right and circular, while delivering a punching technique. The boxer should be comfortable changing his pattern of movement and the

pattern of punches to remove any degree of predictability that might exist.

We have provided some drills, but we need to emphasize that the only blockage to success is the boxer's own imagination.

Use of Treadmill for Developing Footwork Movement

The foundation of a good boxer is footwork and movement. One of the challenges facing coaches is maintaining punching power and variety, while maintaining movement and footwork. After studying different systems used for

Treadmill-based Training

Objective	How to use the treadmill	Output
Hit and move	From standing position, drop into stance and deliver punch. Move away in stance after delivering punch	Footwork
Developing hand speed	Increasing the number of punches in the combination to the pad holder, while in stance. Following combination move back to stay on treadmill	Hand speed and punch variety
Lateral footwork	Working combinations while moving left to right, and vice versa	Multi-direction movement
Developing reaction speed	Increasing the speed of treadmill forces the boxer to become more instinctive in reacting to different situations	Reaction and intuition
Moving with fluidity	Increasing the speed of the treadmill, to force a faster, instant reaction and embrace the forward flow of energy into your own technique	Body moving as one
Moving feet with all technique	Increase the complexity of the combinations while on the treadmill with increasing speed	Hit and move

Quick foot ladder drill 1: hook with step.

Quick foot ladder drill 1: starting position.

Quick foot ladder drill 1: lead hand jab with step.

Quick foot ladder drill 1: rear hand with step.

Quick foot ladder drill 1: uppercut with step.

Quick foot ladder drill 2: starting position.

Quick foot ladder drill 2: lead hand with forward step.

Quick foot ladder drill 2: rear hand stepping back.

Quick foot ladder drill 2: hook with forward step.

Quick foot ladder drill 2: uppercut with step backwards.

Quick foot ladder drill 3: start position.

Quick foot ladder drill 3: step forward with rear leg.

Quick foot ladder drill 3: slide front leg back to rear leg.

Quick foot ladder drill 3: slide rear leg across ladder with rear hand punch.

Quick foot ladder drill 4: lateral footwork start.

Quick foot ladder drill 4: lateral footwork move to left.

Quick foot ladder drill 5: changing stance start.

Quick foot ladder drill 5: changing stance completion.

Quick foot ladder drill 6: side step (1).

Quick foot ladder drill 6: sidestep (2).

Quick foot ladder drill 5: sidestep (3).

sports such as basketball, we looked at how the treadmill can be used to increase the mobility of the boxer. The key principle that the treadmill can encourage in the boxer is to keep moving once techniques have been delivered. We found that the most effective way of achieving this is to have the boxer moving backwards on the spot, and then dropping into stance to deliver a variety of pad-based combinations. This serves two objectives:

* Forces the boxer to increase the pace of the combination, otherwise the boxer will fall off the treadmill as the number of techniques increases.
* Forces the boxer to move backwards once the combination is complete. Again, if he does not he will fall off the treadmill.

The treadmill is an excellent tool to develop and nurture the mentality of 'hit and move'. Footwork can be developed by increasing the speed and also the gradient of the treadmill. Once the boxer applies the learning in the ring, a more free-moving, free-thinking boxer is developed.

The treadmill also encourages a more intuitive response from the boxer, providing the coach does not make the pad holding segment too predictable.

The simple rules for using the treadmill for improving boxing are:

* Be specific what you are training:
     Maintain stance while completing hand techniques and then move
     Maintain movement whilst punching
     Ability to switch stance and deliver same techniques
* Focus on forward/backward and lateral movement
* Focus on developing fast twitch fibres in leg and calf muscles by increasing speed and gradients of treadmill
* Deliver multiple punches as if they were one punch
* Maintain stability while moving feet and hands

Making Combinations Effective

Within the tvp framework the area that represents the most challenging to development and progression has to be predictability. Even when someone gets to being unpredictable, a degree of predictability is developed. For example, Prince Naseem was probably the most unpredictable fighter of recent times. When you expected him to deliver a rear hand, he would deliver a front hand hook – defying all logic of physical movement and force generation. However, the fact that we expected him to do something unusual in itself suggested that there was a degree of predictability. The real challenge was for his opponents to prepare for the unexpected. This requires extraordinary coaching. The temptation of most coaches would have been to continue coaching in the areas in which they were comfortable, making their fighter work harder at the things that were going to be least effective!

One area where coaches might review their own performance would be in the training of combinations. The tendency is that once a fighter has developed good punching technique his programme begins to focus on combinations. The truth is combinations are introduced earlier in his development, perhaps too early, but that is another subject. Combinations on a bag or on pads are sexy. They energize the fighter and stimulate the feeling of being in a fight, with one important difference – there is no retaliation.

The positive aspect of performing combinations is that it encourages the fighter to think about a flurry of techniques as opposed to the 'one hit, one kill' scenario. Another important benefit of combination training is that it forces the fighter to train the hips to contribute to the generation of power in the hitting techniques. However, in the midst of performing combinations people do forget the intricacies of the technique, allowing their hands to drop prior to delivering the following techniques and

Using a treadmill to develop technique.

perhaps also allowing their hands to stick on contact with the target.

Positive and Negative Aspects of Training Combinations

Positive aspects	Negative aspects
Encourage use of hips to generate power	Encourage bad habits, such as hands dropping in between techniques
Encourage continuity of attacks	Can lack thought
Build stamina and endurance	Encourage predictability
Build rhythm	Combinations always tend to comprise either three or four punches
Develop coordination	Loss of stability after completion of combination
Develop ability to change	Failure to recognize that the same punch can be used in succession as part of a combination

A key aspect of the delivery of the combination is the beat. This is the sound that the techniques make as the fighter hits his selected target. A gap in the beat suggests an opportunity for the opponent to deliver a technique of his own. There is generally a tendency for huge gaps to exist between techniques in the delivery of combinations. This 'skip in the beat' will allow the opponent to hit the fighter.

Additionally, people have a tendency to practise the same combinations, which begin to create a sense of predictability. The fighter begins to expect the next technique. This is seen most effectively when a pad holder is holding pads for a fighter. Limitations in the ability of the pad holder will encourage the pad holder to offer the same targets again and again, thus developing a predictable response from the fighter. This situation can be overcome by training with different pad holders.

In the majority of cases predictability is due to the fact that the fighter practises the same combination, which usually follows an alternating sequence, for example, a left hand, right hand and left hand technique is the most common three-punch combination. Some of the mistakes in performing this combination are:
*   The first two techniques are hit with too much power. In reality, the opponent will have moved back after the first technique forcing the fighter to make up distance. This would require intense footwork.
*   The punches stick on the target leaving the fighter open to counterattack. The objective should be to

deliver the combination as 'one punch'. There should be no gaps between the techniques. For example, the second technique should be making contact as the first technique is beginning to be retracted.
*   The left-right-left combination or alternating sequence lends itself to becoming predictable, which means that the opponent will be able to read the fighter in most cases.
*   The fighter will tend to extend over the centreline, causing a loss of stability after the delivery of techniques. For example, the fighter might overreach with the first technique, causing him to be in a less than optimal position for delivery of the second technique. He may extend his hip too far after the second technique, which means he will have to recover centreline before the final technique can be executed, so losing time. After the final technique the hook will cause the hip to take the hand beyond centreline, again causing a loss of stability and a lack of preparedness for the opponent's response.

In training it is possible to see the lack of thought that goes into the training session as people continue practising the same combinations. The session is like a form of relaxation, where the fighter goes through the motions. This may be an effective physical workout, but unfortunately it does not develop the thought processes and instinct to become unpredictable. If the fighter were in a more thought-orientated mode, he would have the awareness to 'break the beat' at a critical moment or even, better still, respond to the coach breaking the beat. For example, one way of developing unpredictability would be for the coach to offer the usual pattern of pads such as left jab, right hand, left hook, and then change one of the pads without warning, encouraging the fighter to change his flow of hitting midstream.

Through continuous practise this ability can be made instinctive. However, without practise this will never develop, except by accident. The accompanying table shows a sample of tempos that can be used to deliver different sequences. The table can be used to develop a full range of combinations. (For a more comprehensive table, see *tvp: Comprehensive Boxing Concepts*.)

Tempos

Sequence	LRLRLR	LLRRLL	RRLLRR	RLRLRL
Punches	112233	112233	112233	112233

Key:
L – left, R – right
1 – straight punch, 2 – hook, 3 – uppercut

Another common fault in training combinations is that they tend to comprise three or four techniques. What happens in the fight if the opponent is still hitting back after this combination? Perhaps the reason for using three- or four-punch combinations is our ability to remember. One way to overcome this deficiency is to practise combinations over a period of time, for example five second bursts.

Have you noticed how combinations rarely have the same punch in succession? The fact is the quickest and most surprising attack is one that contains repeated techniques. However, there is considerable difficulty in delivering repeated techniques with power and confidence due to the fact that the hip has to be taken out and then driven back in. All of these challenges are overcome through practise.

Attributes That Combinations Should Develop and How

The key attributes that the practise of combinations should develop are:
* Ability to deliver a continuous sequence of techniques
* Stamina to deliver a number of techniques with sufficient power and timing
* Ability to deliver a number of techniques as 'one punch'
* Ability to deliver appropriate techniques, not predetermined techniques, with power and timing
* Ability to deliver a comprehensive range of techniques effectively, not just preferred techniques
* Ability to recover after each technique in a stable, ready-to-go position

Combination: lead jab, lead hook, rear hand, lead hand hook.

Training Combinations

In training combinations the fighter will need to identify why there are faults in technique. Usually the lack of timing is down to overextension of the hips beyond centreline. This is probably caused by the desire to deliver the tech-

Combination drill 1: (1) lead hand jab.

Combination drill 1: (2) lead hand retraction.

Combination drill 1: (3) lead hand hook.

Combination drill 1: (4) lead hand uppercut.

Combination drill 1: (5) lead hand jab.

Combination drill 1: (6) rear hand.

Combination drill 1: (7) lead hand hook.

Combination drill 1: (8) rear hand uppercut.

Combination drill 2: (1) lead hand.

Combination drill 2: (2) rear hand.

Combination drill 2: (3) lead hand hook.

Combination drill 3: (1) lead hook to the body.

Combination drill 3: (2) lead hook to the head.

Combination drill 3: (3) rear hand to head.

Combination drill 3: (4) lead hook to the head.

nique with power, as we tend to relate more distance with greater momentum, and thus force. However, force is delivered through acceleration of the technique, that is the increasing speed of the punch as it approaches the target. A conscious effort is required by a fighter to stop overextending after each technique in the combination.

Key steps in training combinations
* Establish the purpose of the combination
* Design an appropriate combination to fulfil the purpose
* Practise the combination slowly, with correct body mechanics on punch bag, followed by floor-ceiling ball.
* Speed up the delivery of combination on punch bag and floor-ceiling ball

SEQUENCE 1 LRLR	SEQUENCE 2 LLRR	SEQUENCE 3 RLRL	SEQUENCE 4 RRLL
1 2 3 4	1 3 2 4	2 1 4 3	2 4 1 3
2 3 4 1	1 3 4 2	2 3 4 1	2 4 3 1
3 4 1 2	3 1 2 4	4 3 2 1	4 2 1 3
4 1 2 3	3 1 4 2	4 1 2 3	4 2 3 1

Punch combinations.

1 – LEAD JAB
2 – CROSS
3 – LEAD HOOK
4 – UPPERCUT

SEQUENCE I LRLR	SEQUENCE 2 LLRR	SEQUENCE 3 RLRL	SEQUENCE 4 RRLL
U D U D	U D U D	U D U D	U D U D
D U D U	D U D U	D U D U	D U D U
U U D D	U U D D	U U D D	U U D D
D D U U	D D U U	D D U U	D D U U

Further punch combinations.

I – LEAD JAB   U – UP
2 – CROSS   D – DOWN
3 – LEAD HOOK
4 – UPPERCUT

* Using the floor-ceiling ball, deliver the appropriate technique in response to the position of the ball
* Get your coach to hold a pair of focus pads offering the practised combination
* Coach should be looking for gaps in delivery of the technique. Coach should deliver attack of his own in the gaps

* Coach then changes the techniques in the combination offering single different techniques
* Coach offers random pads
* Carry out 10 second bursts of punches at random on punch bag, counting number of techniques offered
* Practise with opponent in pre-arranged drills.

Summary of Attacking and Defensive Tools

	Lead hand jab to the head	Rear hand hook to the head	Head hook	Head uppercut	Lead hand to the body	Rear hand to the body	Body hook	Body uppercut
Block	X			X	X	X	X	X
Push away	X	X	X	X	X	X	X	X
Outside parry	X	X			X	X		
Inside parry	X				X	X		
Dip	X	X	X					
Inside slip	X	X						
Outside slip	X	X						
Roll in-out	X	X	X					
Roll out-in	X	X	X					
Inside wedge		X	X	X	X	X	X	X
Outside wedge				X	X	X		
Layback	X	X	X	X	X	X	X	X
Step across	X							
Shoulder defence		X						

Reprinted with permission from *tvp: Comprehensive Boxing Concepts* (BMC Global Services Publishing, 2005)

Attribute Development and Footwork

Attribute	Current score	Development in boxing training
Coordination		Deliver techniques and combinations while moving
Precision		Focus on hitting pads and select small target on bags. Also, hitting moving targets and hitting targets from unusual starting positions
Force		Focus on hitting through the target by engaging the whole body
Endurance		Design practise around Tabata intervals
Balance		Deliver techniques from an unstable platform, such as a bosu ball
Body feel		Personal body awareness
Form		Deliver techniques slowly and continuously, and record on DVD. Review movement
Vision awareness		Measure techniques against reaction time. Receive target from unusual angles to test peripheral vision
Speed		Deliver techniques without power
Timing		Delivering techniques on moving targets
Attitude		Increase stress and tiredness levels, increase complexity level if training and monitor performance

Timing Attributes and Development

Attribute	Description
Reaction time	Measure techniques against reaction time. This is the time taken to respond to a stimulus.
Movement time	Measure time of all techniques. How long does it to take to deliver the actual technique?
Cadence	Delivering techniques with a rhythmic beat to encourage flawless movement and coordination with hand techniques
Broken rhythm	Deliver combinations with triggers for alternative sequences
Tempo	The number of beats delivered in a combination
Counter time	Time taken to deliver a counter technique in response to an attack from your opponent

Speed Attributes and Development

Type of speed	Level	Description
Perceptual or perception speed		How quickly you recognize the need to move or punch, in boxing terms. Perceptual speed is the quickness of the senses to (1) Monitor the stimulus provided, (2) Interpret the stimulus, and (3) Convey the reaction to the brain in readiness for a reaction. For example, the perceptual speed is the time from when your opponent presents a target to when you notice the target. This speed is developed with a partner or coach offering totally random targets
Mental speed		How quickly your mind reacts with an effective physical reaction to an incoming, threatening stimulus from the opponent.
Reaction speed		The speed to deliver a technique in reaction to a stimulus from the opponent
Initiation speed		The speed taken from stimulus to initiation of the delivery of the technique
Performance speed		Time taken to deliver the technique. This is the movement speed to deliver the technique.
Adaptation speed		The speed it takes for the mind to select which technique to deliver in response to the opponent's attack or opening
Alteration speed		This is the speed it takes to alter the direction or delivery of a technique in mid-delivery
Recovery speed		The speed at which your technique recovers back to its start position after the technique has been delivered

Sample Workouts

The following shows some sample workouts with different objectives and outputs:

Speed drill: Throw punches as fast as possible with a minimum of four punches per combination. This routine will develop speed and anaerobic endurance. Increase the number of punches in the combination as you become comfortable with the existing number.

Outside drill: Throw a jab and straight power punch combination. Circle and jab. Throw your combination and move. Circle in both directions. This develops footwork and staying power for the fight.

Inside drill: Get in close with hooks and uppercuts. Slip, bob and weave. This develops inside power and stamina.

Change directions: If you usually circle left, circle right. Throw jabs while mixing in different combinations as you move. This develops coordination, endurance and change-up ability.

Jab: Do an entire round only throwing jabs. Snap out a series of single, double and triple jabs. Mix in feints. Move in both directions. This develops quickness, stamina and coordination.

Practice

The accompanying table shows some alternative combinations that demonstrate tempo changes. These should be practised regularly. As the body will not be accustomed to the rhythm of all these combinations there is a possibility that stiffness will result.

Measuring and Developing Boxing Performance

The following tables are an excellent means of improving the performance of the boxer and the intrinsic characteristics of good technique. We have taken some key aspects of different sports and martial arts and embraced them in the boxing training method. The tests and qualities are based around attributes, speed and timing.

Speed
A good boxer is able to deliver techniques on his opponent quicker, harder, and with less effort than his opponent, while avoiding being hit. A good, faster boxer has the following:

* a pair of fast hands, feet and body movement
* non-telegraphic moves and instantaneous reactions
* good coordination with hands and body moving as one unit
* perfect balance in motion in all directions
* awareness of your own body movement and performance.

Timing
An important factor for the boxer is the timing of delivery of the technique. There is little point in delivering the perfect technique in terms of power, for example, if the timing is totally wrong. The accompanying attributes are key to assisting the boxer to improve the timing of their technique.

CHAPTER 7

PAD HOLDING

All coaching is, is taking a player where he can't take himself.
Bill McCartney

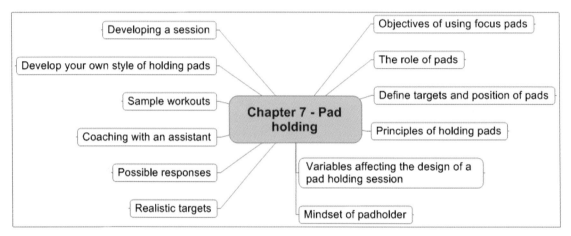

Mindmap overview of Chapter 7.

One of the key development tools for boxers is the focus pad. This very simple tool can be very influential in the development of fighters due to the degree of chaos they can create. However, in many cases they can also be quite destructive in the sense that they reinforce, and encourage, bad habits in the wrong hands. As with any other developmental tool, it is essential that focus pads are used correctly.

This chapter will look at the art of pad holding and where the focus of the coach should be in developing the most complete fighter. The coach needs to be very clear about the objectives and role of the pads in developing the attributes needed to create the most complete fighter. An important aspect of pad holding is the mindset of the pad holder. The pad holder needs to be thinking like an active fighter and not as a passive pad holder. Creativity is also vital and this is nurtured through understanding some basic principles of pad holding to allow the pad holder maximum flexibility in using the pads. We will also look at the application of pad holding to the tvp framework.

Benefits of the Focus Pad

* They allow and encourage a completely random response from the boxer, thus replicating a more realistic response than any other piece of equipment.
* They allow the pad holder to interact with the fighter, as a fighter, with minimal threat to the pad holder, thus encouraging greater creativity on the part of the pad holder.
* They encourage development of speed and reaction times on the part of the boxer.
* They simulate realistic attacks and defences, thus increasing the level of interaction and engagement with the boxer.

The potential benefits of focus pads are enormous, but their effectiveness is dependent on one vital factor: the pad holder. On their own, the focus pad is a piece of leather that can encourage repetition and the development of habit, both good and bad. For the focus pad to be a good developmental tool, it is essential that the pad holder is clear about the objectives of the workout. The danger with the focus pad is that in large gyms it is an ideal substitute for punch bags. Each pairing of fighters will have their own pair of pads, and thus it gives the impression of activity. However, in most cases those holding the pads tend to play no greater role than a punch bag, staying static and predictable – just like a simple bag.

Using Focus Pads

The key objectives of using focus pads are to:
* Simulate a real fight comprising attack, defence and counters
* Encourage accuracy of hitting a moving target that is of a similar size to key targets on a human being (the head and parts of the body)
* Develop unique combination of punches in a dynamic form, at unusual angles

The primary role of holding pads is to develop the following boxing based attributes:

Primary

Introduction of new techniques: By using coach spar gloves, rather than pads, a coach can introduce new techniques in a more realistic manner. This also allows the coach to semi spar with the boxer.

Development of speed: Specifically the pads are a great way to increase the speed of the boxer, but only if the pad holder is one step ahead of the boxer. The pad holder needs to ensure that his transition from one technique is smooth and that the targets are offered for a short period of time, thus encouraging the boxer to hit as fast as possible.

Accuracy of hitting a small target: The reality of hitting a target is that not only is the target small, but it is only on offer for a short period of time. The combination of these two factors makes it imperative that the boxer hits the target quickly and accurately. Therefore, the pad holder needs to present a dynamic target that also happens to be limited in size.

Development of reflexes and reaction times: Pads are an excellent way of developing reflexes and automating responses to different situations. In addition, by limiting the time that the pads are presented, the reaction times of the boxer are also enhanced quite significantly.

Develop an appreciation of range and distance: A major benefit of using the pads versus any other form of boxing equipment is the ability of the effective pad holder to recreate typical fighting distances, thus enhancing the boxer's appreciation of range and distance.

Develop recovery after an attack: By engaging with the boxer, the pad holder can deliver attacks that force the boxer to recover with attacks of his own.

Develop an ability to throw instantaneous counters: Dynamic pad holding encourages rapid responses.

Fault correction
There are many ways to use the pads to correct technique, thus giving positive feedback of the right technique. Examples may be found in the accompanying table.

Fight preparation
Pads can sharpen a boxer prior to entering the ring. The pads also sharpen the timing, accuracy and judgement of the boxer. Pads are excellent for working tactics. In

Fault Correction Using Pads

Fault	Method used by pad holder to correct
Flaring out of arms when punching	Use the other pad to highlight the arms flaring out. Stand the boxer adjacent to a wall or obstacle so that the elbow makes contact with a surface as a warning of the arm flaring out
Movement of body towards target when throwing rear hand punch	Pad holder can position one hand on the sternum so that the boxer receives feedback when the body is moving too far forward.
Insufficient curve on the hook	The pad holder places the other hand in front of the target so that the boxer has to curve his punch around the obstructing hand
Lack of head movement	The pad holder uses the other hand to initiate head movement
Finishing at the end of the technique, thus leaving himself exposed for a counter	The pad holder needs to think like a boxer and throw a counter immediately after the combination on the pads has been completed
Slow retraction of punch	As soon as the pads have been hit, the pad holder returns a counter to speed up the retraction of the technique

Fault correction: ensuring curve on hook. *Fault correction: keeping elbows in.* *Fault correction: over-commitment of body.*

addition, the boxer will feel the crispness in his punches before stepping in the ring.

Secondary

General cardio session
Many people train but do not necessarily want to compete, so pads can be very effective for providing a workout. One of the reasons for this is that the boxer does not need to do much thinking, as he will largely respond to what is offered to him.

Interval work
Pads are a very effective of way increasing the heart rate over a 2 or 3 minute round. In fact adopting a Tabata approach (see Chapter 8) is very effective in maximizing the workload on the boxer. Punching in clusters of 4, 5, 6 and 7 punches is very effective in producing a high work rate.

Defining Targets and the Position of Pads

One of the challenges for the coach is to position the pads in a realistic and relevant position to recreate the real-life scenario. In addition, the coach needs to be thinking one step ahead of the boxer, so that there is minimal time for the boxer to change the trajectory of the position. The pad holder needs to be able to recreate the real-life scenario with little distraction. A key question for anyone holding the pads is to decide what value is added using the pads, rather than just hitting a series of combinations on a punch bag or any other fixed target.

Firstly, the pads provide a dynamic, moving target that will be similar to an opponent. This means the pad holder needs to be in the mindset of a boxer or fighter.

Secondly, the pads can present a constantly changing and dynamic set of targets that can be changed at the last

minute, thus encouraging greater versatility on the part of the boxer.

Thirdly, the pad holder needs to remember that pad holding is programming certain responses from the boxer that can become predictable, so variety and change is essential to maximize the benefits of pad holding.

The key rules for holding the focus pads are:
* Keep the target as close to the original target as possible to encourage the appropriate body dynamics in the technique. The pad holder needs to be absolutely clear as to what the target is.
* The pad holder needs to ensure that they have thought about the following technique and ensured they are not slowing down the boxer by not offering the pad at the right moment.
* The pad holder needs to ensure that they incorporate the right angles and footwork patterns, and not just the hand combinations.

The accompanying photos show the positions in which the pads should be held to maximize the realistic perspective.

Principles of Holding Pads

Targets
The first key concept of pad holding lies in understanding what the pads actually represent. The pads represent targets on the head and body. Therefore, the pads need to be positioned in such a way that they allow the boxer to deliver appropriate punches to these targets.

A vital part of pad holding is developing an appreciation of what the pads signify, and how these are represented by the pad holder. The great advantage the pad holder has is that he possesses two hands, which happen to be shoulder width apart, allowing replication of the body. However, the pad holder needs to ensure that the following rules are never compromised:
* The focus pads should never be held outside of shoulder width. This is due to a lack of reality. It also increases the chances of injury to the pad holder as

Body and face target for switch attack. *Body target for right body punch.* *Face target.* *Face target for double hook.* *Face target for left hook.*

Face target for left uppercut. *Face target for right hook.* *Face target for right uppercut.* *Face target for straight and hook punches.* *Face target for uppercut and hook.*

Targets and Appropriate Techniques

Target	Most appropriate techniques
Front of head	Lead hand punch Rear hand punch
Jaw	Lead hand punch Rear hand punch Lead hand uppercut Rear hand uppercut
Side of head	Lead hand hooks Rear hand hooks
Front of body	Lead hand punch Rear hand punch Lead hand uppercut Rear hand uppercut
Side of body	Lead hand hook Rear hand hook

the body cannot be leveraged for the pad holder.
* The focus pads should be held a minimal distance (just safe distance) from the target they are simulating. This builds an innate appreciation of the target and where it is, which is vital in developing intuitive responses.
* The pad holder needs to ensure they are not presenting two heads by offering two consecutive punches to two different targets that are meant to represent one target, like the head.
* Ensure the pad holder is capable of replicating the same pattern on both sides, that is for both orthodox and southpaw

Variables Affecting the Design of a Pad Holding Session

Level of movement
* Low: static – pad holder remains in static position removing the dimension of distance in the boxer's decision-making process. This is ideal for technical development.
* Medium: unidirectional movement – pad holder encourages movement in either linear or lateral direction, thus introducing the notion of hitting a target that will be moving.
* High: multi-directional movement – pad holder encourages movement in all directions introducing a degree of randomness.

Level of technique
* Low: single techniques
* Medium: multiple combinations

Giant 1.

Giant 2.

Two heads!

Unrealistic body.

Unrealistic for hooks 1.

Unrealistic for hooks 2.

* High: multiple combinations following a defensive movement
* High: multiple combinations combined with counters. A very interactive movement

Level of chaos
* Low: very predictable
* Medium: combinations are known but not when to be delivered
* High: totally random responses

Level of decision training
* Low: low cognitive effort. Instructional
* Medium: preset scenarios. Variable practise
* High: random drills with considerable feedback and self-analysis

Mindset of the Pad Holder

A key to ensuring the success of achieving objectives with focus pads is for the pad holder not to think of themselves as a pad holder, but actually as an opponent. This creates a mindset and edge that is critical to ensuring that techniques delivered against a static target can actually be made to work against a real-life opponent.

The padholder needs to interact with the boxers as if he was attacking them. Clearly the level of attack will be dependent on the standard of the boxer.

Realistic Targets

Realistic targets are a key factor when holding pads. The pads must be held as close to the body and head as possible. This ensures that there is realistic response from the boxer. The correct positioning of the pads also ensures that the boxer adopts the correct, and appropriate, body mechanics for delivering his technique. If the target is positioned too high and wide, then the boxer attempts to compensate for this by adopting inappropriate body

Fault correction 1: (1) low non-punching hand.

Fault correction 1: (2) low non-punching hand.

Fault correction 1: (3) low non-punching hand.

Fault correction 2: (1) flared elbow.

Fault correction 1: (2) flared elbow.

Fault correction 3: (1) rear hand over-commitment.

Fault correction 3: (2) rear hand over-commitment.

Fault correction 4: (1) loose hook.

Fault correction 4: (2) loose hook.

Fault correction 4: (3) loose hook – alternative view.

mechanics. In addition, the boxer will also move his eyes from the target (the opponent) thus disabling his peripheral vision.

The pad holder must also constantly move around the boxer, so as to replicate the real-life scenario: rarely will the boxer fight an opponent who stands in a static position, offering open targets! The pad holder needs to adopt a mindset of fighter, not trainer. The only difference being that the pad holder cannot physically get hit. The pad holder is also predetermining the responses from the boxer.

In many instances the pad holder sees their role as purely one of target provision. However, the most skilled pad holders are very good at attacking their boxers. Throwing attacks at different angles and heights forces the boxer to combine defence with attack, thus replicating reality more closely.

Possible Responses

The role of pad holder is similar to an actor. The pad holder needs to replicate the typical responses of a fighter when the boxer throws the most common techniques.

The different levels of pad holding, as shown in the acconpanying table, are:

Basic: This is the most elementary level of pad holding. The pad holder tells the boxer exactly what the technique is and allows the boxer ample time to hit the pad and recover. The primary objective of the pad holder at this level is the development of technique and accuracy. Considerable time is given to correcting technique and ensuring the technical principles are adhered to. The focus of the pad holder at this stage is the development of technique and variety of technique.

Intermediate: At this level the pad holder begins to introduce some movement to ensure the boxer gains appreciation of range. Additionally, the pad holder begins

Unrealistic targets.

Double jab with partner and pads (1).

Double jab with partner and pads (2).

Double jab with partner and pads (3).

Double jab with partner and pads (4).

Response 1: lead hand punch to pad.

Response 1b: pad holder moves back.

Response 2a: rear hand punch to pad.

Response 2b: pad holder moves back.

Response 3a: pad holder throws lead hand to ensure correct turn of body for technique.

Response 3b: lead punch to head.

Response 4a: left uppercut to body.

Response 4b: body curls over.

Response 5a: left uppercut to body.

Response 5b: pad holder covers up.

Response 5c: uppercut to head.

Response 6a: left hook to head with pad holder moving target.

Response 6b: pad holder moves back and attacker delivers hook to head.

Response 7a: rear hand to body with pad holder moving away.

Response 7b: uppercut to head.

Response 8a: lead hand to body with pad holder bending over.

Response 8b: uppercut to head.

Response 9a: lead hand to body.

Response 9b: pad holder moves back.

to introduce visual cues, such as raising the pads to act as a cue for the delivery of the technique. At this stage the pad holder starts to become more interactive with the boxer. The cognitive input of the boxer now begins to increase.

Advanced: At this stage the pad holder takes the boxer into the ring, ideally, and starts to move around in multiple directions. The pad holder also throws punches of his own to ensure the boxer adopts an appropriate mindset. There are cases where boxers become so used to attacking the pads that they forget the opponent will also throw punches back, and that the mode of delivery of technique might need to be quite creative to allow for defence. The amount of time offered for the boxer to hit the pads is minimal. The pad holder is now trying to build appropriate responses to many different situations. At this stage the pad holder will also start to attack the boxer and offer pads simultaneously to build reactions and a countering mindset.

Competitive: The competitive stage is almost fight mode. The pad holder interacts with the boxer in the ring at full speed as if they are involved in a fight. The only difference

Typical Boxing Responses to Various Techniques

Technique	Typical response of opponent	Application in training
Jab/rear hand to head	Move backwards	Get boxer to throw a double jab to the head. Pad holder retreats after first jab, thus encouraging boxer to follow up with a combination of footwork and punch
Jab/rear hand to head	Block punch	Get boxer to throw a counter to build awareness in boxer
Jab/rear hand to head	Lean back	Get boxer to follow up with punch to the body
Hook to the body	Body curls over	Get boxer to follow up with a bent arm punch to the head
Hook to the head	Move head to body level	Place the focus pad at body height for a hook to the body
Hook to the head	Lean back	Pad holder steps back offering a pad for a stepping or rear hand punch
Uppercut to head	Head moves upward	Pad holder offers a body shot
Jab/rear hand to body	Body curls over	Pad holder offers uppercut to bring opponent up

Pad Holding Levels and Complexity

Level of interaction	Level of movement	Form of initiation of technique	Attitude of padholder	Time to hit pads
Basic	Minimal	Verbal command	Instructional	No restriction on time
Intermediate	Medium paced in single directions	Visual cues by raising the pad	Instructional	Slow to medium timing
Advanced	Medium paced in multiple directions	Pad holder attacks initially	Attacker/ defender	Limited, as in a realistic situation
Competitive	Fast paced in all directions	Visual and random	Fighter	Minimal

Improving Boxing Technique Through Pad Holding

Element	How?
Position of non-punching hand	Pad holder should use opposite hand to fire reminders to the boxer that the other hand should be up when in fighting range
Bodyweight transfer when punching	Every now and then the pad holder should remove the pad as the boxer throws the punch to test if the bodyweight transfer is in control
Break off from inside position	The pad holder throws a punch as a response to the boxer's combination to encourage an appropriate break off
Quality of punching	There are many ways of improving the quality of punching using focus pads
Line of delivery	Introduce restrictions in movement, such as a wall
Retraction	The pad holder should throw a punch after the attack to encourage appropriate retraction
Use of hips, feet, elbows and shoulders	Place the pads at the knees, hips, elbows and shoulders to encourage correct body mechanics
Body lock off on opposite side to delivery	Restrict movement of one side of body with a wall or using opposite hand
Position of head and chin during delivery and recovery	Pad holder needs to throw an appropriate punch when a gap appears to remind the boxer of the faults in technique
Relaxation and acceleration of punching	Offer the focus pad for minimal time to encourage acceleration

is that the pad holder will not be hit, except on the pads. Pads are offered for a minimal period of time, but enough to encourage the boxer to punch and grow. Again, there is considerable emphasis on attacking and encouraging counters.

As the accompanying table demonstrates, the various tvp elements are improved at different stages of the boxer's development. The reason why this is so important is that the role played by the pad holder has to change fundamentally. At the basic level the focus is very much on demonstrating and improving technique, while at the advanced and competitive level the pad holder needs to become significantly more interactive and possess the mindset of a boxer and competitor, otherwise the benefits gained from pad holding are not maximized.

The pad holder needs to be clear as to what his role is at the different stages of the boxer's development and ensure this focus is maintained in training.

Coaching with an Assistant

One exercise that is possible if an assistant is available is for the assistant to blow a whistle every 20 seconds giving the boxer feedback when the round is nearing the end.

Improving Boxing Variety Using Pads

Element	How?
Preferred attacking tools	Observe preferred attacking tools on punch bag and then design combinations based on broad variety of attacking tools
Preferred defensive tools	By studying preferred defensive tools of the boxer, create simulations on pads that increase the variety of defensive tools used
Mannerism of style	Observe on punch bag and in sparring, then simulate on the pads with responses from the pad holder to utilisze and focus on the weaknesses created by the mannerisms
Tempo changes	Change the pattern of punches creatively on the pads
Preferred movement of direction	Change the pattern of movement when holding the pads. Simulate like a fighter.
Footwork patterns	Introduce variety of footwork into the drills

Improving Boxing Unpredictability Using Focus Pads

Element	How?
Danger punch	Pad holder should focus on openings offered by the boxer and exploit them when offered.
Movement of head	By observation and by the pad holder throwing punches in between techniques
Movement patterns and mannerisms	Pad holder has to think like a boxer in the ring, with the exception being that the other boxer can only punch the focus pads
Change of movement speed	Pad holder needs to be able to change the speed of responses expected from the boxer

Importance of tvp Elements at Different Complexity Levels

L – Low, M – Medium, H – High

Element	Basic	Int	Adv	Comp
Position of non-punching hand	H	M	L	L
Bodyweight transfer when punching	L	H	M	L
Break off from inside position	L	M	H	H
Quality of punching	H	H	M	L
Line of delivery				
Retraction				
Use of hips, feet, elbows and shoulders				
Body lock off on opposite side to delivery				
Position of head and chin during delivery and recovery				
Relaxation and acceleration of punching	L	M	H	M
Preferred attacking tools	L	M	H	M
Preferred defensive tools	L	M	H	M
Mannerism of style	L	L	L	H
Tempo changes	L	M	H	H
Preferred movement of direction	L	L	M	H
Footwork patterns	L	M	H	H
Danger punch	L	L	M	H
Movement of head	M	M	H	H
Movement patterns and mannerisms	L	L	M	H
Change of movement speed	L	L	M	H

This will enable the boxer to judge the round and increase or decrease his workload, thus allowing him to better gauge the timing of the round.

Weaknesses of Pad Holding

Despite the many advantages of using focus pads, one should be aware of some of the limitations in the system:
* lack of counters from pad holder

* learning bad habits when holding pads
* limited number techniques

Being Creative: Develop Your Own Style of Holding Pads

As has been noted, the mindset of the pad holder needs to be that of a boxing opponent, otherwise the benefits gained from holding the pads are no different to punching

Focus Pads: Development Sequence

No.	Level of movement	Level of technique	Level of chaos	Level of decision training	Examples	Objective
1	Low – static	Low – single techniques	Low	Low	Jab, rear hand, uppercut, hook	Development of accuracy in technique
2	Low – static	Medium – combination techniques	Low	Low	Jab, rear hand jab, hook, rear hand, hook	Development of speed in transition from one technique to another
3	Low – static	High – multiple combinations from a defensive position	Medium	Low		Turning defence into attack
4	Low – static	High – combinations with counters	Medium	Medium		
5	Medium – unidirectional movement	Low – single techniques from linear and lateral movement patterns	Medium	Medium		
6	Medium – unidirectional movement	Medium – combination techniques from linear and lateral movement patterns	Medium	Medium		
7	Medium – unidirectional movement	High – combinations from a defensive position	Medium	Medium		
8	Medium – unidirectional movement	High – combinations with counters	Medium	Medium		
9	High – multidirectional movement	Low – single techniques moving in multiple directions	Medium	Medium		
10	High – multidirectional movement	Medium – combination techniques moving in multiple directions	High	High		
11	High – multidirectional movement	High – combinations from a defensive position	High	High		
12	High – multidirectional movement	High – combinations with counters	High	High		

Sample Workouts Using Pads for Development

The following workouts are sample three-round sessions that develop the key attributes for boxing.

Basic

Round number	Drills	Objective
1	Basic straight arm punching	Improve technique in punching
2	Basic bent arm punching	Improve technique in punching
3	Basic combinations with basic footwork	Improve technique in punching and footwork

Intermediate

Round number	Drills	Objective
1	Basic punching – straight and bent arm punches	Improve body mechanics and power in basic punching
2	Low number combinations with footwork and defending returns	Improve transition from one style of punching to another, with diverse footwork
3	Low number combinations with return techniques from pad holder	Deliver appropriate techniques in response to attacks from pad holder

Advanced

Round number	Drills	Objective
1	Combinations with diverse footwork	Improving techniques with emphasis on improving quality of punching
2	Variety of combinations moving in different directions	Delivering variety of techniques with movement
3	Variety of combinations with different footwork and responding to attacks from pad holder	Increased interactivity and cohesion with opponent

Competitive

Round number	Drills	Objective
1	Interactive boxing with punches and combinations with pad holder. Moving in all directions, increasing the challenge in terms of attacks and defences	Improve ability to think creatively and intuitively.
2	As above	
3	As above	

the bag or any other target. Using focus pads can be a phenomenal resource or they can be an excuse for the boxer not having to think, as the pad holder will just create different combinations that then become predictable. Pad holders need to visualize themselves as boxers and ensure that clear goals and objectives of development are discussed and highlighted in the workout. Pad holders might look at creative boxers and see if they can recreate scenarios on the pads. In addition, the pad holder should look at the situation in unique perspectives and create responses with the boxer that will stretch and challenge the thinking of the boxer.

All pad holders should keep asking themselves, 'Why are we hitting focus pads? Can we get the same benefit punching the punch bag? What is the value of punching the pads?' If these questions cannot be answered appropriately, then the pads are unlikely to be used effectively. A common response is fitness, but this is not maximizing the benefit of using focus pads.

Developing a Session

The key rules to designing a good session involve the following principles:
* Articulate the objectives of the session
* Identify what level (L, M, H, C) the session is to be geared at
* Identify if the session is geared at training technique, variety or (un)predictability
* Start simple and build up the complexity of the session
* Record the outcomes of the sessions and key learning points

Designing/Planning a Session

The accompanying table contains a checklist of key elements to consider when planning a pad holding session.

Element	Level	Areas of focus
Level of movement	L/M/H	
Level of technique	L/M/H	
Level of chaos	L/M/H	
Level of decision training	L/M/H	
Level of pad holder interactivity	L/M/H	
Construct a picture of the outcome		
Highest level possible		
Record session to outcome		
Key lessons learned		

CHAPTER 8

PHYSIOLOGICAL CONDITIONING

It isn't the mountains ahead to climb that wear you out; it's the pebble in your shoe
Muhammad Ali

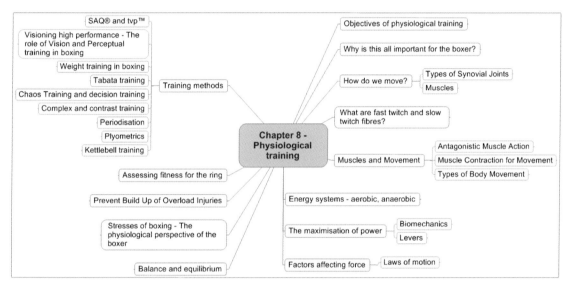

Mindmap overview of Chapter 8.

The field of sports science has grown significantly since about 1990. Major sports have adopted many of the concepts and theories, and reflected these in their training methods. Professional football and tennis, for example, now focus training on very specific elements such as reaction time to improve very specific elements of an athlete's capability. This focus has provided an opportunity to significantly raise the standard and quality of the athletes. An example would be the 100m sprint, where considerable attention has been given to the athlete's ability to react to the starting gun. This degree of specificity is essential in improving the overall quality of boxing and move it to even higher levels.

The key areas of specificity for the boxer are:
* Reaction speed
* Power
* Tempo and rhythm
* Fitness
* Strength
* Speed
* Agility
* Quickness
* Decision making

There are many different aspects to physiological training that can enhance the capabilities of the boxer. The key is ensuring that specific objectives are identified and that the training methods are adapted specifically for boxing. In many instances, training is carried out in these areas and the outcomes are purely accidental. However, by adapting the methods specifically for the boxing scenario progress can be accelerated.

Objectives of Physiological Training

* Develop more power
* Improve fitness and stamina
* Increase speed and strength
* Increase sharpness – increase responsiveness
* Improve accuracy

By understanding how the body works and how power is generated the boxer can be more specific in training the key elements needed to maximize boxing performance. For boxing the key areas to train are the whole body and in particular the legs, as these allow stability and hence a better axis, leading to more accurate and powerful punching and movement.

The boxer needs to understand how to engage the relevant muscles and energy systems to ensure optimal body performance. Additionally, a detailed understanding of the principles of balance, axis and force will allow the boxer to transmit the greatest power over the shortest distance.

A vital element of training is to understand how to optimize the benefit of the training time available by focusing on specific body systems, not just specific muscles, as sometimes happen. This chapter is designed to develop an understanding of these systems and provide an overview of the different training methods that may be used by the boxer.

Components of the Body

Before looking at how we move, we need to understand the different components that make up the human body.

Skeleton

The skeleton is a framework of bones that are held together by ligaments and joints, and has the following four functions: movement, protection, support and blood production.

There are four types of bone and each is given a name dependent on its shape or size:

Long bones   e.g. the humerus (upper arm)
Short bones   e.g. the phalanges (fingers or toes)
Flat bones   e.g. the scapula (shoulder blade)
Irregular bones   e.g. vertebrae (segments of the backbone)

There are three kinds of joint and their classification is dependent on how the bones are joined together.
* Fibrous joints, where fibrous tissue holds the bones together.
* Cartilaginous joints, linked by cartilage; there is some movement, but it is very slight.
* Synovial joints allow for greater ranges of movement; the type of movement depends on the type of joint between the bones. There are several varieties of synovial joints:

Ball and socket joint: found in the shoulder and hip, this type allows the greatest range of movement.
Hinge joint: found at the elbow and knee. Movement is limited to one plane (just like a door hinge).

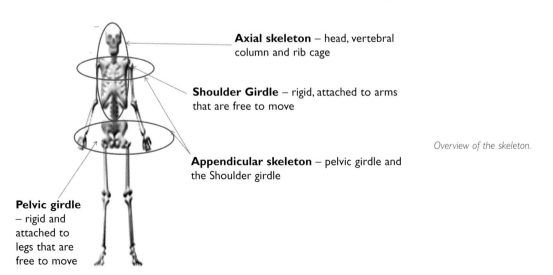

Axial skeleton – head, vertebral column and rib cage

Shoulder Girdle – rigid, attached to arms that are free to move

Appendicular skeleton – pelvic girdle and the Shoulder girdle

Pelvic girdle – rigid and attached to legs that are free to move

Overview of the skeleton.

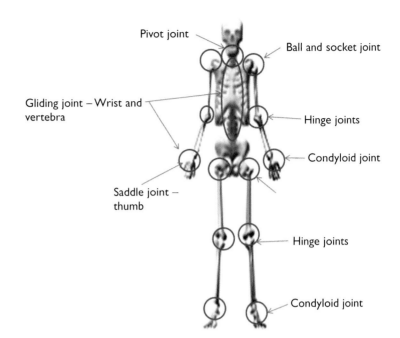

Joints of the skeleton.

Pivot joint

Ball and socket joint

Gliding joint – Wrist and vertebra

Hinge joints

Condyloid joint

Saddle joint – thumb

Hinge joints

Condyloid joint

Condyloid joint: found at the wrist and ankle. Movement is in two planes, but not as great as the ball and socket.

Pivot joint: found in the neck where part of the bone fits into another ring of bone, as in the atlas and axis, allowing rotation of the head.

Saddle joint: found at the base of the thumb. Allows the thumb to be moved in two directions.

Gliding joint: found in the wrist and vertebral column.

Muscles

Muscles are contractile tissues that are capable of extension and contraction to generate movement. There are three main types of muscles in the body; each has a special purpose that is vital to the normal functioning of the body:

Smooth or involuntary muscle: Found in the bowel, the

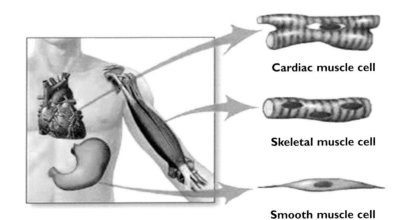

Types of muscles. (Medline Plus)

Cardiac muscle cell

Skeletal muscle cell

Smooth muscle cell

Characteristics of Fibres

Fibre type	Type I fibres	Type IIa fibres	Type IIb fibres
Contraction time	Slow	Fast	Very fast
Size of motor neuron	Small	Large	Very large
Resistance to fatigue	High	Intermediate	Low
Activity used for	Aerobic	Long-term anaerobic	Short-term anaerobic
Force production	Low	High	Very high

gut and internal organs. There is no direct control of this muscle, that is, it works automatically.

Cardiac or heart muscle: Specialized muscle that contracts constantly and automatically. Some factors can affect the speed of the contractions, such as exercise and the release of hormones such as adrenaline.

Skeletal muscles: These are the ones that can easily be seen as a shape under the skin. Unlike smooth muscle or cardiac muscle, we can control skeletal muscles and because of this it is sometimes known as voluntary muscle. Skeletal muscle, also known as striated muscle, is the type that constitutes most of the muscle mass within the body.

Skeletal muscle is constructed from densely knit fibres, which are built from the nutrients necessary for their function by capillaries, tiny blood vessels extending from the arteries of the cardiovascular system. The muscle fibres are bound into bundles, called fascicles, to form a working unit.

Muscle Control

Ultimately the control of the muscles is through the brain, through the messages that it directs to the body through the central nervous system. These messages start from the brain, go through the spinal cord and through nerve pathways to neurons located within every muscle. As these neurons control physical movement, they are known as motor neurons. The speed with which the neurons communicate with their related fibres in the muscles dictates whether the fibre are 'fast-twitch' or 'slow-twitch'.

Fibres and Appropriate Training Methods

Fibres	Type of training	Description
Fast-twitch fibres – require faster repetitions. Used during the concentric phase of movement	Isometric training	Muscle is held in a resistance-generating position for set periods. The clasping of both hands and pulling them with equal force from each arm is a simple isometric movement. A goal of isometric exercise is to ensure that the targeted muscle is contracted and extended in a disciplined fashion, which encourages an optimal relationship between each neuron and the muscle fibre group
Fast-twitch fibres	Weight training	Lifting significant weight with short rest intervals in each set
Fast-twitch fibres	Plyometric training	Intense jumping and interval sprint training for legs, for example. The muscle becomes conditioned to respond to the stimulation provided to the neuron as demanded by the demands of the exercise. When the body senses that the numbers of fast-twitch fibres available to perform the movements are insufficient, neighbouring fibres will be co-opted into assisting the existing fast-twitch fibres
Slow-twitch fibres – used during the eccentric phase. Responsible for the build-up of bulk in muscles	Endurance training	Long distance running, running, cycling, rowing, light sparring etc
Slow-twitch fibres	Slow, negative lifting	Focus on eccentric phase
Both	Pyramidal sets	Start lifting at a weight that will allow 15–20 reps, then gradually go down to a heavier weight for fewer reps

All muscles possess both fast-twitch and slow-twitch fibres.

Fast-Twitch and Slow-Twitch Fibres

Fast-twitch fibres: These are activated by their neurons at a rate ten times faster than the rate of activation for slow-twitch fibres. These are further subdivided into two sub-categories:

* fast-twitch fibre (IIa): resistant to fatigue, but not as much as slow-twitch fibres
* fast-twitch fibre (IIb): fatigue easily and used for short bursts of intense activity

Fast-twitch fibres are used by the body to propel it in short, intense bursts, such as those required in punching and reacting to being hit.

Slow-twitch fibres: These possess a greater quantity of mitochondria, the portion of the human cell that acts as a powerhouse within each cell in the production of energy. These can process greater amounts of oxygen to create more adenosine triphosphate (ATP), the body's fuel for the production of energy. For this reason, slow-twitch fibres are relied on when the muscle must extend and contract repetitively, as in a long fight. Slow-twitch fibres are the units employed by the body to provide the power for a sustained fight over three, ten, twelve or fifteen rounds.

Distribution of fast- and slow-twitch fibres
The distribution of fast- versus slow-twitch fibres in the muscles is primarily an inherited characteristic, determined by the genetic coding of each person. Usually people have muscles with a relatively even distribution of fast- and slow-twitch fibres. Some, however, inherit a significantly greater number of one type of fibre over the other. These tend to excel in the sports best suited to their muscular composition.

Fast-twitch fibres and slow-twitch fibres possess the same capacity to generate muscular power.

Muscles and Movement – Antagonistic Muscle Action

Muscles can only contract and pull. Therefore, joints have to have two or more muscles working opposite each other. This is known as antagonistic muscle action. For this to occur, one end of the muscle must be fixed. This is known as the origin. When the muscle contracts, the other end of the muscle then moves towards the origin. The end that moves is known as the insertion. A good example of this is the upper arm, where the triceps and biceps are on opposite sides of the humerus. The origins of both the triceps and the biceps are at the top of the humerus near the shoulder joint. As the bicep contracts the lower arm (radius and ulna) moves up towards the shoulder. The triceps relax to allow this movement to happen. The bicep

Movement of muscles – contraction of the biceps – Antagonistic muscle action

Movement of muscles.

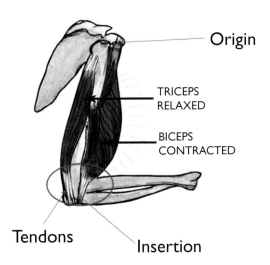

Origin

TRICEPS RELAXED

BICEPS CONTRACTED

Tendons

Insertion

is the prime mover or agonist, while the tricep is the secondary mover or antagonist. Muscles are attached to bones at either side of the joints by tendons.

Muscle Contraction for Movement

There are three types of muscle contraction:
* Isometric: muscle remains the same length.
* Isokinetic: the speed of the contraction remains constant throughout the movement.
* Isotonic contraction can be divided into two types:
  > Concentric: the muscle shortens as it contracts.
  > Eccentric: the muscle lengthens but is still under tension.

Types of Body Movement

Due to the range of movements required in sport, it is useful to be able to describe them technically:
* Flexion: bringing two parts of a limb together – bending at the joint.
* Extension: moving two parts of a limb away from each other – straightening at the joint.
* Abduction: moving limbs away from the centre of the body.
* Adduction: Moving limbs towards the centre of the body.
* Circumduction: the movement of a limb around a joint.

In summary, the human body comprises a skeleton connected by a network of muscles that are stimulated by a series of messages sent from the brain via the spine.

Energy Systems – Aerobic, Anaerobic

There are three sources of adenosine triphosphate (ATP), the body's main energy source on the cellular level.

ATP-PC System (Phosphogen System): This system is used only for very short durations of up to ten seconds. The ATP-PC system neither uses oxygen nor produces lactic acid if oxygen is unavailable and is thus said to be alactic anaerobic. This is the primary system behind very short, powerful movements, such as a fully powered punch or sharp movement away from an attacking opponent.

Anaerobic System (Lactic Acid System): Predominates in supplying energy for exercises lasting less than two minutes. Also known as the glycolytic system. An example of an activity of the intensity and duration that this system works under would be the two- or three-minute rounds in a boxing match.

Aerobic System: This is the long duration energy system. By five minutes of exercise the oxygen system is clearly dominant. This begins to kick in after about the second round of a fight.

Muscles power all movements made by the human body through a series of contractions. In understanding how the body works we should be able to create a more focused training programme.

The Maximization of Power

Biomechanics

Biomechanics analyses and assesses human movement. Through the knowledge of mechanics and physics, biomechanics looks to optimize the impact of body movement. In short, in terms of boxing, biomechanics is looking at how body movement is optimized to generate the most effective punch.

Biomechanics can help with boxing through:
* Increasing speed
* Increasing strength
* Increasing power
* Minimize risk of injury

Levers

To maximize movement for sports such as boxing, we need to understand how to maximize the levers in the body. Levers are:
* Essential for optimizing human movement
* Rigid bars (in the body, bones) that move around an axis of rotation (a joint) or fulcrum
* Forces (supplied by muscles) cause the movement to occur

The key functions of a lever are to:
* Magnify a force to create a simple crow bar effect
* Increase the speed and range-of-motion (ROM). A small amount of muscular contraction close to the fulcrum can produce lots of movement further down the limb
* Change direction of force

The key parts of the lever are:

The axis: the point of movement or pivot, generally at the centre of a joint.

A resistance: the body's weight or some external object.

A force: a muscular force to move the load.

Lever types

There are three different types of lever: first, second and third order. The classification is determined by the arrangement of the applied force, the fulcrum, and the resistance. It is the classification that determines the lever's strengths and weaknesses.

First order: The axis is between the resistance and force. Both are in the same direction. An example of this is the head, where the head pivots on the axis. The resistance is

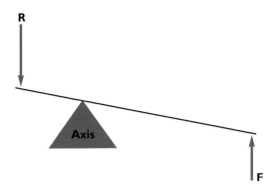

First order levers.

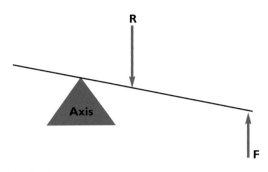

Second order levers.

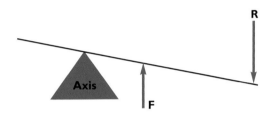

Third order levers.

the weight of the head going down. The force or effort is the muscles at the back of the neck pulling down.
* FAR (force, axis, resistance)
* When the axis is close to the force, it produces speed and range of motion, when close to the resistance, it produces power

* About 25 per cent of the muscles in your body operate as first class levers

Second order: The axis is at one end of the lever. The resistance is in the middle of the lever. The force or effort is at the opposite end of the lever to the axis with the direction of force opposite the resistance. An example of this is stepping up onto your toes. The axis is at the toes. The resistance is that of the body going through the middle of the foot and the force is in the calf muscles pulling the body up onto the toes. This is the most effective lever as a relatively small force can move a large weight.
* ARF (axis, resistance, force)
* Very few occurrences in the body
* Gain resultant force (you can lift more), lose distance

Third order: The axis and resistance are at opposite ends of the lever but the force is offcentre of the lever towards the axis. This is not as efficient as with second order levers but small muscle movement creates long lever movement. An example of this is a biceps curl. The resistance is in the

The levers in action.

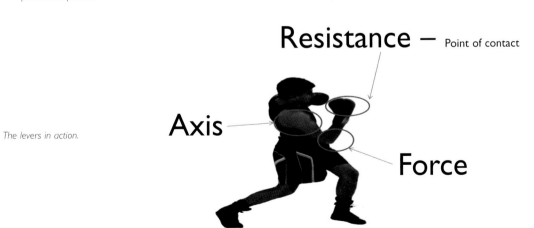

hand, the axis is at the elbow and the biceps make the force.
* RFA (resistance, force, axis)
* As much as 85 per cent of the muscles in the body function as third class levers
* Usually produce speed at the expense of force
* Greater lever length = greater speed

Factors Affecting Force

Torque: turning effect of an eccentric force
    T= Applied Force * Force Arm
    Force arm is the perpendicular distance between the applied force and the axis of rotation
    Eccentric force: applied in a direction not in line with centre of rotation of non-moving axis
    Resistance arm: distance between axis and point of resistance (not the perpendicular distance)
    Inverse relationship between force and force arm
    Inverse relationship between resistance and resistance arm
    Force components and resistance components proportional
        F × FA = R × RA
    Angle of pull
    Rotary component, dislocating component and stabilizing component
    When line of force (inserting tendon) is perpendicular to the bone it is inserting on (90 degrees), dislocating and stabilizing components = 0, therefore all force is rotary

Laws of Motion

A good understanding of the laws of motion will assist the boxer in generating greater power and force in their techniques. There are three elements that comprise the laws of motion: inertia, acceleration, force and reaction, and balance and equilibrium.

Inertia: Newton's First Law of motion
* 'A body in motion tends to stay in motion at the same speed in a straight line unless acted upon by a force. A body at rest tends to remain at rest unless acted upon by a force.'
* Mass is the measure of inertia
* Greater mass = greater inertia
* Implications for sport movement
* Decreased mass *usually* means you are easier to move (less inertia)
* Agonist/antagonist reciprocal inhibition

Acceleration: Newton's Second Law of motion
* 'The acceleration of an object is directly proportional to the force causing it, is in the same direction as the force, and is inversely proportional to the mass of the object.'
* Force = mass × acceleration
* Impulse
* Without time, it is impossible to generate force and change velocity
* Momentum = mass × velocity
* If masses are different, deficiencies can be compensated for by increasing speed
* Implications for sport movement, for example bodyweight and follow through

Reaction: Newton's Third Law of motion
* 'For every action there is an equal and opposite reaction.'
* Ground reaction force, for example using the ground to generate punching power

Balance and equilibrium

Equilibrium is the state of zero acceleration (static or dynamic)
    Balance is the ability to control equilibrium
    Stability is a resistance to the disturbance of equilibrium

The factors affecting balance are:
* Location of the centre of gravity in relation to the base of support
* Size of the base of support
* Mass of the person
* Height of the centre of gravity
* Traction/friction
* Sensory perceptions

Stresses of Boxing
The Physiological Perspective of the Boxer

The key objective for the fighter is to work to reduce weaknesses in style and body shape, while improving strength in adopting a particular style. To maximize the benefit of training, the boxer also needs to ensure that the risk of injuries is minimized. There are a number of factors that can contribute to the boxer's ability to maximize the benefits of training, including style and body shape.

The short fighter
Advantages: the centre of gravity of the body is closer to the floor, meaning balance is more solid. This allows quick movements into a defensive or offensive position. The short fighter is often strong through the legs and core, with good footwork. This is due to the low centre of gravity, which enables minimal upward movement with fast lateral movement.

Disadvantages: has a shorter reach with a tendency to overextend. Usually the advantage of being able to generate power through short distances with the arms is offset by the muscle tone building up, and creating an excess tightening of soft tissue.

The tall fighter
Advantages: has a reach advantage and superior levers and therefore can create more power, if there is time to generate it.
Disadvantages: stiff thoracic, which is due to lots of daily activities or through the rigours of training. If a joint in the spine stiffens the muscles can't move through their full range. Therefore trunk rotation is reduced and there can be overload of the low back. Additionally, the arms are required to provide more power as natural mechanics become restricted leading to an overload of arm muscles and joints. The tall fighter also has problems with reaction time due to the longer levers (arms and legs) and the centre of gravity is higher, causing speed of movement difficulties.

Factors Affecting a Fighter

Training and fighting places different demands on the body. These demands ask the body to cope with movement stress, static stress and shock absorption stress. Of these the fighter will ask 100 per cent of each system. Should one system be inadequate he is at greater risk of injury.

Shock absorption system failure will occur if the muscles have not been trained to dissipate stress from a punch or from a kick. If training is not a gradual build-up, the spine stiffens to assist the muscles, but this will overload other systems. Even if training is gradual there are occasions when this will cause overload and stiffening of the muscles.

Movement/fast reaction and static system failure occurs if there has been a concentration on power without adequate attention to the muscles that stabilize the rest of the body. For example, holding a weight in your left hand, with the arm stretched out, not only uses the arm muscles but you will feel the right side of the low back also working. Therefore any weight training for power (low reps, high weight) should be complemented with medium weight, slow movements for assisted stability.

The weakest part of a muscle contraction is the beginning, for example when the arm is straight and stretched out in front. The muscles at the front of the elbow and at the back of the shoulder are weak. If the arm is blocked or hit at this point, injury is likely in the back of the shoulder muscles as the support is weak. In order to overcome lazy technique, maximize this with light weights at the extreme of movement.

Prevent Build-Up of Overload Injuries

Weight training will cause muscles to tighten. Stretch the affected body part after training to encourage blood into the region, therefore removing waste products and bringing healing cells to the region.

Regular sports massage also assists in preventing injury, although timing is important to fit in with training intensities. For example, lying on the floor over a rectangular block in the upper back helps stretch the spine joints. This should be done daily to help maintain flexibility.

Assessing Fitness for the Ring

One of the key questions prior to entering the ring is 'Is the fighter fit enough?' The key elements that need to be tested are the aerobic fitness and anaerobic fitness of the fighter, but these have to be assessed in very sports-specific terms. Some of the running-based tests that exist might suggest the fighter is capable of coping with the number of rounds in a fight – if he were running, but not necessarily if he were throwing punches. Additionally, one of the key elements of the fitness test should be the level of recovery, which is critical in the ring environment. How rapidly does the fighter recover to continue with the fight?

The test that we are going to demonstrate needs to be adapted to the specific fighting situation: how many rounds and what duration of rounds is the fighter preparing for. This will facilitate a change in the number of 'rounds' that are incorporated in the test and the duration of these 'rounds'.

We will assume that the fighter is preparing for a boxing match of three two-minute rounds (an amateur bout). The equipment needed is a partner and punch bag. The test itself involves the fighter stepping in and out of punching range, delivering a series of punches. First the fighter delivers a jab to the bag and steps out. This is followed by the fighter stepping back in and delivering a jab and rear hand, followed by stepping out. The fighter then steps back in and delivers three punches: a jab, rear hand and jab again. This process is continued until ten punches have been delivered in a front–rear hand combination format.

On completion of the ten punches the time taken and the pulse rate of the fighter are noted. Why? The time taken provides an indication of the speed of delivery of the fighter and the pulse rate provides an indication of the aerobic capacity of the fighter. After a one-minute break the pulse is noted again before the test is repeated, with the time taken and pulse being noted in exactly the same way as before. This is repeated three times in total (replicating the three rounds to be fought).

After the test the fighter will have the following results:

Measure	Round One	Round Two	Round Three
Time taken			
Pulse rate on completion			
Pulse rate after one minute			

The coach needs to be examining from the following points:

1. The time taken to complete the series of punches. After measuring a number of boxers at the tvp Institute we have found that the following times are a good indication of the speed that should be expected for fighters at different levels of attainment:

Time Range	Assessment
30–35 seconds	Excellent
36–45 seconds	Very good
46–55 seconds	Good
56+	Room for improvement!

2. The variation in time between rounds provides an indication of the anaerobic capacity. If the variation is greater than 5 per cent then this suggests more work needs to be done on building the anaerobic capacity.

3. The pulse rate recovery is the difference between pulse rate at end of test and after one minute. This provides an indication of the ability of the fighter to be able to cope with performing at a high level consistently over all of the rounds in a fight.

4. The change in recovery from one round to another gives an indication of the basic fitness level of the fighter.

The action to be taken by the coach is captured in the accompanying table:

The basic rules for changing the test to be more appropriate are:

*   Add five punches for every one minute of duration of round, for example a three-minute round will build up to fifteen punches
*   Add one round for every round to be fought, for example a five-round fight will have five rounds of punches
*   Include kick-based combinations for kick boxing events

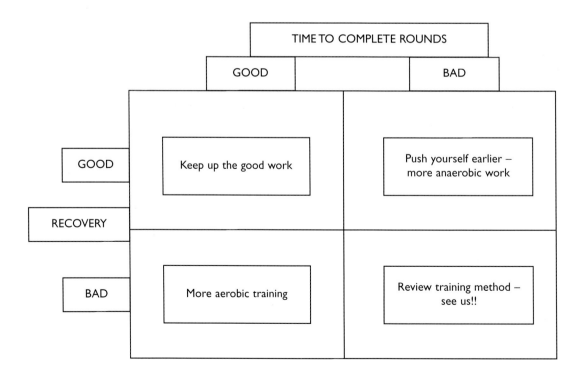

Coaching reactions to ring fitness test results.

Training Methods

There are a number of training methods adopted by different sports, based on the latest thinking in sports science, that may be applied to the boxer's training arsenal. The different methods that we feel are most appropriate for boxing are listed below, with further explanations later in this chapter.

* SAQ and tvp
* Vision and perceptual training
* Weight training
* Tabata training
* Chaos training and decision training
* Complex and contrast training
* Periodization
* Plyometrics
* Kettlebell training

SAQ and tvp

Have you ever wondered how a football team in this era would have fared against a team from the 1960s? Our view is that they would have battered them. I am not sure the same applies to the average boxer today versus the average boxer from the 1960s. There is little chance that today's heavyweights would stand a chance against the likes of Ali, Frasier, Norton and Foreman. Why is it that in certain sports great progress has been made, while in others we seem to have remained stagnant? Perhaps it is down to increased professionalism, as portrayed in rugby, or perhaps it is down to training methods.

There is much that boxers can learn from professional sports such as football and rugby. SAQ International have worked with these sports for many years and have teamed with us to apply these concepts to boxing through their training method called SAQ (Speed, Agility and Quickness) and our tvp (Technique, Variety and Predictability) framework.

The primary objectives of adopting these approaches in boxing are:
* punch harder
* move quicker (in all directions: left, right, forwards, backwards, up and down)
* increase creativity
* increase responsiveness to a greater variety of situations
* make training more diverse and enjoyable

SAQ definitions

Speed means the maximum velocity a boxer can achieve and maintain through an action such as the delivery of a punch. For most humans the ability to maintain maximum velocity is limited to a short period of time or disstance. This includes footwork speed, hand speed and reaction speed.

Agility: generally described as body control and incorporates balance, coordination, timing and rhythm. These can be developed using programmed agility, which means performing drills that are planned, and random agility, which places the fighter in a pattern and sequence that they have to respond to with no prior knowledge. Both are important in the development of a fighter's ability.

Quickness: covers all aspects of acceleration including foot, hand and body movement. SAQ training improves the neuromuscular system that impacts on this process so that whatever the initial fighter's movement – linear, lateral, vertical, dodge, weave, step back – it is automatic, explosive and precise. This is probably the most important aspect of the fighter's make-up. Boxing, martial arts and all combat sports are multi-speed, multi-directional explosive sports and therefore involve a great deal of acceleration and deceleration. The better the quickness of a fighter the more likely they will be harder to hit, and will also be able to hit harder at all different angles.

SAQ training is best delivered while the athlete is fresh and alert. By using high intensity, short interval based sessions with high quality recovery the athlete can perform at a higher level of intensity for longer periods. The sets and reps can be altered to ensure sessions constantly challenge the athlete. Fighting is made up of rounds of high and low intensity activity. The athletes that can maintain a higher level of intensity for longer are the more successful. Long, slow training and training that is designed to provide 'tongue hanging out' fatigue without rest and recovery is more likely to produce a one-paced slower athlete. If you train slow and tired you will fight slow and tired.

(For details of tvp, see Chapter 5.)

SAQ Continuum

The key stages of the SAQ method are described as the SAQ Continuum. This is the sequence and progression of components that make up an SAQ training session. The Continuum is flexible and adaptable to specific fighter requirements. The component parts of the Continuum and how they relate to combat sports are:

Dynamic flex warm-up: warming up on the move involving specific fighting movements. Research has proven that warming up with dynamic flex prepares the fighter for all the rigorous movement required within the combat sports. Essentially dynamic flex does the following:
* increases body and deep muscle temperature
* increases heart rate and blood flow
* increases breathing rate and oxygen supply
* increases activity and coordination in neuro-muscular system and improves mental alertness

Make-up of Training Sessions for a Range of Abilities

	Beginner	Intermediate	Advanced
Dynamic flex	20%	20%	20%
Mechanics: incorporating a variety of techniques from tvp	40%	15%	0
Innervation: incorporating unusual movements as well as the obvious movements (predictability from tvp)	25%	25%	15%
Accumulation of potential: incorporating all elements of tvp	0	20%	25%
Explosion: incorporating a variety of techniques from tvp	15%	10%	25%
Expression of potential: incorporating all elements of tvp	0	10%	15%

Static stretching before training, as generally practised by many martial arts clubs, has been shown to be detrimental to the performance of the fighter.

Mechanics of movement: the development of correct movement form for the different aspects of fighting. Foot movement in combat sports provides balance, co-ordination and transfer of power. Correct foot placement helps the economics of movement and makes the fighter become more efficient.

Innervation: the development of fast feet, agility, co-ordination and control for fighting and combat sports. This is a transition stage from warm-up to high intensity foot and hand work that activates the neuro-pathways, in other words you get the nerves to fire the muscles as quickly as possible. The quicker the feet are placed up and down on the floor, the more control the fighter has and more power is generated in punching and kicking.

Accumulation of potential: the bringing together of the previous components in a SAQ training fighting circuit.

Explosion: the development of explosive multi-directional acceleration for fighting. This stage develops explosive power in punching and kicking. It is only added when the fighter has sound and competent movement techniques.

Expression of potential: short competitive fighting games that prepare fighters for the next level of training.

Dynamic flex warm-down: due to the high intensity levels achieved during training, time should be allocated for the athlete to reduce the heart rate gradually to near resting levels. This will help to disperse lactic acid, prevent blood pooling, return the body systems to normal levels and assist recovery. Dynamic flex warm-down begins with performing a selection of dynamic flex drills starting at a medium intensity and gradually becoming less intense and using smaller movements. Quality of movements should always be maintained.

Designing SAQ training sessions
The SAQ Continuum provides a format for designing training sessions, depending on the required focus. It is important to remember that these training methods are not designed to replace existing systems and arts, but to integrate and advance these systems based on extensively researched training methods from the field of sports science.

The design of the training session is customized to individual needs and the accompanying table might be a typical split of sessions:

The end result from the combination of SAQ and tvp is a complete, efficient and powerful fighter with the capability to be totally unpredictable.

Visioning High Performance: The Role of Vision and Perceptual Training in Combat Sports

Recently there has been a considerable influx, and rightly so, of sports science in the combat sports arena. For the first time the combat sports are learning from other sports and science, combined.

Watching top athletes from different sports is always interesting to see what makes them different. What distinguishes the stars from the average players? Is it their fitness or is it their skill level? Actually, the question is what do we really mean by skill level? We have one view: skill is the ability to apply appropriate techniques to situations that demand a response in a high pressure situation, in a limited time.

Vision plays an important part in combat sport. Coordination, concentration, balance and accuracy are just a few of the visually related abilities used during fighting and competing. The term 'vision' and the growing field of 'sports vision' apply to more than just 20/20 eyesight, glasses or contact lenses. Vision involves many subtle and sophisticated links between your brain, muscles and eyes. When you train for boxing, you probably work on aerobic capacity, endurance, strength, muscle tone and flexibility. Another key element of training is that of improving the elements of vision. The stamina, flexibility and fine-tuning of your visual system can sometimes provide you with the split-second timing needed to excel at boxing.

Integrating SAQ and tvp Techniques

	Technique	Variety	Predictability
Dynamic flex warm-up	Warm the body up specifically for the kicks and punches to follow	Warm the body up for variety	Get the body on the edge of optimal performance
Mechanics	Understand the correct mechanics and the role of the body and feet in delivering the optimal technique in terms of movement and power	Mechanics need to be understood and developed for a full spectrum of techniques, *not* just your preferred techniques. In fact more time is spent developing the areas the fighter is least comfortable with. For example, how many people actually train their weaker side?	This is where your competitive advantage lies. Can you apply *appropriate* mechanics at will? Note we do not say the theoretically correct mechanics. Remember Prince Naseem!
Innervation	This works on the principle that all punches and kicks are driven from the feet. The emphasis is on developing agility in technique from the feet first	Applied to a variety of techniques ensures that the fighter develops a broad range of skills and power	Innervation ensures that the fighter can move in unpredictable ways in a fast and efficient manner
Accumulation of potential	Combination of above	Combination of above	Combination of above
Explosion	Generation of maximum power in the technique with correct mechanics	Generation of power in a variety of techniques ensuring the development of complete fighter	Generation of power in different techniques from unusual and diverse positions
Expression of potential	Combination of above	Combination of above	Combination of above
Dynamic flex warm-down		Similar to warm-up	

Top athletes, irrespective of the sport, are characterized by their ability to give the impression that they have more time than mediocre practitioners. This can be seen quite clearly in the combat sports, where fighters like Muhammad Ali and Prince Naseem always appeared to have so much time, seeing punches early, anticipating their opponents' moves. The key word is 'appeared'. They appear to always be in the right place at the right time. The truth is their perceptual processes or mental quickness, as a result of their vision, was better than that of the opponent.

Perceptions are improved, and hence performance, in the combat arena by improving visual skills. Almost 80 per cent of perceptual input is visual. Generally the eyes lead and the body follows. Combat vision refers to a number of different skills, which we have divided into primary and secondary. The primary skills are critical to the fighting environment and the secondary are useful to the fighters' development.

Primary vision skills

Dynamic visual acuity: allows you to see and differentiate objects clearly while in motion. This is critical in seeing very fast fighters who tend to be very close and offer very little in the way of targets and openings.

Peripheral vision: seeing people and objects out of the corner of your eye while concentrating on a fixed point. A fighter's ability to attack from different ranges and different angles means that peripheral vision needs to be well developed. Boxers are particularly well versed at attacking from a variety of angles.

Depth perception: quickly and accurately judging the distance and speed of objects. Due to the fact that fighters, particularly boxers, move in and out of range so quickly there is a great need for fighters to be able to judge distance and speed very rapidly.

Spatial location: knowing your position relative to other objects while you are moving. This is critical as it is unlikely the fighter is going to 'plant' before dealing with an opponent. Continuous movement is essential while still being able to deliver techniques in an effective manner. Prince Naseem was renowned for being able to land techniques from positions most fighters would not have even thought of.

Secondary vision skills

Eye tracking: the ability to 'keep your eyes on the ball, or fist or kick', no matter how fast it may be travelling from the opponent.

Eye focusing: changing focus quickly and accurately from one distance to another. Fighters move in and out of range very quickly offering small targets, which means focusing skills need to be well developed.

Pursuit eye movement: the ability of the eyes to follow a moving object smoothly and accurately. Keeping, and following, an eye on your opponent and his 'weapons' is fundamental to the fighters' performance.

In addition to the above, we feel that there is another perspective of vision that can be a differentiator in the fight scenario.

Visualization: picturing events with your 'mind's eye' or imagination. Studies show that when you visualize yourself performing a particular activity, your brain doesn't know the difference between performing the activity or imagining (visualizing). Visualization can boost your confidence and aid in greater focus on your athletic goals.

Many coaches have a tendency to hold pads in a static manner that does not actually develop any of the above vision attributes. The result is that you have fighters who are very good at hitting static targets, but are considerably less effective when fighting in a ring, as they 'cannot see what they are hitting', and lack practise at hitting realistic targets that are moving in all different directions.

Improving perceptual capability

The development of vision skills leads to considerable improvement in the perceptual capability of the fighter. Each of the elements of vision need to be focused on during training, utilizing different pieces of equipment. This diversity of equipment ensures that the different elements are considered.

A key question many fighters have is can this mental agility as a result of perceptual skills or anticipation be trained and improved, or is it just simply down to experience? The truth is that it is possible to train and improve these skills over time using the right training methods.

Before we can begin improving our perceptual ability we need to understand how our brain processes information when a punch or kick is thrown, for example. The key stages are:

1. A punch or kick is thrown into the fighter's visual field (i.e. the entire area that can be seen when the eye is forward)
2. The punch or kick is detected by the eyes
3. The information about the punch or kick is transported from the receptors (part of the sensory system that recognizes a stimulus in the internal or external environment) via the sensory neurones (in this case the optic nerves) to the central nervous system (i.e. the brain and spinal cord)

Accuracy drill (1).   *Accuracy drill (2).*   *Accuracy drill (3).*

Accuracy drill (4).   *Accuracy drill (5).*

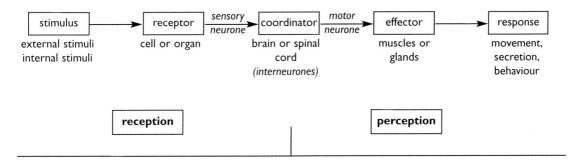

The reflex arc.

Applying the Reflex Arc

Stage of reflex arc	Critical success factors	Developing capability
Reception		
1. Punch is thrown into visual field	Peripheral vision	Broadening visual field
2. Punch is detected by eyes	Eye tracking Eye focusing	Maintain contact with eyes Concentration
3. Information to brain	Relaxed mindset encouraging free flow of information to brain	Meditation
Perception		
4. Information is processed by brain	Depth perception Spatial location Dynamic visual acuity	Multi-dimensional training with equipment
	Analytical stage of process	
	KEY STAGE OF PROCESS	
5. Information is compared to past experience	Past experience scenarios	Training with different sparring partners
	Developing options and choices	Watching videos of different fighters and styles Practising different scenarios with the coach
6. Response decision made	Visualization Creativity	Practising many different responses to the same situation with the coach
	Decision making	Watching videos of different fighters and studying their responses
7. Relevant information to muscular system	Relaxation Intuition	Visualizing different responses.
	Beginning of execution stage of process	Relaxation during complex movements. Performing movements slowly in a relaxed state
8. Physical response	Timing	Repetition
	Completion of execution stage of process	

4. The information is processed in the central nervous system
5. Information is compared to past experience, which is why experience is an important factor
6. Response decision is made
7. Motor neurones transport relevant information to the muscular system
8. A physical response is made

The above stages are sometimes referred to as the reflex arc, as it represents an automatic response, and can be shown diagrammatically.

Stages 1–3 represent the *reception* of information by the senses, which is the same for everyone. However, stages 4–8 represent the *perception* of information by the brain, which is dependent on factors such as experience and training. This is the area that can be enhanced through appropriate training.

One of the primary goals of coaching is to focus on improving the quality of perception of the fighter, especially at the analysis stage of the delivery process.

A key output from perceptual training is the athlete's ability to respond more quickly by seeing situations earlier through improved vision and to possess faster response times, thus gaining a decisive advantage against other fighters.

The key success factors in developing perception skills can be grouped into two categories:

Prior information about an opponent: this involves studying the opponent to explore and examine body posture, delivery mechanisms and movement patterns under different scenarios.

Prediction based on assumptions of the opponent: this may be based on experience of training or fighting boxers of different body types and understanding their body movement and body posture prior to throwing a punch or a kick. This requires the fighter to study as many different styles of fighter as possible and study body posture and other factors. Another prerequisite is that the best fighters are also prepared to take a risk. They may fail occasionally, but they will be successful most of the time.

Weight Training in Boxing

How do you use weights to enhance your boxing skills? Traditional weight training programmes undoubtedly make the boxer stronger and faster, but do not necessarily make him a better fighter, technically. The attributes that make up the tvp framework can be trained through the use of weights. The principles of tvp can be used in the performance of the weights programme to challenge and

Tools and Techniques to Improve Combat Vision and Perceptual Ability

	Focus pads	Peripheral stick	Visual acuity ring	Floor-ceiling ball
Dynamic visual acuity	Coach holds two pads of different types. Fighter has to hit specified pad with appropriate technique when offered as target	Move two peripheral sticks around fighter, who has to hit selected ball	Throw ring in the air. Fighter has to catch the relevant coloured ball Fighter has to hit the relevant coloured ball	Develop rounds on floor-ceiling ball, with a small ball
Depth perception	Position 2 pads at different distances and have fighter hit selected pad	Move stick around at varying distances from fighter and have fighter hit ball		
Peripheral vision		Coach stands behind fighter. Fighter touches ball when in sight.		
Spatial location		As above		Moving in at close distance to ball and make adjustments to feet to accommodate different positions of ball.
Pursuit eye movement		Coach moves stick around the fighter at different speeds. Fighter has to touch the ball		Hitting small floor-ceiling ball while moving around the ball

Developing tvp Techniques Through Weight Training

Tvp principle	Weight training application
Technique	
Position of non-punching hand	Controlled movement of weight
	All exercises completed with hands shoulder width apart
Body weight transfer	1. Keep back on bench
	2. No use of back in techniques
	3. Feet used as stabilizers
	4. Movement with weights from the core
	5. No jerking movement
Break off	1. No use of spotter – use reasonable weight
	2. Control and awareness during eccentric motion
	3. Alert mental state during all movement of weights
Quality of punching	1. Focus on correct form
	2. Focus on detail and style
Relaxation/acceleration	1. Preciseness of movement
	2. Movement under control
Variety	
Defences	1. Practise variety of grips, e.g. reverse grips
	2. Slow up, fast down and vice versa
	3. –ve movements
	4. One arm exercises
	5. On floor v. bench
	6. Standing v. sitting
	7. Assisted partner work
	8. Change patterns of reps
	9. Change order and frequency of reps
Mannerisms of style	Vary the types of movement adopted
Attacking tools	As defences
Footwork patterns	Perform dumbbell exercises while moving in different directions
Tempo changes	Perform movements with weights at different tempos, e.g. a set of ten might be performed as: 1, 12, 123, 12, 1, 1
Predictability	
Preferred direction of movement	1. Change angle of movement
	2. Change order of reps
Danger punch	
Head movement	
Change of movement speed	Perform movements at different speeds: slow, relaxed, fast
Mannerisms of style	

stimulate the mindset required to be a more creative and explosive fighter.

A typical weights programme to help in the development of the fighter is dependent on the following:

* Weight to be used
* Rest period between exercises
* Frequency of training

Weight Selection Table

Month	1	2	3
1RM	50%	60%	70%
Rest	2 minutes	1 minute 30s	1 minute
Frequency	2 × weekly	2 × weekly	2 × weekly

Technique

The technique of a boxer can be greatly enhanced through the appropriate adoption of technique when performing the weight exercise. The key elements are:

* shoulder width: encourages the appropriate development of muscles needed to develop punching power and consistency
* elbows tucked in when performing the exercises: this encourages the position of elbows needed to ensure good defence
* slower movement: develops focus and awareness of all muscles needed in punching and defending
* feel muscle back to starting position: creates awareness of total muscular movement
* relaxed shoulders in all techniques: develops speed through relaxation of shoulders

Training programme sessions

We have divided the programmes into quarterly sessions. All sessions should include the following elements:

* Warm-up: 10 minutes stretching
* Ground work/abs: 15 minutes curls/crunches/back extensions/–ve extensions/knees to chest/leg raises/ V-shaped sit-ups
* Wrist curls: 1 minute

Weight Training Programme: Months 1–3

Objective: platform building

Frequency: 3 × per week

	Sequence	Set 1	Set 2
Warm up – push ups			
Weight		50% × 1RM	50% × 1RM
Rest		2 minutes	2 minutes
Primary			
Bench press	1	12	12
Squats	3	12	12
Front press	5	12	12
Dead lift	7	12	12
		12	12
Secondary			
Bicep curls	2	12	12
Lateral raises	4	12	12
Bentover rows	6	12	12
Leg curls	8	12	12
Warm down – dips		12	12

Weight Training Programme: Months 4–6

Objective: anaerobic capability

Frequency: 3 × per week

	Sequence	Set 1	Set 2	Set 3
Warm up – push ups				
Weight		60% × 1RM	70% × 1RM	70% × 1RM
Rest		1 minute	1 minute	1 minute
Primary				
Hack squat	1	10	8	8
Press behind neck	3	10	8	8
Dumbbell bench press	5	10	8	8
Power clean	7	10	8	8
Deadlifts	9	10	8	8
Secondary				
Bicep curls	2	10	8	8
Tricep extension	4	10	8	8
Dumbbell flyes	6	10	8	8
Single arm punches	8	10	8	8
High pull-ups	10	10	8	8
Warm down – dips				

Weight Training Programme: Months 7–9

Objective: muscular endurance

Frequency: 3 × per week

	Sequence	Set 1	Set 2	Set 3
Warm up – push ups				
Weight		50% × 1RM	55% × 1RM	60% × 1RM
Rest	Partner finishing	1 minute	1 minute	1 minute
Primary				
Bench press	1	20	20	20
Shoulder press	3	20	20	20
Squats	5	20	20	20
Incline dumbbell press	7	20	20	20
Close grip bench press	9	20	20	20
Secondary				
Leg curls	2	20	20	20
Bent over row	4	20	20	20
Upright rowing	6	20	20	20
Leg extension	8	20	20	20
Incline bicep curls	10	20	20	20
Warm down – dips				

* Ankle mobility/calf raises: 1 minute
* Wrestlers bridge: 1 minute
* Neck lifts

Weight Training Programme: Months 10–12

Objective: combination of muscular endurance and anaerobic capability

Frequency: 3 × per week

Week number	Muscular endurance sessions per week	Anaerobic capability sessions per week
1	1	2
2	2	1
3	1	2
4	2	1
5	1	2
6	2	1
7	1	2
8	2	1
9	1	2
10	2	1
11	1	2
12	2	1

The second part of our annual programme of weight training for the development of competent boxing attributes will focus on improving muscular endurance and anaerobic capacity.

Tabata Training

The Tabata protocol is a high-intensity training regimen that produces remarkable results. A Tabata workout (also called a Tabata sequence) is an interval training cycle of 20 seconds of maximum intensity exercise, followed by 10 seconds of rest, repeated without pause eight times for a total of four minutes.

Credit for this simple and powerful training method belongs to Dr Izumi Tabata and a team of researchers from the National Institute of Fitness and Sports in Tokyo, Japan. Their groundbreaking 1996 study, published in the journal *Medicine and Science in Sports & Exercise*, provided documented evidence concerning the dramatic physiological benefits of high-intensity intermittent training. After just six weeks of testing, Dr Tabata noted a 28 per cent increase in anaerobic capacity in his subjects, along with a 14 per cent increase in their ability to consume oxygen. These results were witnessed in already physically fit athletes. The conclusion was that just four minutes of Tabata interval training could do more to boost aerobic

Benefits of Weight Training on Technique

Attribute	Objective	Impact of weight training programme
Technique		
Position of non-punching hand	Quick delivery of follow-on technique	Controlled movement of weight
		All exercises completed with hands shoulder width apart
Body weight transfer	Internalized movement	Controlled movement with total awareness of hand position
Break off from inside position	Always ready!	
Quality of technique	Optimal power and ready for next technique	Complete movement
Relaxation and acceleration in technique delivery	'Out at 50, back at 100!'	Weights pushed slowly and brought quickly back
Variety of tools		
Preferred attacking tools	Variety	Exploring full range of variations of all exercises
Preferred defensive tools	Variety	Exploring full range of variations of all exercises
Mannerism of style	No predetermined mannerisms	
Tempo changes	No pattern	Complete movements using weights at different speeds during sets and between sets
Predictability		
Preferred direction of movement	No preference	Perform dumbbell exercises while moving in different directions
Footwork patterns	No pattern	Feel pushing of weights with feet
Danger punch	All punches should be potentially danger punch	
Movement of head	Continually moving	
Movement patterns and mannerisms	No pattern	
Change of movement speed	Comfortable shifting from one speed to another with total control	Alter speed of movement with weights

and anaerobic capacity than an hour of endurance exercise.

Although Dr Tabata used a mechanically braked exercise cycle machine, you can apply this protocol to almost any exercise. For example, a basic Tabata workout can be performed with sit-ups. The more muscles used the better, so use full knees-bent sit-ups. Sit-up non-stop for 20-second intervals, followed by 10 seconds of rest. Repeat for a total of eight cycles.

How effective can just four minutes of exercise be? You will be amazed at how intense those four minutes will feel. The intervals tax both your aerobic and anaerobic energy systems. To be clear, this isn't 'eight sets of eight', although the goal of doing eight reps in each of the 20-second clusters is about right. Instead it's 'as many reps as I can get in' during the twenty seconds, followed by ten seconds rest.

It helps to be able to see a wall clock with a second hand during your four minutes of fun. Stop at twenty seconds, rest ten seconds, and go again. Watching the clock helps with your focus and also in keeping count of the eight cycles.

A longer Tabata workout example might consist of 4 separate Tabata Intervals, each 4 minutes. The total workout will last 16 minutes. Always begin with a moderate warm-up and cool down session.

Note that the 10-second rest periods in the Tabata workout are important, both physically and mentally. Not only do they allow partial recovery, they also provide psychological relief. Switching back and forth from work to rest makes the workout go quickly. The intervals also allow you to train at a higher level of intensity.

C	Conscious to sub conscious	Boxer should be made aware of what is goind on in terms of technique and position. Through the use of video key points should be discussed to create an inate understanding of technique and process.
H	Harness unpredictability	Make the drills unpredictable and variable by adding triggers.
A	Active to reactive	Start off with set drills then introduce these drills as reactions to triggers.
O	Open drills	Create drills based on open situations where any of the combination of drills will be required.
S	Slow to fast	Start with simple open drills, then progress to more challenging ones

The CHAOS training system.

A Tabata boxing workout
This groundbreaking training philosophy is ideally suited to the boxing environment:
* All training is completed in terms of four-minute rounds. Structure your training around 10 × 4-minute Tabata rounds. This can be your weights sessions, your bag work or even your sparring.
* Each 4-minute Tabata round comprises 8 × 20-second bursts of high intensity activity followed by 10 seconds recovery time.

The application of these concepts can be used in the following contexts: pad holding workouts, bag sparring, or in the ring sparring

CHAOS Training and Decision Training

A key feature of boxing, and in fact most invasive sports, is chaos. It is very difficult to predict what will happen. Yet if you look at much of the training that takes place in gyms the sessions tend to be very structured and predictable. The format of sessions is predictable and changes very little. The content is very similar from one session to another. The one reason why this may not be as detrimental as it could be is that the chances are that most gyms use the same methods.

The key aspect of chaos training is the development of decision-making/reaction time in a chaotic environment. It is essential that the boxer has the ability to deliver relevant techniques in quick time. CHAOS training is a progressive system that confronts the boxer with different challenges that are constantly being elevated.

Stages of chaos training
Develop strength: Follow a boxing-based strength programme with weights and kettlebells helps build a strong core and foundation for your boxing techniques.
Closed drills: These are useful to encourage the body memory to retain the key moves and techniques required for different situations. Follow the quick foot ladder drills to programme these responses.
Basic reaction training: Use visual/auditory or physical cues to activate responses. This is really the start of chaos training. Reaction balls are also very useful for this.
Verbal, physical, visual simple patterns: Different patterns are used to activate responses as around a box with set, simple numbers.
Verbal, physical, visual advanced patterns: As before, except you add a degree of unpredictability, for example by using opposites.
Visual, physical rabbit patterns: Follow the unpredictable behaviour of another person like a mirror drill.

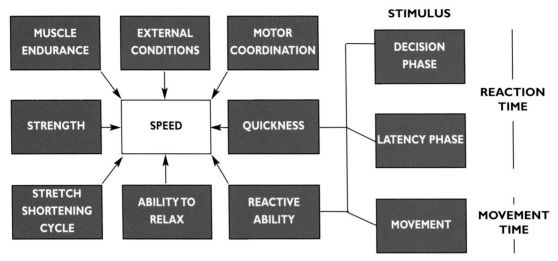

Factors affecting speed of movement.

Decision training model
Boxing has a tendency to use blocked repetitive practise as a training method, where specific responses are practises over and over again. Specific responses are practised over and over again until perfect. There are obvious strengths in this process of learning, but there are also considerable weaknesses. The main one is the inability of the boxer to perform in the ring when the pressure is on,

and also when there is a greater degree of unpredictability, especially when fighting people from different backgrounds and therefore different training methods.

Decision training looks to develop the cognitive skills, as well as the physiological and technical skills that are needed in a competitive situation. Blocked repetitive practise is also important, but needs to be supplemented with CHAOS and decision training.

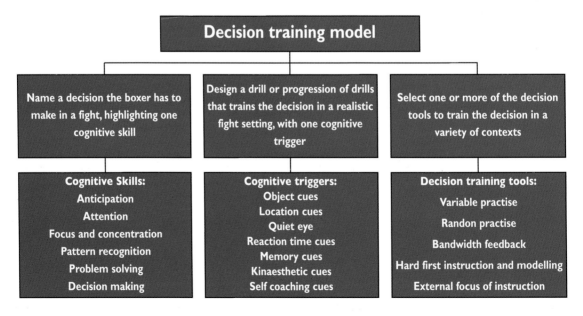

The decision training model.

Behavioural training (physical, technical, non cognitive)	Decision training (physical, technical, cognitive
Instruction – Part to whole training – Easy first instructional – Complex drills – Technical emphasis – Internal focus on instruction – Low use of video models	Instruction – Tactical whole training – Competition like thrills – Hard first instruction – Technique within tactics – External focus on instruction – High use of video models
Practise – Blocked practise – Low variability	Practise – Variable practise – Randon practise
Feedback – Abundant coach feedback – Low use of questioning – Low use of video feedback – Low athlete detection and correction of errors	Feedback – Bandwidth feedback – High use of questioning – High use of video feedback – High athlete detection and correction of errors
Overall Low levels of cognitive effort	Overall High levels of cognitive effort

Behavioural v. decision training.

Decision training makes complete use of video technology to help the boxer articulate why they made certain decisions and also why other fighters make the decisions they do. This discussion helps develop the cognitive skills needed to improve the quality of decision making through reflection and through learning from mistakes.

Decision training also involved the use of triggers, both visual and auditory, to stimulate specific responses to a variety of situations.

Complex and Contrast Training

Complex and contrast training combines weight training and plyometric training to enhance fast-twitch muscle fibre power and boxing performance. Exercises are paired to work the same muscle fast-twitch groups, and thus improving the plyometric performance. This is known as the potentiation effect, enhancing the training effect of one training method on another. The key purpose of the workouts is to improve the performance of type IIb fibres, which increase power.

Complex training involves performing sets of weight training exercises just prior to related plyometric exercises, which work the same muscle groups.

Contrast training involves alternating between the weights-based exercises and plyometric exercises.

Periodization

Periodization is the use of training systems that cycle various aspects of training throughout monthly or yearly

schedules. This recognizes that you cannot train everything at the same time, so you need to prioritize according to your requirements. (For further development of this theme, see Chapter 13.) The key advantages of this type of training programme are:

* Maximal recovery of the boxer
* Maximal progress for the boxer
* Maintains interest
* Maintains motivation and focus on the longer-term programme
* Minimizes the risk of injury

Plyometrics

Plyometrics is training designed to produce fast, powerful movements and improve the functions of the nervous system, so increasing performance in sports such as boxing. Plyometrics involve loading the muscle and then contracting in rapid sequence, using the strength, elasticity and innervation (see SAQ section above) of muscle and surrounding tissues to jump higher, run faster, throw farther or hit harder. An example of plyometrics exercise is jumping off one platform and straight back up onto another platform. This type of training should be carried out for a short period of time, typically 20 minutes, to avoid injury.

Kettlebell training

Kettlebells are an excellent way of enhancing boxing attributes for fighters. Kettlebells are designed to

Kettlebell drill 1: swings (1).

Kettlebell drill 1: swings (2).

Kettlebell drill 1: swings (3).

Kettlebell drill 2: snatch (1).

Kettlebell drill 2: snatch (2).

Kettlebell drill 2: snatch (3).

Kettlebell drill 3: two-handed clean and jerk (1).

Kettlebell drill 3: two-handed clean and jerk (2).

Kettlebell drill 3: two-handed clean and jerk (3).

Kettlebell drill 4: snatch and squat (1).

Kettlebell drill 4: snatch and squat (2).

Kettlebell drill 4: snatch and squat (3).

Kettlebell drill 5: two-handed squat and push press (1).

Kettlebell drill 5: two-handed squat and push press (2).

Kettlebell drill 6: punch drill (1).

Kettlebell drill 6: punch drill (2).

encourage full body, explosive movement that will enhance the boxer's ability to engage the full body to deliver maximal power, from the feet through the body and out via the hands to the target.

The real benefit of using kettlebells, over dumbbells, lies in the ball at the end of the handles. This means that, when completing any of the explosive lifts, the lifter has to make extra effort by engaging the forearm muscles, which is clearly very beneficial for the boxer. The objective of lifting kettlebells, to maximize the benefit to boxers, is to balance the kettlebell at the top of the lift.

The key principles to be applied to lifting kettlebells to maximise the benefit to boxers are:

* Lift the kettlebells from the floor
* Engage the body core to start and complete the lift
* Make the move explosive
* Carry out the exercise on both sides
* Ensure the movements are generated from the legs
* Ensure the correct technique is performed

The main lifts for boxing are:
* The snatch
* The clean
* The clean and jerk
* Complex 1 (two kettlebells, curl and shoulder press, one up, one down)

Applications of Training Systems for Attribute Development

A. Reaction speed

B. Power

C. Tempo and rhythm

D. Fitness

E. Strength

F. Speed

G. Agility

H. Quickness

I. Decision making

J. Accuracy

K. Recovery

Training system	A	B	C	D	E	F	G	H	I	J	K
SAQ	X	X		X		X	X	X			
CHAOS and decision training			X						X	X	
Weight training	X	X		X	X	X					
Kettlebell	X	X		X	X						
Complex and contrast	X	X		X	X	X					
Tabata	X	X		X						X	
Plyometrics	X	X									
Visioning									X	X	
Periodization											X

RING SCIENCE

Knowing is not enough; we must apply. Willing is not enough; we must do.
Johann Wolfgang von Goethe

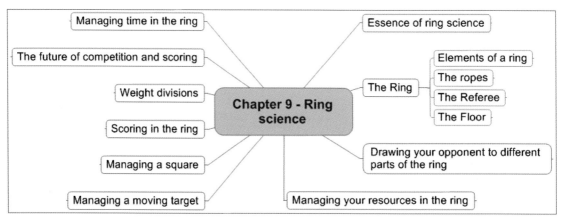

Mindmap overview of Chapter 9.

Essence of Ring Science

Ring science comprises the environment, ring craft and ring generalship. It is essential that the boxer fully understands the environment in which he operates. He needs to understand how to use every space in the ring to create an advantage for himself against his opponent.

Ring craft is the ability to meet and successfully solve problems as they arise in the ring and the different environments that are likely to exist. Ring generalship is a general plan of battle thought out in advance of the fight, which attempts to gain advantage over the opponent. Ring generalship is the boxer's ability to lead and control the match.

Some basic rules to succeed in the art of ring strategy may be expressed as follows:

Psychological (Mental Perspective)
* Think and outsmart your opponent. Boxing, at the highest level is a mental game that requires the boxer to outsmart and outthink his opponent.
* Relax and become one with your opponent. Thinking is important, but the thought process needs to become intuitive. This requires relaxation.
* Appear confident. The boxer needs to portray an image of confidence, irrespective of whatever is going on in his head.
* Be creative. This still is the true essence of man. Creativity is the ability of the boxer to do things that are outside the thought processes of his opponent.
* Move your body forward as you punch. This may appear physical, but we are referring to this from a mental perspective. Even when moving backwards, mentally the boxer should be thinking forward and attack.

Physical
* Be in good physical condition. The maximization of the performance of the boxer is dependent on the boxer being in optimal, physical condition.

Boxing Specific
* Know and fully understand the basics. All techniques should become totally intuitive.

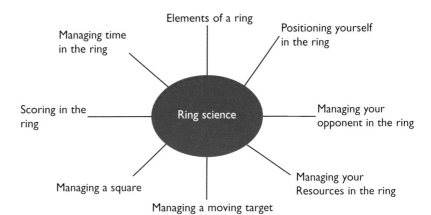

Overview of ring science.

* Keep moving in all directions. Consider the space around you as your playground for expression.
* Carry your hands in the position most appropriate for your distance from the opponent. Your hands are like a radar system able to gauge the level of threat posed by the opponent.
* Keep your chin tucked in. As well as its protective factor, the position of the chin also ensures optimal biomechanics in the delivery of boxing techniques.
* Use a good variety of techniques. Be comfortable delivering all appropriate techniques.
* Punch and move. All techniques should be accompanied by movement.
* Use the whole ring. This is your playground.
* Once the inside position has been reached, keep both hands punching.
* Remain unfazed by your opponent.
* When you punch, snap through your target.
* Straight punch will beat a hook. Simple physics.
* Outside position is the easiest place from which to launch an attack.

Ring science is essential for helping the athlete understand their operating environment. Just as footballers have to understand the football pitch and the roles different parts of the pitch play, the boxer has to understand the ring and make friends with every part of the ring. Some parts of the ring are seen to be threatening to the boxer. The training of the athlete has to focus on developing that intuitive feel for the ring and how to alter tactics in different parts of the ring. Key skills are required to develop the association with different parts of the ring.

Athletes also need to understand the decision-making process they go through to optimize the impact of their inputs in the ring.

Boxers spend considerable time on the bags and pads,

learning and refining techniques and combinations. So why does this go wrong in the ring? A key element of our training is to focus on the ability to attack a moving target and also attacking while moving. Most of the training carried out in the gym is on a static target of some description, whether it be the punch bag or focus pad. In fact, the only tool that really represents a true target is the floor-ceiling ball, but much of this practise also involves little movement, with the exception of the upper body.

The reality is that in the ring, the minute you decide to throw a punch in most cases your opponent will be looking to avoid your punch. Therefore you have to demonstrate an ability to adapt your technique for a moving target. Timing and range become vital features. In addition, the ring imposes restrictions in movement for yourself, especially as you get close to the ropes and corners.

Another difference between fighting in the ring and training in the gym is that in the gym we train against a mindset that appears to advocate a mentality of two-, three-, four- or five-punch combinations. Sometimes we will need to go beyond this. The way we train these combinations also assumes that there is no return of technique from our opponent. The reality in the ring is that we have to punch until the job is done, while responding to our worst nightmare – someone who does not know when to stop. Every time you throw a punch, they throw one back. Now if we analyse most of the training methods employed, they actually are very effective in that boxers take their training approaches into the ring: what they practice is what they do in the ring – not surprisingly. Many people are very effective at putting simple combinations together and then these come out in the ring. Unfortunately the opponent has not read the script and they have their own agenda.

We suggest that our training from the very beginning

should focus on developing an intuitive feel for attacking and defending, with little premeditated planning other than the desired outcome. The initial stages of the fight are used for analysis before getting into the relevant tactical mode. From a strategic perspective, the fighter needs to be a decision-maker and also needs to be adaptable and flexible. Boxing really is a true thinking man's game. The variables that the boxer has to really understand are:

* **Environment:** ring, temperature, fluids, crowd, opponent
* **Resources:** ability, thinking, decision-making, confidence

This mindset can be developed from the very start of training programmes. Clearly the boxer needs to learn basics, but they should learn the basics from a practical perspective from day one. The tvp boxing framework has been designed to provide this unique training perspective. In addition, the boxers should learn to be familiar with the ring from day one. They should be able to move around the ring comfortably in all directions, they should be comfortable defending themselves in the ring and responding with techniques of their own. In addition, the boxer should be able to sense his closeness to the ropes and feel quite comfortable changing his techniques and approach as he gets closer to the ropes.

The Ring

A useful starting point in any science is to fully understand the environment you are playing with. The following from the *2008–2009 USA Boxing Rulebook* (available at http://usaboxing.org/member-services/rulebook) is a very complete description of the ring:

The ring shall not be less than 16 nor more than 20 feet square within the ropes; the apron of the ring floor shall extend beyond the ropes not less than two feet. The ring shall not be more than four feet above the floor of the building or grounds of an outdoor arena and shall be provided with three sets of suitable steps for the use of boxers, coaches and officials, one in each boxer's corner and one in a neutral corner for use by doctors and referee . . .

The ring shall be equipped with at least four ropes. All rings will have two spacer ties on each side of the ring to secure the ropes. The rope shall not be less than one inch in diameter. Such ropes shall be manila rope, synthetic, plastic rope or any similar material, and shall not be made of metal of any type. All ropes shall be wrapped securely in soft material. Of the four ropes used, the lower rope shall be 18 inches above the ring floor, the second rope 30 inches, the third

Ring Variations

Size	Typical dimensions	Primary purpose	Attributes developed
Small	9 × 9ft – 2 × 12ft	Attribute development Sparring	Intricate footwork Full body movement Creative punching Awareness Rope fighting Opponent manoeuvring Space management Blocking Reactions
Medium	12 × 12ft – 15 × 15ft	Transitional/progression training Competitive sparring	Adaptability Fitness
Large	16 × 16ft	Amateur (punchers' ring) Amateur international (boxers' rings)	Competition familiarization Style development Style adaptation
	18 × 18ft	Pro	Strategy development
	20 × 20ft – 24 × 24ft		

Key Areas of the Ring: Pros and Cons

Part of the ring	Attacker advantages	Attacker disadvantages	Defender advantages	Defender disadvantages
Centre of ring	Controlling pace Control distance	Losing control of ring High likelihood of missing shots	Scope to move Potential control	Lack of control pace Inappropriate response (running)
Corners of ring	Less mobile target	Overconfidence	Turning opponent Limited decision making	Limited space Increased work rate Limited choices
Ropes	Less mobile target	Overconfidence	Turning opponent Limited decision making	Limited space Increased work rate Limited choices

rope 42 inches, and the fourth rope 54 inches above the ring floor. The ring floor shall be padded with a one-inch layer of ensolite AAC or AL closed cell foam rubber (or chemical equivalent). The padding shall be covered with canvas, duck or similar material, tightly stretched and laced securely in place, preferably under the apron. If the ropes are coloured red, white and blue, red is the top rope, followed by white, blue, etc.

Ring posts shall extend from the floor to the height of 58 inches above the ring floor. The ropes shall be connected to posts. The turnbuckles must be covered with a protective padding . . .

Plastic bags shall be fixed in the two neutral corners outside the ring in which the referee and doctor shall drop the cotton or tissue pads for bleeding.

Elements of a Ring

The ring is a unique area of space with real and imaginary boundaries. This space can be viewed as restrictive in real terms, but is actually the boxer's world, where the only limiting factor is the boxer's imagination. To maximize the impact of the ring we need to understand the different areas and features of the ring.

There are many different sizes of rings, designed both for training and for different levels of competition (for details *see* the accompanying table).

Key areas
The centre: This is the area of the ring that is most talked about in positive terms. Controlling the centre suggests

The ring: the centre.

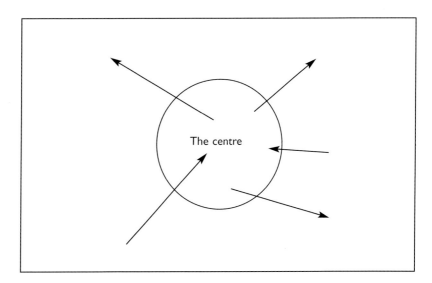

The centre

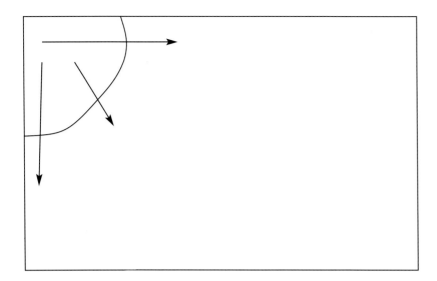

The ring: the corners.

the fighter has control of the fight. From the centre the fighter has space to move in all directions. Space is available to make mistakes. One of the dangers of the centre is that it can sometimes give a false sense of security. Controlling the centre allows the individual to look good, but sometimes without achieving anything. Fighting from the centre of the ring generally makes the fight a long-range fight.

The corners: The corners are quite restrictive as movement is restricted due to the limited space available. However, it does force the fighter into positive action and demands quite explosive movement in unusual directions. The corners also allow the fighter the opportunity to use an upward/downward movement to maximize the advantage of being in the corner. On many occasions coaches will give the fighter a feeling of apprehension when in the corners. The corners should be seen as an opportunity so

as to convey a positive mentality to the fighters wherever they are in the ring. Specific work needs to be carried out to help prepare the fighter to work in the corners. At this point the fight is most likely to be close quarter and will demand a very intuitive style of fighting that needs to be trained specifically for.

Specific work needs to be done on the defensive elements of fighting from the corners.

Ropes
Muhammad Ali made the 'rope a dope' famous in his fight against George Foreman. He used the ropes to support his fight strategy. What was remarkable was his appreciation of how to use what was available to him to his advantage, after considering all the pros and cons of his situation. A key element of the ring is the tension of the ropes. An increased tension in the ropes can allow extra

	Loose ropes	**Tight ropes**
Pros	**Good for soaking punishment, if required.**	**Good for rebound Can act as trigger for rapid movement away from the ropes.**
Cons	**Can be quite draining as there is no give.**	**Opponent can also rebound back onto you when attacked.**

The ropes.

force when rebounding off the ropes. Loose ropes can actually make it difficult to maintain a valid attack on your opponent.

Referee

The referee is essentially an obstacle and external figure that has the potential to move in an unpredictable manner. Awareness of the referee needs to be considered and therefore training needs to include a third person moving in the ring in unique directions. A great way of getting the same impact is by having two or three pairs performing in the ring at the same time.

Floor

One element of the ring that sometimes people do not take into consideration is the floor of the ring. This is usually made of a cloth mat that has a number of characteristics:
* Heavy duty: Quite a bit of friction causing restriction in movement, which increases the effort required to move. This can also cause slipping in the ring.
* Loose boarding: Position yourself in the ring and do not let the boarding spoil your movement.

Ring Performance

Drawing Your Opponent to Different Parts of the Ring

All boxers should be comfortable leading opponents to different parts of the ring. The ability to manoeuvre the opponent into key parts of the ring can be very beneficial in opening different responses from the opponent. This can be achieved through footwork, punching and body movement.

Managing Your Resources

The boxer needs to understand what the key resources are and how to maximize their effect. The key resources are:
* Energy: food intake, drinks, nervous state, rate of burn, mental state
* Power: energy, mechanics, relaxation
* Air: quality of air, humidity, smell, gum shields, nasal breathing

Managing a Moving Target

The key resource for focusing on a moving target is feel and sight. Very rarely will the boxer be offered a static target. The key targets on the human body are differentiated by size, mobility and impact potential. Essentially there are three primary targets that a boxer can legitimately hit: face, body and arms.

To assist with the development of skills for hitting a moving target, focus pads are ideal, providing the pad holder is constantly moving the focus pads so that they are presented as moving targets. Floor-ceiling balls are excellent for developing the appreciation for changing range, but a good coach who is able to move the focus pads in all different directions and place the pads in different locations is the ideal solution. These skills need to be specifically built on and not left to chance through sparring.

The understanding of the different targets and which ones are easier to hit is critical when taking into account how fights are scored (see below).

Managing a Square

One of the major skills to be developed is the art of moving in a square ring. This means we need to understand how the ring is shaped and how we might categorise its different sections.

The different types of footwork that may be used to move around the ring are:
* Forward/backward

Managing Moving Targets

Target	Size	Mobility	Impact potential
Face	Small	Highly mobile due to range of motion of head. Head also has complete range of movement in lateral, linear and circular direction	Can be very damaging if hit on correct spot on the head. The face allows multiple targets to be hit from multiple directions: uppercut, hooks, rear hand and lead hand punches
Body	Large	Limited mobility. Very dependent on footwork. Without footwork it is very difficult to move target away from opponent	Can be very damaging if hit with the right punches. The body is very difficult to protect and can lead to head being vulnerable as the body's resistance is broken down. All punches to body can be effective
Arms	Medium	Limited mobility, unless body is moved	Limited damage potential

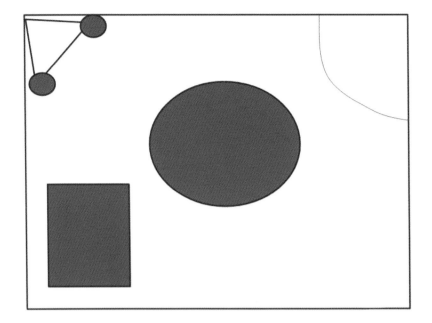

The ring: areas for movement.

* Lateral steps
* Spinning on a foot
* Sidestep
* Forward step

Appropriate Footwork for Different Areas of the Ring

Footwork	Corners	Centre	Ropes
Forward/backward		X	
Lateral steps	X	X	X
Spinning on foot	X	X	X
Sidestep	X	X	X
Forward/backward step		X	

Scoring in the Ring

One of the most intriguing things that we find is how many boxers actually know how they will win a fight. This is like trying to win a game and not knowing how you can actually win it. A key aspect of boxing is understanding how to score. Unfortunately, much of this is still left to chance, unless there is a knockout, but sometimes a more tactical fight has to be followed. Therefore it is essential to know how you are scored.

The scoring of a professional fight is based on four basic criteria: clean punching, effective aggressiveness, ring generalship, and defence.

Professional fights are scored on a Ten Point Must System in which the boxer who wins a round must be awarded ten points, with his opponent receiving nine or less, usually nine. A fighter loses a point for every knockdown he suffers. Thus a boxer who is winning a round and scores two knockdowns during that round will earn a score of ten, while his opponent gets a seven.

The four scoring criteria are used to determine the winner of each round. Once the fight is over, the scores from each of the three ringside judges are tallied and the results announced.

While clean punching is generally given greater weight by most judges, the other three are also vital.

Clean punching
A clean punch is one that lands on a scoring area (face or side of head, not including the back of the head; the front and sides of the torso) with the knuckle portion of the glove. In amateur boxing, the scoring portion of the glove is white. Though a professional glove lacks such markings, the scoring portion of the glove is basically the same.

Clean punches will land flush, not glancing or partially blocked by one's opponent. 'Slapping' or 'backhanding' is not allowed.

Effective aggressiveness
Effective aggression is demonstrated when a fighter presses forward and, in doing so, scores more clean punches, or more damaging blows, than his opponent. If a boxer is a particularly hard puncher, even blows that are

not landed particularly cleanly, but obviously affect his opponent, are given scoring weight.

Ring generalship
The ability to control the pace and style of a fight is ring generalship. For instance, a high volume-punching brawler will attempt to force a 'stick and move' boxer into a slugfest. Conversely, the pure boxer will attempt to slow the pace of the fight by keeping his opponent at the end of his jab and use angles and feints in order to set up his heavier punches.

It is imperative that professional judges comprehend each fighter's respective style in order to understand who is controlling the action and demonstrating superior ring generalship.

Defence
The fourth criteria used for judging is defence, the ability to avoid an attack. A boxer with greater reach than his opponent may stay on the outside and use his footwork to avoid punches. Other options are to stay inside and slip punches or block an opponent's punches with one's gloves, arms and shoulders. A highly skilled fighter may choose to use a combination of defensive techniques, depending on the situation.

If two boxers are awarded the same number of points, the judges decide a winner by assessing such factors as which boxer took the lead and showed better style. If those factors are also found to be even, the judges turn to the competitor who showed better defence.

Punches to an opponent's arms, or punches judged to have no force behind them, do not score points.

Common fouls that are penalized include hitting below the belt, holding, pressing an arm or elbow into the opponent's face, forcing the opponent's head over the ropes, hitting with an open glove, hitting with the inside of the glove and hitting the opponent on the back of the head, neck or body. Others include passive defence, not stepping back when ordered to break, speaking offensively to the referee and trying to hit the opponent immediately after the order to break.

Weight Divisions	
There are eleven weight divisions (with maximum weights) as follows:	
Light flyweight	(48kg)
Flyweight	(51kg)
Bantamweight	(54kg)
Featherweight	(57kg)
Lightweight	(60kg)
Light welterweight	(64kg)
Welterweight	(69kg)
Middleweight	(75kg)
Light heavyweight	(81kg)
Heavyweight	(91kg)
Super heavyweight	(more than 91kg)

Decisions
Unanimous decision: All three judges score the same boxer as the winner.
Split decision: Two judges score in favour of one boxer (the winner) and one judge scores in favour of the other.
Majority decision: Two judges score for one boxer (the winner) and one judge scores the match a draw.
Draw: One judge scores in favour of one boxer, one judge scores in favour of the other, and one judge scores the match a draw. Neither boxer wins the match.
Majority draw: A very rare result given when two judges score a draw and one judge scores in favour of one boxer.

If a fighter is penalized by the referee, for example for multiple low blows, the referee will instruct each ringside judge individually to deduct a point for that fighter from their score card for that round.

The future of competition and scoring
Scientific experts at the Australian Institute of Sport (AIS), working in collaboration with a range of partners, including the Commonwealth Scientific Research Organisation (CSIRO), are exploring ways to use microtechnology monitoring sensors in the development of new automated scoring systems that could aid the future judging and safety of both men's and women's boxing.

Round Objectives by Assessment

	Punching	Aggressiveness	Ring generalship	Defence
Early part	Reconnaissance Familiarization Identifying mannerisms	Low to high Dependent on a number of factors	High Identify gaps and opportunities	Space management
Middle part	Increase work rate	As above	Change according to assessment in early part of round	Use more defensive choices
Final part	Push the boundary	High rate	Tighter use of space	Keep compact, but think attack

Managing Time in the Ring

Different tactics should be applied for different phases of the fight and different phases of the round. In its simplest form we should think of both the rounds and fight in terms of the first third, second third and final third. The only reason for this categorization is the three-minute round. You may find that for a two-minute round you split the fight into four phases, for example.

The accompanying table shows where the priorities might lie in terms of objectives for punching, aggressiveness, ring generalship and defence. The obvious reason for this selection is that our strategy and tactics should relate to what the fighter is being assessed by.

SPARRING

The wise learn many things from their enemies.
Aristophanes

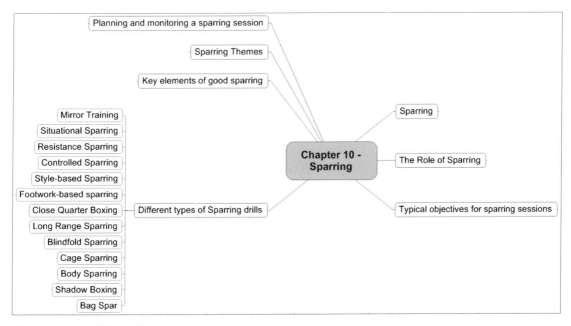

Mindmap overview of Chapter 10.

One of the most frequently asked questions in boxing today is, 'Who would be the champions today, the current crop of boxers or the fighters of yesteryear?'

Most people would say today's boxers would be superior because they are bigger, better, stronger and quicker than those of yesteryear. Do today's boxers have better fundamentals and throw more punches than their predecessors? Certain myths surrounding fighters from the past are stated as fact – they didn't throw combination punches, they didn't move with lateral movement, they were slow, crude, with only one pace and with limited skills – but what is the evidence?

Today's fighters with more knowledge of nutrition and sports science are are supposed to be far superior to those of yesteryear, according to some, but this is simply not the case in our opinion. If you look at the methods of boxing training today, there hasn't been much change from the practises used 100 years ago in most gyms: skipping, running, bag work, floor to ceiling ball, medicine ball and sparring. They have all been around since the nineteenth century. The many training improvements from sports science and nutritional supplements have not helped today's crop of fighters box any better than the past champions. Despite all the available technology, some of today's fighters still can't make it to the final bell, or even to the twelfth round.

The only significant change in the game is that fighters today box fewer rounds than those in the past, with styles remaining pretty much the same. A swarmer back then boxes the same as a swarmer today. Whether the fighter be a southpaw or a swinger, a counter-puncher or a hit-and-move artist, they used the same styles back then as they do today. Nothing has really changed.

What has changed is the way the fighters' condition themselves. Jim Jefferies was a heavyweight champion in the 1900s, and his daily training regime was as follows:

* Each morning he ran 14 miles, alternating from a jog to a 100 yard sprint, without stopping to rest or walk.
* In the afternoon he played three games of hand-ball.
* He punched a bag for 25 minutes straight.
* He then skip-roped between 1,500 and 2,000 times.
* He would then box for 12 to 16 rounds or toss an 18 ounce medicine ball!

Even without the advances in sports science this type of workout would make a fighter tireless in the ring, even today. Going back to the conditioning side, fighters of the past lived in an age where there were fewer cars, people walked a lot more and food was not sprayed with chemicals. Many boxing fans are under the impression that the old-timers, although tough and strong, lacked the boxing skills to compete with the more modern fighters. An early twentieth-century swarmer lightweight champion, Battling Nelson, might lose every round in a twelve-round fight against a fast and elusive Floyd Mayweather. But in fairness, how would Floyd perform against Nelson if he had to pace himself for a forty-five round fight to the finish? Or how would he fare with 5oz horsehair gloves, no mouthpiece, no padded canvas, no protective cup and a referee who was quite liberal with fouls? Floyd Mayweather would never have seen the thirtieth round, let alone the fortieth, and would almost certainly have succumbed to Nelson's fierce body punches as he slowed down, because Mayweather isn't conditioned to fight for longer than twelve rounds. Jess Willard defended his heavyweight title against Jack Dempsey in 1919 and continued to fight for three rounds despite horrific injuries that extended to four broken ribs, cheekbone fractures in three or four places, a broken nose, both eye sockets smashed and damaged ear drums. Then consider Sonny Liston in his first fight with Cassius Clay in 1964, conceding after six rounds with a slight shoulder injury by quitting on his stool.

During the olden days, the fighters fought four or five times a week. Clearly there are medical constraints and health issues today, but the point is that the fighters of yesteryear were conditioned for a totally different and more brutal fight game, in which today's fighters would not stand a chance, in our opinion.

The early twentieth-century boxers were also much better at infighting than the current crop. The reason for this is that modern referees separate fighters as soon as they get close to the clinch. It has been said that fighters in the early twentieth century fought at a slow pace and

their punch statistics don't equal that of modern fighters. This is a myth. Consider the following. The fight between Ad Wolgast and Battling Nelson for the lightweight title, held on 22 February 1910, was described as concentrated viciousness, the most savage bout ever witnessed. They fought to the forty-second round. Nelson, a swarmer like Ricky Hatton, averaged eighty-five punches a round and threw ninety shots in the thirtieth round. These guys threw just as many punches per round as we see in modern bouts but they did the same over forty rounds.

People say fighters back in the old days didn't punch as hard or as cleanly, and scored fewer early round KO's, but this isn't the case. The vintage fighters fought more scheduled rounds so the average fight lasted longer.

We underestimate the talents of the boxers from the early twentieth century, before fights were televised.

So what can we learn from the old fighters in today's training environment? Perhaps, reflecting on the capabilities from the olden days, our training regime needs to toughen up. Firstly, much of the equipment used today in modern gyms is actually responsible for not maximizing the potential of fighters. Weights made up of awkward, everyday shapes such as tree trunks and sand bags force all muscles and joints to be utilized together, thus working on developing core stability. Muscle isolation by using fancy multi-gyms stops us from maximizing the workout. Additionally, we tend to limit our training to between three and five sets – why not eight sets, to build the resistance and determination? You need to beware, however, of the body warning you of injuries. Full body exercises are demanded to maximize the benefits of the workout.

Repetition is necessary to achieve the mentality, discipline and toughness needed in such rigorous situations. The objectives have to be clear. If we consider our tvp framework, for example, restricted time should be spent on developing quality of delivery. However, once refinement has taken place repetition on bag, floor-ceiling ball and sparring will develop the required levels of performance. Instead of doing 1-, 2- and 3-minute rounds, you should do 5–10 minute rounds, building up intensity in rounds. Instead of doing 10–12 rounds, do 20 rounds. To develop the ability to throw plenty of punches, or kicks for that matter for kick boxing, aim to build a sequence in the rounds of bag work and sparring by starting low and building up to above average performance. The objective of training based around these concepts is that we are trying to increase the number of punches thrown. Some people might see this as not being the same as punches landed, but you have to have the capacity to throw the punches before you land them. A typical weekly workout developed at the tvp Academy would look as follows for building endurance for sparring:

tvp Typical Weekly Workout

Day	Resistance-based workout	Fight-specific workout
Sun		Technique work: 30 minutes 10 × 5min rounds on bag. Punches per minute: 15, 25, 20, 30, 10
Mon	Afternoon: 8 set based exercises at 50%, 60%, 65%, 55%, 70%, 70%, 60%, 80% of maximum load for: bench-press, squat, bent over rowing, dead lifts, shoulder press. Followed by tricep dips and chins. 15 mins abs workout	Morning: 3 × 10 min rounds on floor ceiling ball at controlled pace
Tues	Rest	3 × 5 mins on speedball
Wed		Variety-based workout: 45 mins 5 × 10 min rounds sparring
Thurs	Afternoon: 8 set based exercises at 50%, 60%, 65%, 55%, 70%, 70%, 60%, 80% of maximum load for: bench-press, squat, bent over rowing, dead lifts, shoulder press. Followed by tricep dips and chins. 15 mins abs workout	Morning: 3 × 10 min rounds on bag. Punches thrown per minute: 15, 20, 25, 30, 20, 15, 20, 15, 30, 15
Fri	Rest	3 × 5 mins on speedball
Sat		Predictability work: 60 mins 5 × 10 mins sparring – body sparring

Workout Objective for Period

1. Ability to fight strongly for 15 × 3-minute rounds, hitting an average of 80 punches per round, giving a total of 1,200 punches.
2. Throw 25 punches per minute of every round

Equipment required: Free weights; floor ceiling ball; speedball; punchbag; partner; ring

The accompanying table shows a typical weekly workout programme that stretches the capability of the boxer.

The Role of Sparring

A fundamental part of boxing training is sparring. This section will look at how to get the maximum out of sparring to help with the development of our boxing skills.

The role of sparring is to allow the boxer to experiment with techniques, to experience the challenges of delivering techniques in unpredictable circumstances and to build an intuitive feel for reacting to your opponent, in a broad variety of scenarios.

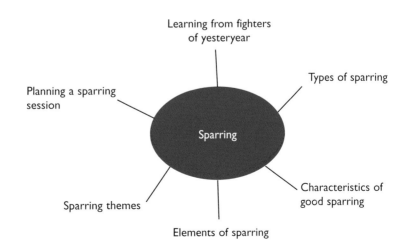

Overview of sparring.

The key requirements for sparring are:

A ring: sparring is designed to recreate the competitive situation as closely as possible, under controlled circumstances, so a ring is a must.

An appropriate opponent or training partner: the key is to find an opponent who will satisfy the basic objectives of your sparring session. You also need to find an opponent who will stretch you during your sessions. The reason for calling your opponent a training partner is that he is there to work with you to improve you, not beat you.

Clear objectives: all sparring sessions should have clearly defined objectives so that you are in control of your development. This also ensures the greatest return from your training time.

Ground rules to achieve objectives: clear rules are needed to ensure that the sparring session does not deteriorate into a brawl.

Typical Objectives for Sparring Sessions

Boxing specific
* Practise technique
* Practise variety
* Practise being unpredictable

Physiological conditioning
* Develop fitness/stamina
* Improving reactions and reflexes

Competition specific
* Learning to read different opponents
* Coping with pressure
* Fight preparedness
* Coping with different styles
* Improving footwork

Sparring Drills

Type of sparring	Objectives of sparring	Skills/competencies developed
Mirror training	Replicate other fighter's skills Learning to observe opponent Learning to read body movement	Variety in technique Intuitive skills Body language
Situational sparring	Develop intuitive responses to specific situations Develop creativity skills in restricted situations	Specific skills
Resistance sparring	Develop power Develop speed Increase responsiveness	Power and speed in hitting punches from multiple situations
Style-based sparring	Learning advantages and disadvantages of different styles Understanding which styles can be combined with your own style	Awareness of how alternative styles fight
Controlled sparring	Continuity in attack Moving smoothly from defence to attack Build confidence to attack and be hit	Ability to keep hitting until fight is over or advantage is gained
Footwork-based sparring	Develop ability to move quickly Become one with the attack	Footwork
Close-quarter sparring	Build intuitive feel of how opponent will move in tight space Learn to feel opponent's movement	Sensory skills
Long-range sparring	Move in and out of range	Covering distance
Blindfold sparring	Develop intuitive feel for delivering techniques and movement	Intuition
Cage-based sparring	Develop leg power for movement and punching	Power
Bag spar	Developing tvp attributes	All-round boxing capability
Body sparring	Building defence and competitiveness	Competitiveness
Shadow boxing	Visualizing different styles	Visualization

Mirror sparring (1).

Mirror sparring (2).

Mirror sparring (3).

Mirror sparring (4).

* Coping with range
* Improving decision making during fights

Types of Sparring Drills

There are many forms of sparring practise. Each of these has a specific objective and is used to develop different skills and competencies.

A key method of training mentioned earlier is decision based training, where video recordings are used to assist the boxer identify strengths and weaknesses (see Chapter 8).

Mirror Training

This involves replicating another fighter or coach. The key to making this form of sparring valuable is to find a good selection of fighters from different backgrounds, with different strengths and weaknesses, and fighters who like to express themselves.

This form of sparring can take place anywhere in the gym, but we suggest that all of these drills should take place in the ring to assist in the familiarization of the ring.

Divide the ring into two, and place the lead fighter in one half and give him three minutes to express himself. The aim of the boxer is to maintain and replicate move-

ment with the fighter. For the next three minutes the boxer will now become the lead. The role of the lead is to outfox the other fighter. This will demand creativity and an increase in movement speed.

Situational Sparring

Situational sparring involves creating specific situations, perhaps based on weaknesses that the boxer is suffering from, and developing responses that are then repeated.

Situational sparring can also be used to restrict the one boxer to one range of techniques and the other fighter to something totally different. Restrictive sparring involves creating restriction for one or both boxers, so as to allow greater focus on a particular aspect of the technique.

Restrictions may apply in terms of the following:
* Who is attacking?
* Who is defending?
* What techniques may be used?
* What targets might be hit?
* What pace the session will take place at?

Resistance Sparring

Resistance-based sparring involves the use of resistance bands tied to the corners, and the use of viper belts, to restrict movement. This method may be combined with any of the other forms of sparring.

Sparring (1).

Sparring (2).

Sparring (3).

Sparring with resistance band and partner (1).

Sparring with resistance band and partner (2).

Sparring with resistance band and partner (3).

Sparring with resistance band and partner (4).

Sparring with resistance band and partner (5).

Controlled Sparring

Controlled sparring is carried out at a lighter pace and power. The objective is to control the hits so giving the boxers the opportunity to learn from attacks and defences that work and fail.

Style-Based Sparring

Style-based sparring is excellent for building a boxer's appreciation of the strengths and weaknesses of different styles. Each boxer will be given a specific style to replicate and will fight incorporating that style. A great way of learning specific styles is to analyse old fights and identify what works and what does not.

Defending with footwork (1).

Defending with footwork (2).

Footwork-Based Sparring

One fighter can punch and the other fighter has to evade using only his footwork,

Close-Quarter Boxing

The objective of close-quarter boxing is to encourage continuity and in some cases even having the fighters close their eyes so they develop the feel of the other fighter.

Long-Range Sparring

The primary objective of long-range sparring is to develop the ability to get in to deliver a punch and immediately move out of range to avoid being hit.

Blindfold Sparring

This requires considerable skill and is really targeted at the experienced boxer looking to develop his feel for close-in fighting. A key feature of this form of sparring is maintaining contact in some form with your training partner. Clearly, the pace of the session should be geared to the experience level of the boxers. Less experienced boxers should be very closely monitored and encouraged to take a very slow pace. The objective of the session is to feel

Partner shadow boxing in ring (1).

Partner shadow boxing in ring (2).

Partner shadow boxing in ring (3).

your opponent and be able to respond instantly to his movement changes,

Cage Sparring

Placing a height restriction on the ring, by using a net for example, forces the boxers to adopt very low stances. This is a great stamina workout, but also develops leg strength necessary to develop power. In addition, the boxers will enhance their body hitting techniques considerably.

Body Sparring

Body sparring allows both boxers to hit in a competitive manner with minimal risk of injury. The target is set between neck and the naval. The method also encourages the development of body defence techniques.

Shadow Boxing

Shadow boxing is a very effective way of developing a feel for delivering techniques with movement, and with minimal risk. Shadow boxing is also an effective way of warming up. However, shadow boxing needs to have specific themes built into the workouts to prevent the workout being a pure cardio workout. Typical themes would be adapting your fighting style for other fighting styles.

Shadow boxing, if performed correctly, can be a very powerful way of developing the creative and concentration skills required in boxing. However, considerable patience is required on the part of the boxer. Boredom may set in and there may be over-reliance on the coach to dictate the content of the session.

The primary objectives of shadow boxing are:
* warm-up: raising heart rate
* technique familiarization

Typical Bag Spar Rounds

Timing	Round 1	Round 2	Round 3
0–20s	Position of non-punching hand	Tempo changes	Freestyle round
20–30s	*Break*	*Break*	*Break*
30–50s	Bodyweight transfer	Preferred direction of movement	Freestyle round
50–60s	*Break*	*Break*	*Break*
60–80s	Break off from inside position	Footwork patterns	Freestyle round
80–90s	*Break*	*Break*	*Break*
90–110s	Quality of technique	Danger punch	Freestyle round
110–120s	*Break*	*Break*	*Break*
120–140s	Relaxation and acceleration in technique delivery	Movement of head	Freestyle round
140–150s	*Break*	*Break*	*Break*
150–170s	Preferred attacking tools	Movement patterns and mannerisms	Freestyle round
170–180s	*Break*	*Break*	*Break*
180–200s	Preferred defensive tools	Change of movement speed	Freestyle round
200–210s	*Break*	*Break*	*Break*
210–230s	Mannerism of style	Freestyle round	Freestyle round
230–240s	*Break – 2 minutes*	*Break – 2 minutes*	*Break – 2 minutes*

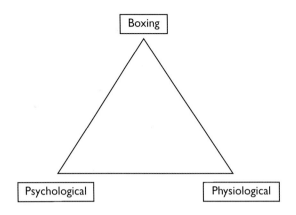

The key elements of sparring.

* creativity
* visualization
* patience
* security
* focus

Bag Spar

Bag spar is simply sparring on the punch bag, but with focused themes. The ideal themes that we work to are based on the tvp framework. Using the Tabata intervals (4-minute rounds comprising 8 × 20s on, 1 0s off), focus on monitoring the boxer for each of the tvp elements.

A bag spar workout would comprise of a creative round of boxing hitting and moving around the bag, with particular emphasis on the following elements in the accompanying table.

Key Elements of Good Sparring

The key elements of sparring may be captured in terms of three areas: boxing, physiological and psychological.

Boxing attributes (based on tvp attributes)
* Attacking
* Defending
* Evading
* Countering
* Confusing

Physiological attributes
* Continuity in sparring – lightweight sparring
* Ability to take a punch
* Varying speed when sparring
* Acceleration in sparring

Psychological attributes
* Getting relaxed when sparring
* Mental state when sparring

Sparring Themes

When designing a sparring session it is important to consider the focus of the session. If you consider the

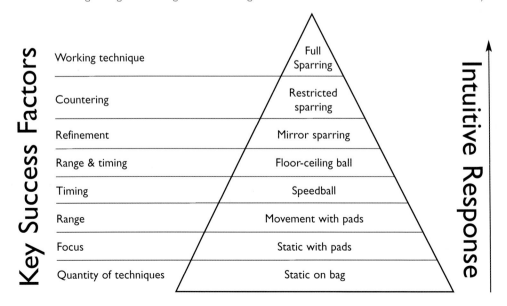

Technical Development Pyramid.

Combining Sparring Themes

	Power	Speed	Aerobic	Anaerobic
Attack	Development of power in punching	Development of speed in punching and moving	Development of the ability to continue punching over the full duration of the fight	Development of the ability to punch with power over a long period of time
Ring generalship	Development of dominating styles			
Effective aggressiveness	Developing confidence	Control of aggression	Fitness	
Defence	Strength in technique	Developing reaction speed to deliver defensive techniques	Development of aerobic capacity to defend	Development of strength in delivering defensive techniques

scoring mechanism used in boxing, it makes sense to incorporate these, in addition to the different attributes required, into the sparring sessions.

Boxing-Based Themes

Attack: a very important part of boxing as this is probably the most recognizable way of scoring points and winning a fight. Though the other elements of scoring are important, without an ability to attack there is no chance of winning.

Ring generalship: a key to gaining points for ring generalship is the ability to understand the advantages and disadvantages of different styles of fighters, and to understand how these styles command the ring.

Effective aggressiveness: is looking at ways in which a boxer controls the fight through aggression and directing this aggression in the right way.

Defence: this is very often an overlooked area. Points may be scored through a demonstration of confidence and control by defending yourself in a technically competent manner.

Athletic-based Themes

Power: development of hitting power
Speed: development of speed in delivering techniques
Aerobic: development of cardiovascular fitness
Anaerobic: development of muscular capacity

Combining Themes

The best way to maximize the benefit of sparring sessions is to combine the themes, as shown in the accompanying table.

Planning and Monitoring a Sparring Session

When planning a sparring session it is important to know what is to be achieved and how this is to be done. Keep to the plan and maintain records of the outcome, as seen below:

Theme of sessions:

Key objectives of session:

Duration of session: mins.

Skills to be developed

		Session Number					
Skill	Method	1	2	3	4	5	6

FIGHT STRATEGIES

All the time he's boxing, he's thinking. All the time he was thinking, I was hitting him.
Jack Dempsey

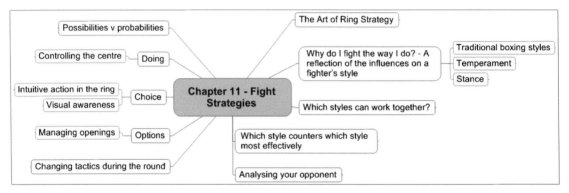

Mindmap overview of Chapter 11.

The Art of Ring Strategy

The art of ring strategy requires the fighter being able to understand his environment (his relative positioning in the ring, the state of the ring and its surroundings), understand the strengths and weaknesses of the opponent and, very importantly, understand his own strengths and weaknesses. An understanding of these three core elements allows the fighter to formulate decisions in a rational and objective manner. In a split second the fighter has to analyse, explore options and decide what his action is going to be, as shown in the decision-making cycle.

There tends to be a huge reliance on the coach in the corner to tell the boxer what to do at the end of the round. Unfortunately that may be too late. The boxer needs to take full responsibility for making those decisions during the round, as well as at the end.

Analyse

Analyse the Opponent

As a starting point the fighter needs to be able to understand the different types of opponents he is likely to be facing. He also needs to be aware of the different ways by which to deal with the different styles.

The fighter needs to be adaptable and versatile. There will be times when you are faced with a taller opponent or a more able counterpuncher, for example, which is why it is so important to include different types of sparring partners to perfect the tactics against the different styles. An important aspect of training for ring strategies is to consider to what degree certain styles can adopt other styles and how effectively these can be embraced by the boxer. The different ways in which you adopt different styles will have an impact on the way the boxer is perceived.

Why Do I Fight the Way I Do?

Many fighters may wonder why they possess a particular style. The key influences in the fighting style of the fighter include body type and physique. Some fighters, however, might be of the same weight but possess contrasting styles. In this section we would like to explore the styles and the impact on your body from a physiological perspective.

A fighter's style can usually suggest whether the fighter is maximizing the impact of his natural attributes. It is all well and good being coached, but there are many exam-

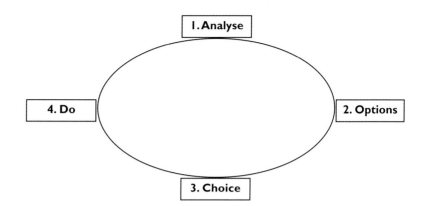

The fighter's decision-making cycle.

ples of fighters adopting styles that actually conflict with their natural attributes, restricting their ability to fulfil their potential, and also causing injury through stresses imposed on the body.

Traditional Boxing Styles

Boxing styles adopted by boxers vary according to a number of key factors:
* body and build
* height of boxer
* temperament

These factors affect the reach of the boxer and his ability to move in and out of range quickly. The traditional boxing styles adopted tend to be those given below.

Slugger	Heavy puncher with low work rate. Generating power from the floor. Relatively tight and compact. Heavy shots. Delivering single shots.
Crouch and weaver	Works on the inside. Liable to hit up using push from the ground. Constantly working with body movement. Constantly presents moving target. Superior drive upwards from legs when attacking. Difficult to hit due to superior head movement.
Swarmer	High work rate based on tempo, relatively low power hitting. Continuous punching.
Persistent jabber	Little control. Fighting technique based on jab and run. No rear hand. Easily defeated once jab has been passed. Ideal to be trapped against ropes, as they are used to looking for space to run into.
Swinger	Slow on feet generally. Generate power from floor, meaning that they tend to be fairly static. Tend to stalk the opponent to a committed position such as the ropes so as to launch an attack.
Counterpuncher	Wait and see character to fighting. Hard to combat unless you specialize in drawing, feinting and countering their counter. Difficult to get the counter-puncher to lead. Bodyweight towards front foot.
Southpaw	Majority are counterpunchers. Dangerous left hand if they are true southpaws. Have an advantage in that they face more orthodox fighters than the other way round. Need to specialize in drawing the southpaw.
Short box fighter	Very strong on the inside position. Successful in working opponents into corners and ropes. Tend to cut the ring off for opponents. Style based on two handed attacks.
Rusher	Normally works in a straight line. Untrained boxer with little lateral move-ment. Explosive off the start and work little off angles.
Heavy puncher	Punches with full commitment of body and mind with all punches.
Switch hitter	Capable of leading off both sides. Hits with confidence with rear hands in both stances. Capable of putting shots together on both sides without compro-mise.

The attributes possessed by fighters that affect what style is adopted are body type, temperament and stance.

Body Types
Body types can be categorized generally by:
* height (tall, medium or short)
* build (well built, medium or slim)

The shorter fighter: The shorter fighter needs to develop the style of the counterpuncher with his weight towards the front foot, but under no circumstances should his body weight be over the front foot as this will move him into striking range of the opponent.

The taller fighter: The taller, thinner fighter will have his weight towards his rear leg, as he should use his height and reach to his advantage. From this position his jab will be his main scoring weapon. The stance of the taller fighter will also be more sideways on to his opponent, emphasizing the reach advantage over his opponent.

Temperament

Another key factor affecting the stance to be adopted by the fighter is the personality of the individual. For instance, a very strong and aggressive type of boxer should not be moulded into a cagey counterpuncher as he will find this a very restrictive style. On the other hand, if the fighter is a natural counterpuncher with a passive personality it will be extremely dangerous to turn him into a Joe Frazier type of character.

Stance

An important aspect of developing a style of fighting is how well a fighter adapts to an orthodox or southpaw style. The key question is who decides: the coach or fighter. Some natural right-handers are encouraged by their coaches to become southpaws regardless, and this leads to the southpaw becoming a one-handed fighter. He has little or no power in his rear hand, he has no control of his rear hand, and most importantly he will have no confidence in his ability to throw his rear hand. The same is true of the left-hander as well. In these cases the fighter will never fulfil his potential, as his development will be stunted forever. One of the key problems is that the fighters feel comfortable when they should not be.

The fighter should decide which is the most appropriate stance to be adopted. The coach can advise the fighter, but the fighter should explore in sparring, padwork and bagwork the limitations of working in different stances.

Selecting Styles

A very damaging assumption made by different fighters is that they can emulate their heroes in terms of fighting prowess. Unfortunately they do not possess the attributes to copy the likes of Prince Naseem. Coaches may end up producing fighters with a certain style and not different fighters. This is seen very clearly with the martial arts where it is relatively easy to spot fighters from certain clubs because of the style and techniques adopted.

All fighters should be able to fight comfortably in both stances with power in either hand, and should also be able to move in both directions. Going back to the question of styles, many bad habits are allowed to form in a fighter's style because the coach is not aware of the fault, or the coach has not shown the fighter, from the beginning, a mechanically sound technique.

Brendan Ingle's fighters appear to be trained in the same way and doing the same thing, but in fact they are not. Brendan sets down a template within which they develop. He lets them explore their potential and develop to fulfil that potential. He does not teach his boxers to be clones, although it appears that way. A study of the styles of Johnny Nelson, Junior Witter and Prince Naseem demonstrates that fact.

A fighter's physical shape can also predetermine the ring style. Short heavyweights like Rocky Marciano, Joe Frazier and Mike Tyson were aggressive fighters out of necessity, who had to get inside their opponent's longer reach and work with close bent arm shots. Ernie Terrell, WBA Champion in the 1960s, at 6ft 6in, could never attempt such a style. He used his height and reach to make himself the most awkward heavyweight of his era.

Ideal Features of the Different Styles

Style	Height	Build	Temperament	Level of adaptability
Crouch and weaver	Short	Stocky	Aggressive	Medium
Persistent jabber	Tall	Lean and slim	Anxious	Low
Swinger	Tall	Heavy	Aggressive	High
Counterpuncher	Medium	Any	Calm	High
Southpaw	Any	Any	Any	High
Short box fighter	Any	Any	Any	High
Rusher	short – medium	Stocky	Aggressive	Low
Switch hitter	Any	Any	Any	High
Swarmer	Shorter	Stocky	Aggressive	Low
Slugger	Shorter	Stocky	Aggressive	Low
Heavy puncher	Any	Any	Any	

Which Styles Can Work Together?

L – Low, M – Medium, H – High

Style	Level of adaptability	CW	PJ	SW	CP	SP	SB	RU	SH	SM	SL	HP
Crouch and weaver (CW)	M		L	M	H	H	H	H	H	H	H	H
Persistent jabber (PJ)	L	L		L	L	L	L	M	H	L	L	L
Swinger (SW)	H	L	L		L	H	L	L	H	L	M	H
Counterpuncher (CP)	H	H	L	L		H	H	L	H	L	L	L
Southpaw (SP)	H	H	H	H	H		H	H	H	H	H	H
Short box fighter (SB)	H	H	H	H	H	H		H	H	H	H	H
Rusher (RU)	L	H	L	M	L	H	H		L	H	H	H
Switch hitter (SH)	H	L	L	L	M	H	L	L		L	L	L
Swarmer (SM)	L	H	L	H	L	H	H	H	L		H	L
Slugger (SL)	L	H	L	H	L	H	L	H	L	H		H
Heavy puncher (HP)	H	H	H	H	H	H	H	H	H	H	H	

Rocky Marciano was one of the roughest and toughest heavyweights of all time. He made his 68in reach, his 5ft 10in height and 13 stone bodyweight work for him by adopting a style that consisted of a 'hit them anywhere' approach. If his punches did not land on the target area then he would punch your arms until blood vessels were ruptured, which would force the fighter to drop his arms, leaving the chin exposed. Clearly his approach worked as he retired the only heavyweight champion with a perfect record of forty-nine wins and no losses.

As the boxer's style is determined by certain attributes (height, build and temperament), some boxers are more adept at changing styles than others. The accompanying table shows which styles are adaptable and which can most easily be adapted to.

The table shows that the typical crouch and weaver will adapt quite easily to the majority of styles, but will struggle to become a persistent jabber and also a swinger, to a certain extent. This is largely down to the mindset and temperament of the crouch and weaver, and also the typical physical profile of this type of boxer.

An interesting observation is that the most adaptable boxers are shorter, mobile boxers, who also need to be very adept at changing their tactics. In addition, their

Which Style Counters Which Style Most Effectively

D   dominated: signifies that the style in the left-hand column dominates

O   overshadowed: signifies the style in the top row is dominant

N   neutral: both styles cancel each other out

Style	CW	PJ	SW	CP	SP	SB	RU	SH	SM	SL	HP
Crouch and weaver (CW)	X	D	O	D	O	O	O	O	N	O	O
Persistent jabber (PJ)		X	O	O	O	O	O	O	O	O	O
Swinger (SW)			X	O	O	O	O	O	O	O	O
Counterpuncher (CP)				X	N	O	D	N	O	D	D
Southpaw (SP)					X	O	D	O	O	D	D
Short box fighter (SB)						X	D	N	D	D	D
Rusher (RU)							X	O	N	O	O
Switch hitter (SH)								X	D	D	D
Swarmer (SM)									X	O	O
Slugger (SL)										X	N
Heavy puncher (HP)											X

Key Tactics Used by Styles

Style	Technique	Variety	Predictability
Slugger	Bent arm shots Linear footwork Slow foot movement rooting	Low level of variety	Highly predictable
Crouch and weaver	Bent arm shots Low stance	Variety of body and head movement	Unpredictable in vertical movement
Swarmer	Mixture of linear and bent arm shots High tempo of punches	Limited range of footwork Changing tempo High variety in combinations	Highly predictable
Persistent jabber	Linear punches	Circular, unidirectional footwork	Highly predictable
Swinger	Long, circular trajectory punches Slow on feet	Limited variety Limited defences	Highly predictable
Counterpuncher	Mixture of techniques Good footwork Precision, quick punches Focus on drawing opponent in	High variety of punches, footwork and defences	Highly predictable
Southpaw	Depends on opponent	Depends on secondary style	Depends
Short box fighter	Compact techniques Good footwork Tight defences Good head movement	Good variety of techniques Good variety of defences	Medium
Rusher	Fast and linear	Limited variety	Limited predictability
Heavy puncher	Strong, good power generation Not good technique as defined by tvp	Limited variety of punches and footwork Limited hand-based defences	Predictable
Switch hitter	Good technique Good footwork	Good variety of techniques, footwork and defences	Unpredictable

temperament will also be very balanced and calm.

Another consideration in terms of styles is which are more likely to dominate over the other styles. The accompanying table demonstrates the anticipated level of dominance that a style might achieve other another.

Analysing Your Opponent

To understand your opponent and their responses, the boxer needs to test the opponent, which requires taking some risk to stretch the opponent. The risk has to involve piling pressure on the opponent through pace and strength. Key techniques to adopt to stretch the opponent are shown in the accompanying table.

Changing Tactics During the Round

Changing tactics during the round is extremely difficult and needs a change in mindset from the boxer. This requires a change of pace and alterness.

Options

There are many choices the fighter has to make. These choices are based on the fighter's need to create and manage the openings that will secure victory.

Managing Openings

What distinguishes the top fighters from the rest is their ability to create and exploit openings. Inexperienced fighters have a tendency to lead with their hearts rather than leading with their minds. Experienced fighters are masters at being able to create openings and make the opponent go where they want them to.

There are many different approaches to creating openings. The distance from the opponent dictates which approach is the most appropriate. Before we look at the tools to create openings we need to ensure that the concept of range is fully understood. Simply, there are three ranges that the fighter is likely to find himself in:

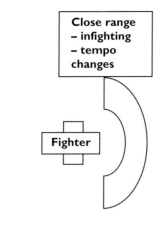

The openings toolkit.

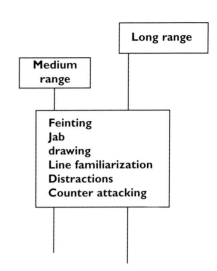

Close range: head touching distance in a normal stance
Medium range: able to make contact with opponent with arms extended 50–75 per cent of full extension
Long range: opponent is just outside the range of full extension of the arms

In addition, a fourth range might be discussed: being out of range.

At medium and long range, the most common approaches to create openings are:
* Feinting
* Use of jab
* Drawing
* Line familiarization
* Distractions
* Counterattacking

To make the above work, the fighter needs to be able to switch attack in a comfortable manner. Switch attack means switching the attack from body to head and vice versa: both are equally effective. The advantage between the two, though, lies with the body attack and then switch to the head, because you've got the leg drive when punching to the head.

Some possible combinations are:
* Jab to body, right hand to head
* Jab to head, right hand to body
* Right hand to head, left jab to body
* Jab to body, jab to head.

For close range fighting the fighter needs to develop a number of skills, including:
Infighting: This is the ability to feel the energy provided by

Choices Preferred Based on Openings and Style

Style	Close range	Medium range	Long range
Crouch and weaver (CW)	2	1	3
Persistent jabber (PJ)	3	2	1
Swinger (SW)	3	2	1
Counterpuncher (CP)	3	2	1
Southpaw (SP)	Depends on secondary style	Depends on secondary style	Depends on secondary style
Short box fighter (SB)	1	2	3
Rusher (RU)	3	2	1
Switch hitter (SH)	1	2	3
Swarmer (SM)	1	2	3
Slugger (SL)	1	2	3
Heavy puncher (HP)	1	2	3

the opponent and be able to counter in a swift move, moving from defence to attack in one swift move. Infighting also requires an ability to minimize space between the two fighters, which demands excellent use of body movement and torque to generate necessary power, while minimizing the opportunity for the opponent to penetrate.

Tempo changes: The ability to 'feel' your opponent and respond accordingly. The development of this 'feel' is easier when the opponent becomes predictable and attacks at the same tempo. By varying the tempo you will introduce another factor, so demanding that your opponent must adopt a higher level of fighting competence.

Choice

Intuitive Action in the Ring

Practise is essential to make responses totally intuitive and automatic in the ring. Anticipation is critical to developing this ability.

By observing different opponents, with different styles, you develop an ability to read body movement, thus improving the level of anticipation. Through sparring it is possible to develop an awareness that leads to improved timing and thus anticipation. Mirror sparring is also a very effective way of developing this appreciation of other fighting styles.

By watching different fighters you are able to think about different scenarios and possibilities that you are likely to encounter in the ring. Scenarios involve being aware of different possible situations and visualizing the different options that are possible, and practising these.

Being able to anticipate correctly involves continuous repetition of the different techniques described under

different circumstances. Watching different types of fighters and fighters from other styles might also be very effective. Anticipation also develops by utilizing the correct form of sparring, ranging from pre-arranged sparring to full-out sparring. Isolation of the element to be practised is critical to success in developing the ability to anticipate.

Visual Awareness

Visual awareness of the ring environment is crucial to success in the boxing game. Visual awareness is needed to be able to see, create and exploit an opening. The fighter needs to be able to see very quickly an opening to be able to launch an attack. The fighter must develop an awareness of the opponent changing his tactics during a fight, and be able to anticipate the techniques delivered.

Visual awareness starts with the fighter being fully aware of his own body movement and behaviour. The fighter needs to be conscious of what his body is doing during different phases of training and during the delivery of different techniques. A coach is invaluable in creating this awareness, as during the rush of adrenaline the fighter may not be aware of what he is doing.

The fighter also needs to create an awareness of his relative position in the ring, and the position of the opponent in relation to the fighter himself. This is why it is useful to carry out many of the drills and training in the ring itself, so that the fighter is familiar with the size of the ring.

A key skill to developing awareness is listening. During the developmental stage of training the fighter needs to be good at listening to his coach and the coach needs to be able to communicate effectively with his protégés.

Doing

Controlling the Centre

One of the keys to success in the ring is the ability to control the centre. What does this mean? Many people interpret this to mean staying in the centre of the ring, which with a normal-sized ring means the opponent is still quite free to move around at leisure.

Controlling ring space or keeping the centre of the ring means dominating the centre and being in charge of it. Dictating the way your opponent moves and directing him off into corners, instead of chasing him around the ring, gives numerous advantages. So often you see a fast-moving fighter running around the ring and his opponent following him instead of closing him down onto the ropes or corners where his movement is restricted. Also this needs to be backed up with plenty of lateral movement with shots constantly coming from different angles. At all times the fighter needs to be changing directions so that

Practise
Observation
Scenarios
Visualisation
Sparring

Developing intuition.

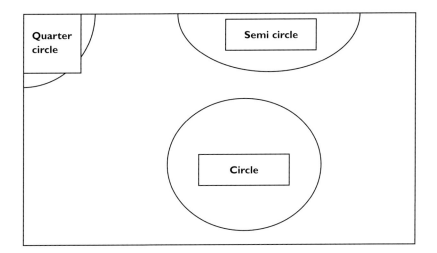

Controlling the ring.

the opponent cannot time his attack against you. To control the centre of ring and cut the ring space down, a fighter must be able to move in all directions, maintaining balance at all times.

The aim of controlling the centre is to restrict the ability of the opponent to move. Therefore controlling the centre actually means controlling the centre of the circle of movement of the opponent. If the opponent is near a corner then his circle of movement is actually a quarter of a circle, which is considerably easier to manage. If he is against the ropes, but away from the corner, then his circle of movement is actually a semicircle. This is a little more difficult to manage, but still easier than a complete circle. If the opponent is standing in open space then his circle is a complete circle.

The variables that determine how the fighter is going to control the centre are:
* Footwork
* Punching speed
* Movement speed
* Tempo changes

Controlling the centre involves messing up the opponent's work rate. All people have a natural work rate that mirrors their natural body rhythm, similar to the person's metabolic rate. Many fighters usually fight or train at this natural work rate. There is a degree of comfort attached to it. The key to controlling the centre is to alter the opponent's natural work rate, taking them outside their comfort zone. For the fighter it is vital that they are comfortable and have practised working out at different work rates. This is where SAQ training, interval training and plyometric training are especially useful as they force the person to train beyond their comfort zone.

Footwork and different footwork patterns, combined with movement speed variations, will cause confusion to the opponent. To make the footwork effective the fighter needs to be able to read the opponent's patterns and be aware of his preferences.

Varying the punching speed and the tempo of the punches will take the opponent outside his zone of familiarity.

Defending against an uppercut in the corner (1).

Defending against an uppercut in the corner (2).

Defending against an uppercut in the corner (3).

Defending against an uppercut in the corner (4).

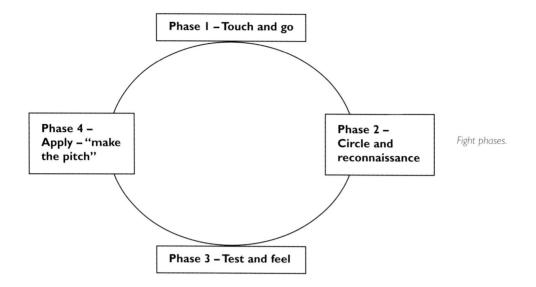

Fight phases.

The variety is developed through the tvp framework. As with all things these areas need to be practised.

Possibilities v. Probabilities

A combat event can be divided into a number of distinct stages.

Phase 1: Touch and Go: this is the opening phase of the fight where the fighters exchange in the touching of the gloves followed immediately by the commencement of the fight. In fact, the touching of the gloves indicates the start.

Phase 2: Circle and reconciliation: this is the surveillance phase of the fight where both fighters try to get to know their competitor.

Phase 3: Test and feel: during this phase both fighters will throw shots to see how their opponent responds.

Phase 4: Application: 'make the pitch' – this is the point when the fighter lets his intentions be known.

These four phases are part of a circle that every fighter

Possibilities and Probabilities

Phase	Possibilities (fighter types)	Probabilities						
		T	CW	SW	CP	SP	R	SH
1. Touch and go	Touch gloves and break off	H	H	H	H	H	H	H
	Touch gloves and steam in	L	M	H	L	L	H	H
	Touch gloves and clinch	L	M	L	M	L	H	H
2. Circle and reconnaissance	Circle in one direction	H	M	L	H	H	L	M
	Circle in multiple directions	L	L	L	M	L	L	M
	Linear movement	L	H	L	M	H	H	H
	Lateral movement	L	L	L	M	L	L	H
3. Test and feel	Throwing non-contact hits	H	M	L	L	L	L	M
	Throwing the bombs	L	H	H	L	L	H	L
	Stand and observe – non-compliant	M	H	L	H	H	L	H
4. Apply 'make the pitch'	React to prompt	H	L	L	H	M	L	M
	Attack from different angle	L	H	H	L	H	L	H
	Increased work rate	M	L	L	L	M	H	H
	Variety of responses	L	L	L	L	L	L	M

T = Tall fighter   H = High probability   M = Medium probability   L = Low probability

Cutting your opponent off (1).

Cutting your opponent off (2).

Cutting your opponent off (3).

Cutting your opponent off (4).

Cutting your opponent off (5).

Cutting your opponent off (6).

goes through, though at different speeds. Some fighters will progress from one stage to the next during a very short period of time, whereas others will move through them very slowly. Our experience suggests that the style of your opponent is a major factor in determining how quickly the fighter will go through each phase. (The different styles that may be adopted can be seen in the table earlier in this chapter.)

The possible actions a fighter might typically take during each of these phases (we have picked the most common)

Moving off ropes 1 (1).

Moving off ropes 1 (2).

Moving off ropes 1 (3).

Infighting: creating space (1).

Infighting: creating space (2).

Infighting: creating space (3).

Infighting: entering (1).

Infighting: entering (2).

Infighting: gaining inside position (1).

Infighting: gaining inside position (2).

Tying your opponent (1).

Tying your opponent (2).

Tying your opponent (3).

Infighting: gaining inside position (1).

Infighting: gaining inside position (2).

Infighting: gaining inside position (3).

Infighting: gaining inside position from different angle (1).

Infighting: gaining inside position from different angle (2).

Infighting: gaining inside position from different angle (3).

and also the probability attached to each of the fighting styles to adopt each specific possibility are demonstrated in the accompanying table. The fighter types are shown by abbreviations representing the different types given in the table above. L suggests a low probability, M suggests a medium probability and H suggests a high probability. This table is a powerful tool in helping fighters analyse opponents and develop strategies to cope with different styles of fighters.

The table shows that potentially a short fighter can be

Double jab with partner (1).

Double jab with partner (2).

Double jab with partner (3).

Double jab with partner (4).

one of the most difficult opponents you can face if they plan their strategies correctly. The rusher and swinger tend to be the most predictable. Additionally, the responses with all high probabilities show the most common responses used by fighters of any styles.

Another application of the table is to try to second guess your opponent's response and expectation of you, thus giving you an opportunity to do the unexpected.

FIGHT ANALYSIS OF THE CHAMPIONS

A champion is someone who gets up when he can't.
Jack Dempsey

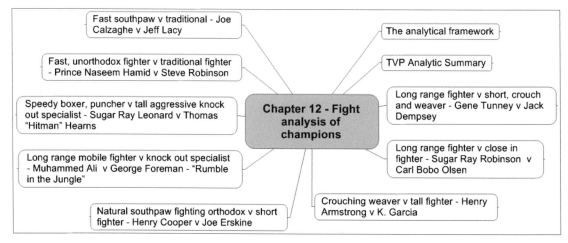

Mindmap overview of Chapter 12.

We have spoken at length about the importance of studying other fighters and learning from experience of what has worked and what has not. This is a vital part of advanced boxing. A key area of learning for the seasoned boxer is watching and learning from the very best.

In this chapter we will provide an analysis of fights involving legendary boxers from the past and present, and see what lessons we can learn, and more importantly how do we develop some of the key attributes of these great fighters.

In analysing the fights we have tried to look at the development of a fight and to identify the fights that most closely resemble a tvp type boxing match. In fact, the closest fight to a tvp performance was Joe Calzaghe v. Jeff Lacey.

The Analytical Framework

In analysing so many fights we were able to create an analytical framework using the tvp approach, which we

found extremely helpful in carrying out the analysis. The following table was used as a foundation for the analysis. By using the tvp framework we discovered we spent a lot of time looking for specific things in the fighter's style and way of boxing. This also made us examine features of different fighters that we did not really see or even look for previously. (For a deeper understanding of each of these components of a fighter's make-up, see Chapter 5.)

It is important to remember that we are not being prescriptive in our analysis. We looked at what worked and what did not work for different boxers. We then tried to analyse why these things did and did not work, thus enabling us to see the degree of application to other boxers.

Each of the analyses is preceded by short biographies of the fighters. This is then followed by a round-by-round commentary and a detailed analysis of each of the fights, finally ending with a short training programme. This framework provides an excellent supply of drills and techniques for developing your skills. We also suggest you watch the fights on YouTube, as this is where we found the source

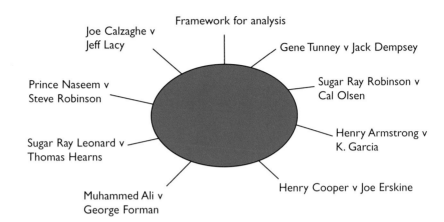

Fight analysis overview.

material. Each analysis is accompanied by a fifteeen-minute training routine to practise the key learning points from the match.

Long-Range Fighter v. Short Crouch and Weaver

Gene Tunney v. Jack Dempsey, 22 September 1927

The Fight: An Overview

The glory that was Jack Dempsey's returned to him in that transient moment in the seventh round of Chicago's extravaganza. The 150,000 saw it. Saw Jack Dempsey with that dreaded left hook punch Gene Tunney on the jaw. Saw Tunney go down to the canvas, felled. Saw Jack Dempsey watch the toll of the referee like he had watched the toll of many another referee – standing, waiting, for his opponent to get up, if he could. Gene Tunney did get up. With the count of nine he rose to his feet a calm, deliberate fighting machine, stunned, but aware, and there Gene Tunney saved the championship. It was Dempsey's only serious threat to regain the title he held for seven years, and Tunney, getting up, preserved his title as becomes a champion. The technical story of the battle can be briefly told. Dempsey, pawing, sniffing, advanced on Tunney from the outset, beckoning him to close quarters, and Tunney danced away, hitting as he danced, and sapping the strength of his foe from the start.

Shirley Povich, *Washington Post*, 22 September 1927

Gene Tunney and Jack Dempsey fought twice for the world heavyweight championship. Gene Tunney won on both occasions. The fight in 1927 is known as the Long Count Fight. Dempsey floored Tunney in the seventh round but refused to go to a neutral corner, according to the rules. The countdown was delayed and Tunney, given this extra respite, recovered sufficiently to outbox Dempsey the rest of the way. The quotation from the *Washington Post* really describes the essence and extent of the 1927 fight.

The fights were really a case of a long, tall fighter versus the shorter, crouching weaver style, which has always captured the imagination of audiences the world over.

Having examined both fights in detail, Tunney's style was

tvp Analytic Summary

Element	Fighter A	Fighter B
Style	What are some of the key features of the fighter's style? What type of fighter is he?	As with A
Technique	Position of non-punching hand Body weight transfer Break off from inside position Quality of technique Relaxation and acceleration in technique delivery	As with A
Variety	Preferred attacking tools Preferred defensive tools Mannerism of style Tempo changes	As with A
Predictability	Preferred direction of movement Footwork patterns Danger punch Movement of head Movement patterns and mannerisms Change of movement speed	As with A

Fighter biographies	Determine background of fighter Look for factors that contributed to style
Round by round narrative	Detailed commentary, round by round Understand the evolution of rounds and factors that contributed to outcome
Tvp based analysis	Detailed analysis of fighting performance
15 minute development plan	Drills to develop learned skills Develop a coaching and development mentality

Fight analysis framework.

very much Ali-esque, with hands down the side, considerable movement in all directions around the ring and fighting from longer range. From a technical point of view Tunney spent much of the first fight moving Dempsey out of position on a frequent basis. Dempsey appeared tired and out of focus in the first fight. Tunney really dominated using his extensive reach for advantage. Dempsey fought with a crouching weaver style, very similar to Rocky Marciano. Dempsey was very much rooted in the first fight, but was considerably more mobile in the second, leaving little opportunity for Tunney to dominate as he did in the first fight.

Dempsey tended to be quite predictable in the first fight and was kept on the edge of the reach of Tunney. Dempsey needed to seize the initiative and use more creativity, which he certainly did more in the second fight. Additionally, in the first fight Dempsey appeared to waste considerable energy bobbing and weaving with no real focus and outcome.

Both fighters, in both fights, tended to be fairly predictable, using a low variety of techniques. What makes the fights interesting were the differences in style, a bit like Ali v Frazier forty or so years later, the long count in the second fight and the domination of Dempsey by Tunney. Tunney used the jab regularly to fend off the shorter bent arm shots of Dempsey. Success for Dempsey was very much dependent on his ability to close the gap with Tunney, but Tunney's footwork and movement in the first fight was noticeably far superior to Dempsey's ability to close the gap. In the second fight, however, Dempsey was better at seizing the initiative, as evidenced by his knockout. Additionally, Dempsey wasted less energy moving around and tended to have more focus in his movement.

15 Minute Learning Plan

Long-range fighter (Gene Tunney)
Objective
* Fight on the edge of range
* Good footwork moving in and out of range
* Maintaining distance

Drills
Padwork
* Stepping forward/backward in stance delivering jabs with pad holder

Fighter biographies

	James Joesph "Gene" Tunney	Jack "Manassa Mauler" Dempsey
Life time	May 25, 1897 – November 7, 1978	June 24, 1895 – May 31, 1983
Weights	Heavyweight	Heavyweight
Country of birth	UK	USA
Style	Long range fighter	Short, crouch and weaver
Famous for	Heavyweight champion 1926–1928	Heavyweight champion 1919 to 1926

tvp Analytic Summary: Tunney v. Dempsey

Element	Gene Tunney	Jack Dempsey
Style	Long-range fighter	Short, crouching weaver
Technique	Long range Hands down Non-conventional jabbing Good footwork	Short range Focus on bent arm shots Footwork better in second fight
Variety	Little variety in techniques and footwork. Movement in same direction most of the time	Little variety in techniques More variety in footwork in second fight More linear footwork movement
Predictability	Little creativity in punches, but marginally more creativity in footwork Great use of appropriate tactics	Little creativity

* Switching feet moving forward and backward delivering jabs with pad holder
* Sliding forward and backward in stance delivering jabs with pad holder
* Moving in, out and around of circle delivering jabs with pad holder

Short, crouching weaver fighter (Jack Dempsey)
Objective
* Get inside fighter with long reach and stay there
* Deliver bent arm shots after entry into range
* Making room for delivery of bent arm shots once entry has been made

Drills
Heavy bag: theme when hitting bag – in close with all shots being bent arm shots

Padwork: rolling into attack, slipping in and out with coach

Sparring: condition sparring
* gaining inside position
* making room for delivering punches
* breakaway safely under cover

Long-Range Fighter v. Close-in Fighter

Sugar Ray Robinson v. Carl Bobo Olsen, 9 December 1955 and 18 May 1956

The Fight – an Overview

Fight 1: 9 December 1955
Round 1: This fight really demonstrated the difference in styles between these two fighters. Robinson spent most of his time dancing round elegantly, moving in and out of range. Robinson had a style similar to Muhammad Ali. Both fighters had a tendency to throw jabs while they were moving out of range. The timing was exquisite, like watching supreme dancers. Olsen was much more predictable, coming in with hooks and staying there, allowing Robinson to throw a good variety of combinations, with no reply from Olsen. Robinson demonstrated excellent timing and a broad variety of punches switching from high to low and vice versa. A difference in class is there for everyone to see.

Fighter biographies

	Sugar Ray Robinson (born Walker Smith Jr.)	Carl Bobo Olson
Birth and era	May 3, 1921 – April 12, 1989	July 11, 1928 – January 16, 2002
Weights	Welterweight	
Middleweight	Middleweight	
Country of birth	US	Hawaii
Style	Long range	Close in figter
Famous for	Frequently cited as the greatest boxer of all time	World middleweight Champion between Oct 1953 and Dec 1955.

Round 2: Robinson continued as he finished the first round, throwing head shots coupled with great movement. Olsen maintained his focus on throwing bent arm shots, but without really making up the distance or causing Sugar Ray any trouble. Olsen threw a right hand over the top that landed on Robinson's face. Sugar Ray demonstrated intricate head movements followed by a broad range of punches making full use of his hips for power. Sugar Ray's mindset was much more relaxed and playful compared to Olsen's 'I'm gonna get ya' attitude. Olsen's mindset showed signs of desperation, as if he had a belief that whatever he threw would not work. Sugar Ray Robinson was beginning to switch to another level combining excellent head and body movement with clever combinations, one of which knocked Olsen out, winning Robinson the middleweight title.

Fight 2: 18 May 1956

The crowd was loud and enormous (20,000 spectators). Olson constantly clinched with Ray, more like a wrestler than a fighter. We wondered why Referee Mushy Callahan didn't break them apart and caution them to move and fight. Sugar had said that he had observed previously that Olson would drop his right arm when he delivered a good punch with his right hand. In two minutes and fifty-one seconds of the fourth round Olson did just that, and faster than lightning, Sugar delivered a punch with his left hand to Olson's right jaw that must have made him see stars as he sagged to the canvas like a bag of cement. The roar of the crowd was music to my ears.

Edna Mae Robinson [Mrs Sugar Ray Robinson]

I was hit well in the body in the third round, and that punch was Bobo's ruination. After he hit me in the body, I lagged my left, and that gave him confidence. He got brave and came on in the fourth, and when he started to punch the body again, I hit him flush on the jaw with the left. It was hard, but I wasn't sure I had him until the count reached ten.

Sugar Ray Robinson

The fight was held in broad daylight at Wrigley Field, Los Angeles. Sugar Ray looked full of confidence, as befitted a world champion. He led with jabs and hooking with the same hand, confusing Olsen. Olsen got in close but tended to do nothing once he was in. His timing just appeared to be off. Sugar Ray started to use more bent arm shots, throwing an exquisite left hook to the head that caught Olsen unawares. There were many relaxed shots from Robinson, while Olsen seemed to be considerably more cautious than he was in the first fight, probably aware of the danger offered by the champ. This caution allowed Sugar Ray to show his full repertoire of rhythm and flair, dancing in and out of range throwing punches at will. Was Sugar Ray this good, or was the approach of the opponent encouraging this style? Robinson then magically threw a right hand to the body, followed by a left hook to the face

tvp Analytic Summary: Robinson v. Olsen

Element	Sugar Ray Robinson	Carl Bobo Olsen
Style	Long-range, mobile fighter	Close-in fighter
Technique	Excellent techniques. Focused punches with good retraction. Excellent footwork moving out of range while throwing effective jabs. Fast delivery of punches from all different angles Hands held high on delivery of punches, protecting the face	Continual bent arm shots closing in but failing to protect himself on retraction
Variety	Superb variety in punches and footwork patterns. Good gliding movement. Excellent combinations made up of same and different hands combinations	Little variety in techniques and footwork. Relied heavily on close-in bent arm shots
Predictability	Totally unpredictable. Very adaptable Different sequence of punches Moving in all different directions Creative combination	Little creativity Very predictable

with full use of his hips maximizing the power generated, knocking Olsen out in glorious fashion.

15-minute learning plan

Objective
* Delivering a knockout combination
* Punching from low to high
* Using the hip to generate power

Drills
Stand in front of your punchbag.

Drill 1   From an on guard position, bend your legs and raise your hands, protecting your face, as you sink ready to throw a body shot.
   Using your hip throw a rear hand punch to the body, keeping your non-punching hand high to protect your face.

Drill 2   Bend your legs with your rear hand extended, touching the bag.
   Relax and launch and yourself, throwing a lead hand hook to the face.

Drill 3   From an on guard position, we are going to combine drills 1 and 2.
   Bend your legs and throw a rear hand punch to the body, and wait.
   Using the power in the bent legs, throw yourself up, throwing a lead hand hook to the head.

Drill 4   With a partner holding focus pads, repeat drill 3 with movement.

Crouching Weaver v. Tall Fighter

Henry Armstrong v. Ceferino Garcia, 25 November 1938

The Fight – an Overview

Round 1: Armstrong came out ready to attack, adopting a wide stance with head constantly moving. His style was very aggressive, extensively leaning on his opponent. The first round was dominated by Armstrong leaning on Garcia and Garcia trying to resist the pressure being applied. Occasionally Garcia would move back, keeping Armstrong at arm's length, but he was being continually sucked into his space.

Round 2: Garcia started the second round with a jab followed by an overhand hook shot. He looked sharp, but then again he became sucked into a 'pushing' match with Armstrong. The second round really carried on from the first with Armstrong adopting this leaning posture. His

stance was fairly wide and square on, but he was getting away with it. Garcia continued to resist the physical presence and was making no real advances. Armstrong moved in continually, hitting Gracia with a series of uppercuts and hooks, while his head stayed close to his opponent's head. Armstrong was dictating the pace. Everytime Garcia attempted to break off, he was drawn into Armstrong's game plan. Armstrong was making contact with more shots.

Round 4: Armstrong came out closing the distance between him and Garcia with some long-range lead hand hooks. His head was constantly moving, making it very difficult for Garcia to land anything effective. Armstrong's stance was really quite wide and square, but he was being supported by Garcia's resistance. It almost looked as if Armstrong would just fall if Garcia stepped back. Armstrong was working really well off the inside of his opponent, landing with uppercuts and hooks. On a couple of occasions Garcia moved back and Armstrong swung wildly, missing his target by a large distance. Garcia tried to hold off Armstrong whenever he was able to create space, with his lead hand, but was unable to sustain this for any period of time. Armstrong refused to let Garcia take advantage of his reach.

Round 7: Armstrong began the round by launching straight into Garcia, covering the distance in a split second. This allowed him to continue his strategy of leaning and delivering a series of bent arm shots. Armstrong belittled his height disadvantage to Garcia by adopting a very low, crouching stance that allowed him to come inside Garcia's lead hand. Armstrong continually attacked with his head down, pounding away at Garcia, with a variety of bent arm shots. Garcia temporarily pushed Armstrong away, but as he was moving back Armstrong landed a couple of long-range hooks. Garcia was taking a pounding without delivering any shots in return.

Round 10: Garcia came out with a spring in his step, but again was sucked into Armstrong's close-range battle. Momentarily Garcia had some range advantage and landed a lead hand, rear hand combination. Garcia now appeared to be more adamant about maintaining the distance between him and Armstrong, thus allowing him to land more effective shots, but Armstrong was persistent in coming forward. It is interesting that all of Armstrong's shots were bent arm shots, irrespective of range. There were signs in this round that Garcia was also starting to adopt a more leaning stance; maybe tiredness was setting in. Armstrong was very effective at pushing Garcia's arms away, creating openings for landing a series of uppercuts.

Round 14: For the first time in the fight Garcia now started moving away from Armstrong as he leaned, deliv-

Fighter biographies

	Henry Armstrong	Ceferino Garcia
Birth and era	December 12, 1912 - October 22, 1988	August 26, 1912 — January 1, 1981
Weights	Featherweight Welterweight Lightweight Middleweight	Middleweight
Country of birth	US	Phillipines
Style	Crouching weaver	Tall fighter
Famous for	World featherweight/welterweight/ lightweight champion	Middleweight world champion

tvp Analytic Summary: Armstrong v. Garcia

Element	Henry Armstrong	Ceferino Garcia
Style	Crouching weaver	Tall fighter
Technique	Effective bent arm punching. Wide, square stance, which might have left him open, but his continuous punching ensured he was never left open. Head down and very well protected as he delivered his bent arm punches	Very sharp when he did fight his way. Very good retraction and line of delivery when he dictated the pace of the fight
Variety	Good variety of bent arm shots with uppercuts and hooks being delivered from a variety of angles. Limited defences as he relied heavily on closing distance. Footwork was also limited	Little variety in fight as his style was being dominated by Armstrong
Predictability	Fairly predictable	Very predictable

ering some effective shots using his power and range advantage. Garcia's movement appeared to be much sharper than in previous rounds.

Round 15: Garcia moved around the ring quickly as he landed a series of shots to the body and head. He made good use of a straight lead hand and rear hand uppercut, though perhaps it was now getting too late. Armstrong was finding it a little more difficult to hit Garcia, but did land an overhand shot, followed by him curling into protective posture, which appeared to be a very effective technique. Armstrong finished the round well by just bull-dozing his way through Garcia.

Result: Armstrong won on points.

15-minute Learning Plan

A key learning point from this fight was Armstrong's ability to open Garcia at close range, by moving his hands as he delivered uppercuts. This will be the focus of our 15-minute plan.

Objective
* Deliver punches to a target from close range where the opponent is well protected with his hands.

Drills
All of the following drills are based on partner work.

Starting position: Both fighters close in, leaning on each other, with hands up protecting the face:

Drill 1   Pull both arms of your partner down and deliver punches.

Drill 2   Pull partner's right arm down, and deliver left uppercut to face. Do opposite arm.

Drill 3   Pull partner's arms apart and deliver punches.

Key points: Do not hold onto your partner's arms. Move them and hit!

Natural Southpaw Fighting Orthodox v. Short Fighter

Henry Cooper v. Joe Erskine, 17 November 1959

The Fight – an Overview

Henry Cooper held the British and Commonwealth titles, after defeating Brian London earlier in 1959.

Erskine, however, had twice defeated Cooper in 1955 and 1957. They met for a third time at Earl's Court Arena, London.

Round 1: Henry Cooper moved well, especially considering his adaptation to orthodox from his natural southpaw stance. Erskine was very mobile but seemed to bounce a lot and moved very much in one direction. Cooper hit with a left hook. He appeared to be very single handed (left), reflecting his natural southpaw tendency. Cooper worked well off his lead punch and appeared very agile in this first round, catching Erskine a few times.

Round 2: Cooper decided to control the centre of the ring and did this very effectively. Erskine continued to move in one direction, trying to avoid Cooper's hook. As a short boxer, Erskine also found himself having to leap in to deliver effective punches. Cooper worked on the inside, counterpunching off his left hand and delivering shots with immense power. This is the benefit of switching away from your natural stance. Cooper slipped in the corner and delivered a combination while in a very deep stance. Erskine hit some low shots, but appeared to do little damage.

Round 3: Erskine attacked immediately as he came out for the third round. Cooper threw a series of body shots and combined these with left uppercuts as he opened Erskine up. Cooper was relying heavily on the left uppercut and hook. Erskine appeared to be less mobile in this round as he stood still trying to find openings.

Round 4: Little change in activity to the previous rounds.

Round 5: Cooper now began to trade lead hand jabs with more power behind them. There appeared to be a determination to make sure this was not a third defeat to Erskine. Erskine was moving around in circles, using all of the ring, whereas Cooper was fairly static in this round. Cooper continued to throw a series of body shots, with the intention of delivering a hook. Cooper looked to be getting stronger, punching with greater power than in the earlier rounds. Erskine was punching more for points. Cooper finished the round hitting Erskine after the bell.

Round 6: As Cooper continued in his non-natural stance, there was a tendency for Cooper to leave his rear leg trailing as he pulled from his front leg, rather than push from his rear leg. This is another common feature of fighters who are not fighting with their dominant side forward. Cooper was now starting to become more dominant, jabbing Erskine as he walked into range. Erskine moved around expending considerable energy, but getting nowhere if we are totally honest. He had a pattern of moving up and down, but did not make any inroads into Cooper. However, he did finish the round landing a good right hand to the jaw.

Round 7: Many of Cooper's shots were now landing regularly. As Cooper delivered his shots, his feet were well grounded, ensuring maximum power from his punches. Cooper was also now very economical with his movement. He was landing regularly with the jab, as Erskine struggled to get close. He appeared to have tired himself out with all the bouncing in earlier rounds. Cooper maintained distance well and also began to switch attack from body to head in a smooth movement.

Rounds 8 and 9: The pattern of round 7 continues.

Round 10: Erskine delivered some good and effective jabs. Cooper threws a right hand, but missed. Cooper cut Erskine off in the corners, looking for the knockout blow.

Fighter biographies (adapted from Wikipedia)

	Sir Henry Cooper	*Joseph 'Joe' Erskine*
Birth	3 May 1934	Jan 1934 – Feb 1990
Weights	Heavyweight	Heavyweight
Country of birth	UK	Wales
Style	Natural southpaw fighting orthodox	Short fighter
Famous for	British, European and Commonwealth champion	British heavyweight title from August 1956 to June 1958.

tvp Analytic Summary: Cooper v. Erskine

Element	Henry Cooper	Joe Erskine
Style	Natural southpaw, fighting orthodox	Short fighter
Technique	Effective punches using excellent body mechanics. Focused punches with good retraction. Footwork was rather limited, especially with the role of the rear leg. Hands held high on delivery of punches, protecting the face. Maintained distance very well	Good technique in the early rounds, but technique started to go when tired. Footwork was very cumbersome with lots of bouncing
Variety	Little variety as most punches were delivered as single punches. However, the 3-punch combination that knocked Erskine was superb	Tried different punches, but his uni-directional movement limited his options
Predictability	Fairly predictable until the last round	Little creativity Very predictable

Erskine struggled in the latter part of the round as Cooper landed a series of left-hand combinations.

Round 11: Erskine again moved around with this bouncing action, wasting more energy. Erskine threw shots to make himself look busy rather than with any belief of doing any damage. Cooper held the centre of the ring well and demonstrated excellent body mechanics as he delivered very effective punches to Erskine's head and body.

Round 12: Erskine threws a jab and uppercut but neither landed. Cooper was operating on the edge, allowing him to cut Erskine off as he tried to move away from Cooper. Cooper was covering up well to make Erskine's efforts quite ineffective. Cooper threw a right uppercut and Erskine fell. He got up and Cooper landed a vicious hook. Again Erskine got up. Cooper looked to have had enough and bombarded Erskine with a three-punch combination. It was over! Cooper won the fight on a technical knockout as Erskine was hanging almost unconscious over the lower rope when the referee stopped the bout.

15-minute Learning Plan

An important attribute of the top fighters is the ability to switch, seamlessly, to 'the other side'. Henry Cooper was naturally a southpaw, but fought orthodox style. Practise is required to be able to switch sides and deliver effective combinations, while still being able to defend. The following workout is very effective at developing this ability.

Objective
* Develop attributes to be able to fight on both sides
* Be able to deliver effective combinations from both orthodox and southpaw

Drills
Equipment needed: punchbag

Drill 1   1. Stepping into the punchbag from orthodox stance by bringing the right foot to the left and stepping towards the bag delivering a lead hand punch, and then stepping in exactly the same motion back to the start. This is one technique. Do this 10 times.
2. As in 1 but now deliver a lead hand and rear hand punch. Do this 10 times.
3. As in 2 but now add a lead hand hook. Do this 10 times.
4. As in 3 but now add a rear hand uppercut. Do this 10 times.
5. Repeat 1 to 4 on the southpaw side.

Drill 2   Do the same combinations as in drill 1, but substitute the step with a rear leg push towards the bag.

Long-range Mobile Fighter v. Knockout Specialist

Muhammad Ali v George Foreman, 30 October 1974

The Fight – an Overview

Muhammad Ali's challenge to recover the world heavyweight title, known as the 'Rumble in the Jungle', was held in the Mai 20 Stadium in Kinshasa, Zaïre.

    The fighters entered the ring at four in the morning, to allow the satellite feeds to the US to be shown Prime Time. The attendance was 60,000, although

Fighter biographies

	Muhammad Ali born Cassius Marcellus Clay Jr.	George Foreman
Birth	January 17, 1942	January 10, 1949
Weights	Heavyweight	Heavyweight
Country of birth	US	US
Style	Long range, mobile fighter	Knock out specialist
Famous for	3 times world heavyweight champion. "The Greatest".	2 times world champion

Mobutu would watch on TV from his compound for fear of assassination. At the opening bell, Ali seized the initiative with an audacious attack. He rushed at Foreman and landed a hard right hand. Then he hit Foreman with punches that confounded the champion. Then Ali went to the ropes and allowed Foreman to hit him. Even Angelo Dundee was unaware of Ali's plan. In between rounds one and two Ali would lead the crowds in chants of 'Ali Boma Ye!'

Boxing-memorabilia.com

Round 1; The searing heat demanded a change in approach from both fighters, but only Ali was able to adapt. Foreman came to the fight with one game plan : this was going to be his moment of glory and nothing was going to change it. Ali looked sharp, however, managing the ring space magnificently, moving around the ring like a lightweight, delivering accurate explosive punches from the go. Foreman was ready to knock Ali out, but Ali came prepared to go the whole distance. Consequently Foreman's technique suffered with his hands dropping regularly and his movement restricted by flat-footedness. Foreman had assumed Ali was finished, but now realized he was dealing with 'The Greatest'.

Round 2: Ali spent the entire round leaning on the ropes, but in control of Foreman. He kept Foreman at arm's length. In the meantime, Foreman was loading each shot, wasting valuable energy and power that he would need later on, missing his target. Ali delivered good techniques when he saw the openings before covering up, letting Foreman destroy himself while taunting him. At the end of the round Foreman went back to his corner looking totally confused.

Round 3: Ali continued to deliver punches at the right time, in between laying on the ropes taunting George. This was fight strategy at its best: Ali was thinking one step ahead of his opponent. Foreman tried attacking the body with swinging shots that were missing the target, and again wasting valuable energy. Ali delivered beautiful right, left combinations that hit their target with a degree of inevitability. Foreman's legs started to look tired, his head moving all over the place. Ali switched on for the last ten

to fifteen seconds with a barrage of shots, each one hitting with deadly accuracy. Ali looked like he knew exactly what he was doing.

Round 4: Ali started the round with three-punch combinations that hit Foreman with speed and fluidity. Ali's technique appeared to have risen a level – even for 'The Greatest'. It was as if he knew there was no margin for error. Ali's placing of shots was spot on – straight line with short, sharp movements. Foreman continued to swing wildly, lacking balance when delivering his shots and missing most of the time. Ali, in contrast, demonstrated the variety in his repertoire and was hitting with 90 per cent of his punches.

Round 5: Ali was not looking for control of the centre of the ring – he was defying logic by looking for the corners or the ropes. He caught Foreman with left hooks as he tried to nail Ali. Foreman demonstrated no variety in technique, swinging wildly from one side to another. Ali hit Foreman with a series of six left, right-hand combinations, hitting the target every time, breaking off brilliantly behind his jab and then countering the wasted responses from a deflated Foreman. Foreman was never expecting this.

Round 6: Ali continued, as he did the other rounds, with a series of beautiful combinations before 'retreating' to the ropes. Foreman was starting to look as though he was out of ammunition – he was looking lost! He tried to pull Ali off the ropes, but Ali just saw it as an opportunity to jab him. Ali even had time to wave his support on.

Round 7: Ali went straight to the ropes this time. He sensed Foreman might be wilting. Ali demonstrated his power of psychology by constantly talking and taunting Foreman and motivating the crowd. Ali moved backward delivering a series of right-hand punches. Foreman went through the ropes – he was just about done – but he did deliver a good uppercut near the end of the round. Was he making a comeback?

Round 8: Again Ali was straight on the ropes and threw a triple right hand. Foreman threw a left hook with no control. The swinger is back! Foreman delivered his most

tvp Analytic Summary: Ali v. Foreman

Element	Muhammad Ali	George Foreman
Style	Long-range, mobile fighter	Knockout specialist
Technique	Excellent techniques. Focused punches with good retraction Fast delivery of punches from all different angles Hands held high on delivery of punches, protecting the face	Technique disappeared quite early in fight Continual wild swinging of punches Hands down by side suggesting tiredness and lack of control
Variety	Superb variety in punches and footwork patterns. Good gliding movement Conserved energy by laying on ropes to allow greater variety when needed	Little variety in techniques and footwork Was lost when his strategy was not working
Predictability	Totally unpredictable. Very adaptable Different sequence of punches. Moving in all different directions	Little creativity Very predictable Confused

technically correct punch, a left, right combination with his hands held high, protecting his face. Ali hit Foreman with a combination. Foreman looked tired and totally out of control. Ali sensed Foreman was nearing his end, throwing punches for the sake of it. Ali slid off the ropes and delivered a right-hand, left hook, right hand, left hook combination as he swivelled away from Foreman. OUT! Foreman was on the floor.

15-minute Learning Plan

Objective
* Good footwork moving in and out of range
* Timing of defence and punch
* Coming out of corners and angles safely

Drills

Drill 1   Set up three lines on the floor, as shown in the diagram
Move between lines 1 and 2, gliding in and out with a constant rhythm in stance
On command, move from line 1 to 2 to 3, and back from 3 to 2 to 1 in stance

Drill 2   As Drill 1, except pad holder stands in front of fighter. Fighter delivers jabs as they move forward and back

Drill 3   Fighter stands in corner facing partner. Partner attacks with hook to body (a) providing energy to fighter. Fighter pushes arm away, allowing partner to continue forward (b). Fighter swivels 180 degrees out of the path of the partner (c). Both fighters face each other (d and e).

Speedy Boxer-Puncher v. Tall, Aggressive Knockout Specialist

Sugar Ray Leonard v. Thomas 'Hitman' Hearns, 16 September 1981

The Fight – an Overview

The bout was held at Caesar's Palace, Las Vegas, in order to decide whether Leonard, the WBC title holder, or

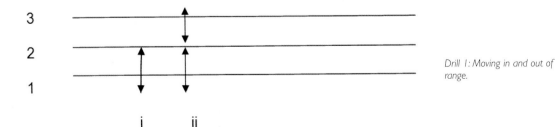

Drill 1: Moving in and out of range.

Fighter biographies

	Sugar Ray Leonard	Thomas 'Hitman' Hearns
Birth	May 17th, 1956	October 18, 1958
Weights		Welterweight super welter middle supermiddle light heavy cruiserweight
Country of birth	US	US
Style	Speedy, boxer, puncher	tall aggressive knock out specialist
Famous for	Fighter of decade for 1980s	Greatest Super Welterweight of all time by Ring Magazine and received the 'Fighter of the year' award in 1980 and 1984

Hearns, the WBA champion, should be the undisputed world welterweight champion.

Round 1: Both fighters came out from their corners on their toes, moving around in multiple directions. Leonard appeared to be moving more smoothly while delivering body shots as he entered into range. Hearns looked to be trying to control the centre. Both fighters used the first round to assess each other's strengths and weaknesses.

Round 2: Very similar to the first round. Hearns was trying to find Leonard, but Leonard's movement was excellent, floating around the ring very effectively. Leonard was moving and hitting with simple, single punches that made some contact with Hearns. There were occasional interchanges between the two fighters, when in punching range, but Leonard's movement was pretty much controlling the essence of the fight. The combinations delivered by Leonard worked as he spent more time in punching range than the previous round. Hearns spent most of the round head hunting, occasionally making contact.

Round 3: Leonard continued to drop regularly to deliver body shots to Hearns. He punched and moved straight back out, not giving Hearns the opportunity to counter, but Hearns did land some shots. At one point Hearns delivered two rear hand punches that rocked Leonard. However, Leonard continued to provide Hearns with a continually moving target. Leonard delivered combinations that created holes in Hearns's armoury.

Round 4: The fight slowed down from the earlier rounds. Leonard delivered punches and moves, but at a slower pace than the earlier rounds. Hearns was holding his lead hand in its infamous low position. Hearns appeared to be limited in his range and variety of punches at this stage of the fight. This round was used by both fighters to attempt to change the tempo of the fight. It looked as though both fighters had strategies in mind. Hearns still struggle in this round to make any contact with Leonard, who was moving more fluidly.

Round 5: Hearns had been predictable and one-dimensional, relying on a big shot dependent on the opponent standing still. Leonard was very dynamic and used the space in the ring effectively. He changed direction, confusing Hearns, and came in to punch low, making it difficult for Hearns to hit him. Although Leonard was moving beautifully, he did not really land many shots in the first five rounds.

Round 6: Leonard came out with the smell of the victory after the first five rounds and was hitting more viciously, causing Hearns many problems in the round.

Round 7: Leonard was now starting to take more control of the centre of the ring, but appeared to be more effective than when Hearns was adopting a similar strategy. Leonard looked to be ready to take the fight to Hearns, exchanging many punches and delivering an excellent body shot followed by a continuous flurry of punches. Hearns was now looking as if he was struggling. The body shots were beginning to hurt. Leonard was delivering a broad variety of shots from every angle.

Round 8: Hearns was trying to recover, staying away from Leonard by circling and moving, but Leonard still seemed in control. Hearns was taking on Leonard's strategy from the earlier rounds, but his motives were different. Where Leonard had been looking for openings, Hearns was trying to avoid being hit. Hearns was moving in a desperate manner. He bounced off the ropes and was running backwards. Leonard was always in control and moving just on the edge of his range.

tvp Analytic Summary: Leonard v. Hearns

Element	Sugar Ray Leonard	Thomas 'Hitman' Hearns
Style	Speedy boxer-puncher	Tall, aggressive boxer, knockout fighter
Technique	Excellent technique. Non-punching hand in appropriate positions. Excellent use of body mechanics	Excellent technique with punches. Able to cover for having a low lead hand. Excellent body mechanics
Variety	Broad range of punches and defences. Good use of tempo changes	More limited than Leonard. Very reliant on the big hit. Fairly one-dimensional in terms of pace and change
Predictability	Very unpredictable due to the variety of movement and punches. Able to change speed	Very powerful, but more predictable

Round 9: A very similar round to round 8. Leonard was starting to close Hearns into the corners. A key lesson is that Sugar Ray was controlling the ring!

Round 10: Leonard was now working off both counter-punching and attacking mode. Hearns wanted to control the centre but Leonard would not give this space easily. Both fighters were punching when they needed to.

Round 11: Both fighters were setting themselves looking for punches. Hearns punches Leonard with a rear hand to the face with a hook, utilizing the power available to him. Both fighters were striving for the centre of the ring.

Round 12: The fight was now becoming a more close-range battle. Hearns had now recovered from the last few rounds and was taking the fight to Leonard, who continued to move well but was less effective than in the previous rounds. Both fighters were trying to stake a claim for the centre with no one really dominating. A fairly balanced round. At the end of round 12 Leonard's trainer, Angelo Dundee, warned him, 'You're blowing it now, son! You're blowing it!'

Round 13: A reinvigorated Leonard came out roaring. He started with a rapid combination and pushed Hearns onto the ropes. Hearns managed to rise, but was dropped again near the end of the round. He was struggling and Leonard unleashed a vicious series of punches that took Hearns to the floor. Leonard had now regained control of the fight. Smelling victory, he laid Hearns on the ropes to take a count. After hurting Hearns with a right, Leonard exploded with a combination of punches and sent Hearns through the ropes.

Round 14: Hearns was spent by the beginning of round 14, and Leonard pinned him against the ropes, where he unleashed another furious combination, prompting the referee to stop the contest.

Result: Leonard won on technical knockout in Round 14.

The fight had lasting consequences. Some months later Leonard discovered that he had suffered a detached retina, which forced him to retire. He would make comebacks, including taking the middleweight title from Marvin Hagler in 1987, but he never sustained consistent success. Hearns went on to win more world championships, but he retained some resentment that his loss against Leonard had reduced the endorsements to which he felt entitled.

15-minute Learning Plan

A key learning point from this fight was Leonard's ability to move around the ring and provide Hearn with a constantly moving target. This will be the focus of our 15-minute plan.

Objective
* Develop footwork patterns that create continuous movement
* Develop ability to punch while moving in and out of range

Drills
All drills will be performed using quick foot ladders.
Drill 1   In stance, move forward punching
Drill 2   In stance, move backwards punching
Drill 3   In stance, move forward two moves and back one move. This develops the ability to punch and retreat out of range
Drill 4   In stance, slide two moves forward and back one move
Drill 5   Facing the ladder from a sideways position, move in and out of the rungs as you move laterally across the ladder, while punching.

A video of the above drills can be seen at www.martial-boxing.com

Fast, Unorthodox Fighter v. Traditional Fighter

Prince Naseem Hamid v. Steve Robinson, 30 September 1995

The Fight – an Overview

The fight was held before Robinson's home crowd at Cardiff Arms Park.

Round 1: Naz came out looking confident while Robinson looked as if he knew he had to defend. Robinson looked tense with his hands protecting his face all the time. Naz looked relaxed and eager to destroy. He fought from a distance that he knew he could explode from, while leaving his hands down allowing him to relax and be totally unpredictable. Robinson threw a series of punches more in hope than with conviction, very rarely hitting Naz. When Robinson moved forward with conviction, Naz had plenty of time to move away and not be troubled by the token gestures. Naz frequently took a crouched position from which to launch a series of attacks. This reminds us of postures taken by fighters from the 1950s and great fighters like Nigel Benn. Naz threw effective punches and opened the space between him and Robinson very effectively. There was certainly a difference in the degree of self-expression between the two fighters: Naz seemed to be enjoying himself and the opportunity to demonstrate his talent, whereas Robinson appeared very cautious. Naz led with a couple of lead hand uppercuts that Robinson struggled with. Naz demonstrated his ability to lead with bent arm shots rather than the traditional straight line punches. Robinson spent most of the round throwing token punches with no intention or belief that they would do anything, fuelling Naz's self-belief that this would be his fight. This first round simply demonstrated Naz's ability to read and act on distance. Towards the end of the round, Robinson threw a few combinations that excited the crowd, but they made little impact on Naz. Naz also spent the round showing he is comfortable fighting from both an orthodox and southpaw stance.

Round 2: Naz came out leading with a few lead hand punches from a southpaw stance, trying to initiate a reaction from Robinson. Robinson advanced with a combination but Naz moved away very sharply, showing off his mobility. Naz appeared to be controlling the space in the ring, moving away from the ropes very effectively. Naz threw his lead hand punches with his hands down by his side, knowing Robinson had no intention of taking the lead. Robinson was starting to look very predictable, whereas Naz was so unorthodox that at one point he wrestled Robinson over to the floor. After this, Naz stood square on with his hands down, inviting Robinson forward. Robinson did not take the bait so Naz started to show off his dance moves. Robinson now became aggressive and advanced with intent, but Naz also demonstrated his agility and speed, moving away from Robinson.

Round 3: Naz came out for the third round looking fairly orthodox, but soon went back to his inimitable style. Robinson managed a rear hand punch that landed on Naz's face, but he moved back taking away the impact of the punch. The rest of the round continued pretty much as in the earlier rounds. Due to Robinson's guard, Naz was working very hard on landing the uppercut and coming through his guard with his lead hand. Robinson again tried to launch himself on Hamed, but the distance that Naz retained ensured he had plenty of time to move away. This was especially the case when he launched four or five consecutive punches as he moved forward – not one shot landed on its intended target.

Round 4: Naz came out with hands up, but still toying with Robinson. Naseem looked for unique angles to open up Robinson's defence, without feeling rushed and leaving himself open. He crouched and tried to open him up with lead hand uppercuts. Naz changed his stance and made complete use of the ring, leading Robinson to different parts of the ring. Again, there was no suggestion in this

Fighter biographies (adapted from Wikipedia)

	Prince Naseem Hamed	Steve Robinson
Birth	February 1974	13 December 1968
Weights	Bantamweight Featherweight	Featherweight
Country of birth	Yemen	Wales
Style	Fast, unorthodox fighter	Traditional fighter
Famous for	Various boxing sources claimed Hamed was one of the greatest British boxers of all time.	WBO World Featherweight Champion. He was a worthy champion with 7 successful defences of his title

tvp Analytic Summary: Hamid v. Robinson

Element	Prince Naseem Hamid	Steve Robinson
Style	Fast, unorthodox fighter, relied a lot on counterpunching	Traditional fighter with good technical capability
Technique	Punches generally comprised of large body movement, which led to loss of balance on many occasions. Hands generally down, but maintained good distance from opponent	Excellent technique with punches. Was not able to close off distance effectively
Variety	Broad range of punches and defences. Good use of tempo changes. Excellent range of movement and agility. Great variety of footwork	Relied on traditional punches delivered along linear line. Low variety in techniques
Predictability	Very unpredictable due to the variety of movement and punches. Able to change speed and deliver techniques from unusual angles	Quite predictable due to degree of caution

round that Robinson was the defending champion. Robinson was not throwing himself at Naseem and appeared to be wanting him to come to him, but without much luck.

Round 5: Pretty much the same as previous rounds. Naz did a bit of play-acting to try to rile Robinson. Again one of the most impressive things about Naz was the way he dominated and used the whole ring, attacking from a variety of angles. Naz threw a four-punch combination that put Robinson on the floor for only the second time in his career. As Robinson got up, Naz could smell the world title and began to let loose, while Robinson appeared to be dazed. Naz threw a number of combinations, with the most effective being the rear hand followed by the uppercut.

Round 6: Naz continues to lead with his front hand uppercut. The round was pretty slow, but exploded halfway through with Naz attacking from all angles once again. Naz was hitting with bent arm shots from all angles and hitting a variety of targets. Robinson was looking to survive. If body language is the most effective means of communicating a message, then Robinson had lost.

Round 7: Robinson changed his posture and came out looking confident, but without really being effective. The only real difference in this round was that Robinson was trying to seize more of the initiative.

Round 8: Nothing much happened, but Robinson slipped and the referee stopped the fight. If anything the end was a bit of an anticlimax. The Prince was now the King.

Result: Prince Naseem Hamid won on a knockout in Round 8.

15-minute Learning Plan

A key learning point from this fight was Prince Naseem's ability to change stance and deliver unusual combinations from either side. This will be the focus of our 15-minute plan.

Objective
* Develop ability to switch stance and deliver unusual combinations
* Develop ability to make creative combinations

Drills
One partner holds two focus pads.

Drill 1	In stance, move forward punching with lead hand. Then switch, and do the same on the other side. Then switch back to orthodox stance and deliver lead hand jab, followed by rear hand punch. Switch to southpaw and repeat combination. Switch and deliver lead hand jab, followed by rear hand punch, followed by lead hand hook. Switch again and repeat combination.
Drill 2	As Drill 1, but change the order of the three punches: lead hand hook, rear hand punch and lead hand jab.
Drill 3	As Drill 2, but change combination: rear hand punch, lead hand hook, lead hand jab.
Drill 4	As Drill 3, but change combination: rear hand punch, lead hand jab, lead hand hook..

A video of the above drills can be seen at www.martial-boxing.com

Fast Southpaw v. Traditional

Joe Calzaghe v. Jeff Lacy, 4 March 2006

The Fight – an Overview

Round 1: Both fighters came out to the centre of the ring, testing each other, Calzaghe in his famous southpaw stance and Lacy in orthodox stance. Within the first minute the two fighters engaged, with Calzaghe tying Lacy up and moving him around the ring while in a clinch. Once released from the clinch Calzaghe fired an effective hook to the head. The first few punch combinations from Calzaghe ended up in clinches. Calzaghe was trying to maintain range while Lacy was looking to make the fight a closer affair. Both fighters were very effective, delivering the jab and moving away. Parts of the first round became quite messy as Lacy tried to tie Calazaghe up, holding his head. Halfway through the round Lacy put an effective combination together that drove Calzaghe into the corner, but Calzaghe delivered a great right uppercut as he was being driven back. Calzaghe followed this up with a number of combinations that suggested he had hurt Lacy. Calzaghe continued to hit Lacy, dropping his hands as he moved away and then firing combinations from a lower starting point, enhancing the power in the punch. Lacy recovered well, but was then caught with a right hook to the head. Lacy was clearly struggling with the southpaw's hook over his guard. The round ended with a flurry of exchanges from both fighters.

Round 2: This round began as the first round did. Lacy was still getting caught by Calzaghe's left uppercut, which was finding the target through the middle of Lacy's guard. Calzaghe was moving his head very effectively, making it very difficult for Lacy to land his shots. Calzaghe was also doing very well to maintain the inside position in the clinches. Calzaghe demonstrated brilliantly the art of infighting. He delivered effective bent arm combinations while in close and then moved away behind a series of straight punches. Lacy was struggling to make any signifi-

cant impact on the fight. Calzaghe was making great use of the whole of the ring, 'dragging' Lacy from one corner to another, not getting stuck on the ropes and thus disorientating Lacy. Calzaghe gave himself the distance, allowing him to deliver effective punches from unusual angles. Lacy's punches appeared relatively ineffective, pushed to their target rather than thrown in an effective manner. Calzaghe finished the round with some classic uppercuts, combining great body and head movement to land damaging shots to Lacy's head. Great movement from Calzaghe and great frustration from Lacy.

Round 3: This round began in very dynamic fashion with Lacy trying to tie Calzaghe up on the ropes, but Calzaghe's head and body movement was mesmerising as he turned Lacy's energy against him. Calzaghe turned Lacy onto the ropes in one swift movement while continuing to hit Lacy. His punching effectiveness moved up another level in this round, hitting from various angles and ensuring his head was never still enough to be hit. Calzaghe moved away in an unorthodox stance with his hands down by his side, but he always ensured he had sufficient distance between him and Lacy. Calzaghe enjoyed delivering a double lead hand jab, rear hand combination on a few occasions, mixed with lead, rear hand combinations. Lacy looked completely lost.

Round 4: The fourth round began with Lacy throwing a jab, but Calzaghe ducked superbly, timing his movement to perfection. Lacy was throwing one punch at a time and relying on making an impact with one hit, whereas Calzaghe was throwing a flurry of hits and moving all of the time. Calzaghe finished the round with a combination of four or five bent arm shots to Lacy's head. The result was that Lacy continued to throw punches that were more pushed than thrown.

Round 5: The most distinctive difference between the two fighters at this stage was the level of head movement. Lacy threw a lead hand jab with his full bodyweight behind the punch and Calzaghe moved smartly away from it by turning on the ball of his front foot. Calzaghe also frustrated Lacy by holding on to him as he tried to get in

Fighter biographies

	Joseph William Calzaghe	Jeffrey Scott Lacy
Birth	born 23 March 1972	May 12, 1977
Weights	Super Middleweight Light heavyweight	Super middleweight
Country of birth	Wales	US
Style	Fast southpaw	Traditional
Famous for	WBO super middleweight title for over ten years	Olympic champion

tvp Analytic Summary: Calzaghe v. Lacy

Element	Joe Calzaghe	Jeff Lacy
Style	Fast, southpaw fighter who relied on hit and move philosophy	Traditional, orthodox and powerful fighter with good technical capability
Technique	Punches generally comprised of large body movement, which led to loss of balance on many occasions. Hands generally down, but maintained good distance from opponent. Sharp punches followed by quick movement. Very good at closing space after punching	Good technique with punches. Movement was restricted and predictable
Variety	Good range of punches and footwork. Good use of tempo changes. Made good use of linear and circular movement patterns. Great variety of footwork. Made good use of combinations comprising bent arm and straight shots	Relied on traditional punches delivered along linear line. Low variety in techniques
Predictability	Very unpredictable due to the variety of movement and punches. Able to change speed and deliver techniques from unusual angles. Danger punch was the uppercut with the lead hand. Constantly changing direction and turning. Excellent head movement	Quite predictable due to being on back foot for all of the fight

close. Lacy attempted an uppercut of his own, but telegraphed it and missed Calzaghe by a considerable distance. What was really impressive about Calzaghe was the number of different punches he was throwing and the way he was moving after punching. Lacy started to throw wild punches near the end of the round, giving more encouragement to Calzaghe.

Round 6: Lacy tried to progress forward in this round, but to little effect. Calzaghe allowed Lacy to tire himself out and then hit him with several combinations before tying Lacy up again. Lacy struggled to the inside position and seemed to be tiring. At this point the thing that stood out was Calzaghe's hand speed and head movement. In addition, Calzaghe was getting below Lacy's punches, making his shots ineffective.

Round 7: Calzaghe continued to use his southpaw stance to his advantage, closing off Lacy's options. Lacy had a couple of good punches, but not to any real effect. Calazaghe made really good use of the whole ring. The round finished with Lacy in the corner being attacked from all different angles with a barrage of punches. Lacy had nowhere to go and no response.

Round 8: Followed a similar pattern to the previous rounds. Calzaghe was way out in front.

Round 9: Lacy seemed to be lacking any degree of explosiveness, and as a result nothing changed.

Round 10: Throughout the fight Lacy's footwork and movement had been very predictable, whereas Calzaghe had been quite creative and unpredictable. Calzaghe littered this round with some different combinations, throwing a rear hand, lead mix that Lacy failed to see.

Round 11: Calzaghe continued as in the previous round. Lacy fell early in the round, but more due to a push from Calzaghe. This seemed to be quite a scrappy round, with stoppages and Lacy falling over a couple of times. The latter part of the round was characterized by great combinations from Calzaghe.

Round 12: Calzaghe dominates this round in a way that he had dominated the fight. Almost all the first minute of the round was Calzaghe pounding Lacy with punch after punch, ending up with Lacy going to the floor for the first time in his career. As Lacy tried to hold on to Calzaghe, he moved away, creating space to continue his barrage of punches. The round was briefly stopped to make glove adjustments to Lacy's hands. Calzaghe also landed some Naseem-like uppercuts from low hands. What a fight – what a one-sided fight.

Result: Joe Calzaghe wins on a unanimous points decision.

15-minute Learning Plan

A key learning point from this fight was Joe Calzaghe's ability to hit and move away from the target. This will be the focus of our 15-minute plan.

Objective
*   Develop ability to hit combinations and move

tvp Analysis Summary

Fight	Styles	Key Learning Points	Practice
Gene Tunney v. Jack Dempsey 1926, 1927	Long-range fighter v. short, crouch and weaver	Fighting at range and closing the gap	Pad- and bag-based drills
Henry Armstrong v. Ceferino Garcia 1938	Crouching weaver v. tall fighter	Close range punching	Partner work
Sugar Ray Robinson v. Carl Bobo Olsen 1955, 1956	Long-range fighter v close-in fighter	Unpredictable punching with power	Bag-based punching from low to high
Henry Cooper v. Joe Erskine 1959	Natural southpaw fighting orthodox v. short fighter	Switching so you can fight orthodox and southpaw	Punch bag drills
Muhammad Ali v. George Foreman ('Rumble in the Jungle') 1974	Long-range mobile fighter v knockout specialist	Footwork Defence and attack Negotiating the ring	Ring- and pad-based drills
Sugar Ray Leonard v. Thomas 'Hitman' Hearns	Speedy boxer-puncher v. tall, aggressive knockout specialist	Punching while moving in and out of range	Quick foot ladder drills
Prince Naseem Hamid v. Steve Robinson 1995	Fast, unorthodox fighter v. traditional fighter	Change stance and deliver unusual combinations	Partner and focus pad drills
Joe Calzaghe v. Jeff Lacy 2006	Fast southpaw v. traditional fighter	Punch and move	Partner and focus pad drills

Drills

One partner holds two focus pads.

Drill 1   In stance, hit pad with lead hand. Partner throws punch back forcing you to slide back out of range

Drill 2   Throw lead hand jab, lead hand hook and lead hand jab. After last jab partner throws punch back forcing you to move back

Drill 3   As Drill 1, but follow with rear hand to body and lead hand to face, with partner throwing punch to force movement

Drill 4   Throw rear hand to body, followed by rear hand uppercut to head, lead hand hook to face and lead hand jab. Partner returns with punch to force movement

Drill 5   Repeat all of the above but replace moving back with head movement

Drill 6   Create three parallel lines on floor, separated by 6in. In stance move in and out of the first line. On the command of your partner, double up with punches as you move in stance

THE CHAMPION'S LOGBOOK

An ounce of performance is worth pounds of promises.
Mae West

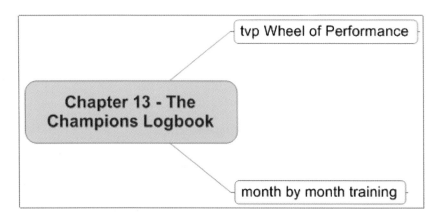

Mindmap overview of Chapter 13.

This chapter provides a twelve-month planning programme, detailing month by month the key areas of development and the drills to maximize the training experience

12 Months to Becoming a Champion in Boxing and Combat Sport

A note of caution: the programme is designed on a twelve-month basis, but we are not suggesting that it takes only twelve months to becoming a champion. We are assuming that the athlete has been training for some years, and we are looking to add the final touches during this twelve-month period.

The starting point for any sports programme is to determine the current level of performance and compare it to the desired level to becoming a champion. This will involve identifying role models and learning from them. Once the gap in the levels of performance has been determined, it will be necessary to create a twelve-month plan.

Create personal vision – where do you want to see yourself in 12 months time, and maybe even longer

Determine current levels of performance using appropriate testing methods

Determine desired levels of performance to becoming a champion based on observing role models and personal vision

Design 12 month training plan incorporating physical, mental and sport specific elements

The 12-month plan process.

The first task in preparing our training programme is to create our personal vision. What is driving us? Our personal vision needs to be meaningful and inspirational. The vision will drive us through our most difficult times. Our vision reflects our values and the way we want to be seen by others. In short, our vision is our dream. In terms of timeframe our vision should be viewed in the longer term, usually five years, but for the purpose of this exercise we will look at the vision for the twelve-month period. Think about the vision carefully. The vision should engage and frighten, while stretching your capabilities to the maximum. See yourself living the dream like a movie. Steve Morris, the world famous karate and combat arts exponent and champion, tells the story of how he would smash through bricks and wood by visualizing himself doing it in the first place. This 'picture' was his confirmation that the act was possible. You need to be able to see yourself delivering the outcome, to succeed.

Month 1

Describe your vision in as much detail as possible. Engage as many of the senses as possible in the description – what you would see, feel, smell, hear and so on. Take your time in expressing this vision. Check the following:

* Is it ambitious?
* Does it engage and frighten?
* Does it stretch me?
* Is it motivational?
* Am I excited by my vision?

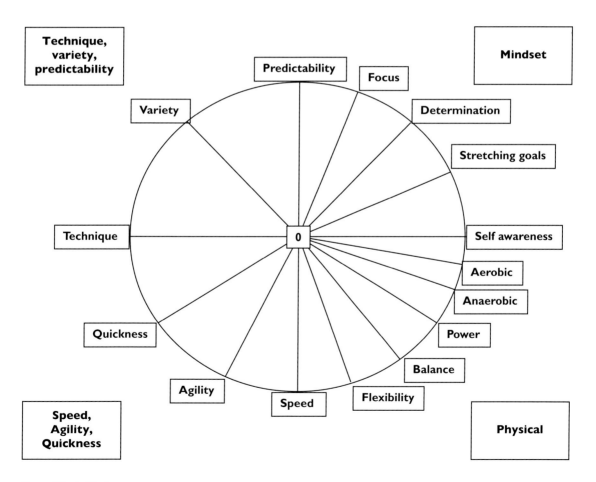

The tvp Wheel of Performance.

Month 2

Before we actually start our training programme we need to know what we want to achieve. We need to create a set of tangible goals for the next year that will drive the design of our training programme. The tangible goals need to be very specific to yield the desired outcomes.

The tvp Wheel of Performance

The second task, which is quite closely related to the vision, is the setting of specific goals. These goals will break down the vision into smaller, more attainable and meaningful measures that provide the athlete with the focus needed to be successful. We also need to set specific targets related to our baseline level. For combat sports, and boxing in particular, the goals need to be divided into four areas that are linked, but need to have a separate focus of attention.

The mindset and physical areas are more generic athletic attributes, whereas the SAQ and tvp are very boxing specific.

Mindset

This is a way of assessing the mental determination and will to fulfil the goals. We see this as a vital starting point, as champions are able to push through their mental barriers in the most challenging of times. Champions are able to continue when physically their bodies have given up. We would go so far as to say that mental capacity is probably the key differentiator between an average boxer and a champion. The key elements to consider in terms of the champion's mindset are: focus, determination, stretching goals, self awareness.

Assessing mindsets
Focus will be assessed by the coach or individual, in a relatively subjective way, by observing the level of concentration and application towards specific goals during training and preparation, prior to competing.

Key questions that will affect the scoring out of 10 are:
* Is the boxer on time for training? This is a test of commitment and seriousness for the competing boxer.
* Does the boxer demonstrate single-mindedness during training or is his mind wandering? This is a test of the level of focus during training.
* Does the boxer own the goals and visit them before each session? Is the boxer really committed to the goals?

Determination is assessed based on the boxer's ability and desire to push themselves during sessions. Key questions are:
* Does the boxer keep pushing themselves until the pre-agreed goals are met during a session?
* Does the boxer demonstrate a spirit and desire while training?
* Does the boxer keep looking to learn during the sessions?

Stretching goals is based on how ambitious the boxer is and how far he believes he can go. Key questions to help with the assessment are:
* How easily are the pre-agreed goals being met? Are they stretching enough?
* What is the attitude of the boxer towards the goals: are they easy, OK or hard?
* How does the boxer feel at the end of sessions? Has he ventured outside his comfort zone during the session at any time?
* Do the goals excite the boxer?

Self-awareness is based on the boxer's ability to identify personal strengths and weaknesses without the input of the coach. Key questions are:
* Does the boxer identify progress in the same way as the coach?
* What are the typical questions asked by the boxer: are they relevant or irrelevant in the eyes of the coach?

Defining Mindsets

Component	Definition	Boxing application
Focus	Level of concentration and application towards a set goal	Attitude and desire to achieve a specific goal during training and competing
Determination	Will to succeed and deliver set goals	Will to win
Stretching goals	Ambition to develop, improve and succeed yourself	Pushing performance boundaries to new limits
Self-awareness	Focus on personal improvement of key areas needed for success	Self-coaching and self-appraisal

Key Components of Physical Fitness

Component	Definition	Relevance for boxing
Aerobic fitness	The heart's ability to deliver blood to working muscles and their ability to use it effectively	Ability to fight continuously for the required rounds, with minimal reduction in performance. Can you last the course?
Anaerobic	Muscle's ability to contract and apply strength time after time	Ability to punch with maximum power for as long as possible during the required rounds. Can you sustain power to the end?
Power	Ability to exert maximum muscular contraction instantly in an explosive burst of movements	Ability to punch with maximum strength quickly
Balance	Ability to control the body's position, either stationary or while moving	Ability to maintain appropriate posture while delivering a tirade of punches. Are you as light on your feet as you should be?
Flexibility	Ability to achieve an extended range of motion	Ability to reach and deliver techniques from a variety of angles without sustaining injury. Are you prone to muscle stiffness or injury?

The coach needs to set scores based on current levels of performance and set monthly targets for improvement based on the coach's subjective assessment and in discussion with the boxer.

Tools that may be used by the coach to improve performance are as follows:

Focus: Focus is maintained and improved by applying discipline to pre-agreed prioritized actions and goals. In addition, the coach and boxer need to monitor the boxer's attitude during training, trying to identify lapses and the cause of these lapses. The coach should demonstrate the relevance and importance of focus to achieving physical goals by setting stretching tasks to test the level of focus in the boxer to succeed in something that may be outside their current capability.

Determination: The coach needs to help the boxer identify their motivation for success and keep reminding them of this as a driver of action. The boxer again needs to prioritize his key motives to help with providing drive during challenging times of training. Role models can be quite useful in providing boxers with motivation when the going gets tough.

Stretching goals: The coach needs to know how to take the boxer outside his comfort zone and also how to bring them back so that their motivation levels are maintained and enhanced.

Self-awareness: Through discussion of performance and appropriate questioning from the coach, the boxer's self-awareness grows considerably. Playback of training sessions and competition can be a great way of increasing self-awareness.

Physical

A key aspect of training in combat sports, as in any other sports, is the need to add physical activity and training to maximize efficiency, improvement and balance. Adaptive body stress is essential to increase the physical capabilities of the athlete. There are a number of elements of physical development that need to be considered in

Key Components of SAQ

Component	Definition	Combat sports application
Speed	Distance covered in a unit of time	Distance covered by a punch or by an individual moving in different directions (linear, lateral, vertical) in the ring in an appropriate unit of time. Can you move as fast as possible?
Agility	Ability to move quickly in any direction and maintain balance	Ability to punch while moving in any direction. Can you make all the necessary moves better than the opponent?
Quickness	Ability to generate a movement in shorter amount of time (acceleration)	Ability to move hands and legs to punch more quickly. Can you react quicker?

Key Components of tvp

Component	Definition	Combat sports application
Technique	The maximal interaction of all appropriate parts of body and mind in delivering a punch or kick	Punching with correct and appropriate dynamics. Are you punching efficiently, economically and effectively?
Variety	A good understanding of the full range of techniques available	Understanding all punches and different applications. What contingencies do you have?
Predictability	Ability to do the unexpected	Creative application of punches and body movements. Can you outthink your opponent?

preparing for competition. These are shown in the accompanying table.

SAQ

SAQ training enables the boxer to move faster and punch harder, and engages the body and nervous system in a way in which specific boxing training might not target specifically.

tvp

This is a valid method for testing relevant boxing attributes.

Applying the Wheel of Performance

1. Agree with your coach the most appropriate areas to be monitored and goals to be focused on for the training programme.
2. Assess your current levels of performance under each of the agreed headings by scoring out of 10. This can be done by carrying out a number of tried and tested methods used by athletes all over the world if you want to go beyond a subjective method. Draw your position on the Wheel of Performance for each of the headings.
3. Determine desired performance profile on a month by month basis. Note that 10 out of 10 may not be appropriate for all situations. Additionally, this may not be realistic in our timescales. Plot your desired profile at the end of the 12-month period, and break this down into monthly profiles.
4. Construct a training programme to deliver desired results over the next three-month period based on the accompanying table by allocating the percentage of time to be focused on during each month.

Sample Framework for an Exercise Plan

Component	Exercises	Month 1	Month 2	Month 3
Focus				
Determination				
Stretching goals				
Self-awareness				
Aerobic				
Anaerobic				
Power				
Balance				
Flexibility				
Speed				
Agility				
Quickness				
Technique				
Variety				
Predictability				

Month 3

Having agreed on our goals and targets in the last two months, we are now ready to start planning the actual training. At this stage of the preparation (ten months prior to competition) we need to ensure the basics and essentials are in place so that we can become more targeted to the event itself during the latter stages of preparation.

The Wheel of Performance will provide the basis for the training encompassing the key elements at the various stages of the preparation. The Wheel of Performance ensures there is balance in the training method between all four perspectives.

For boxing the four areas are linked, but need to have a separate focus of attention at different stages of preparation.

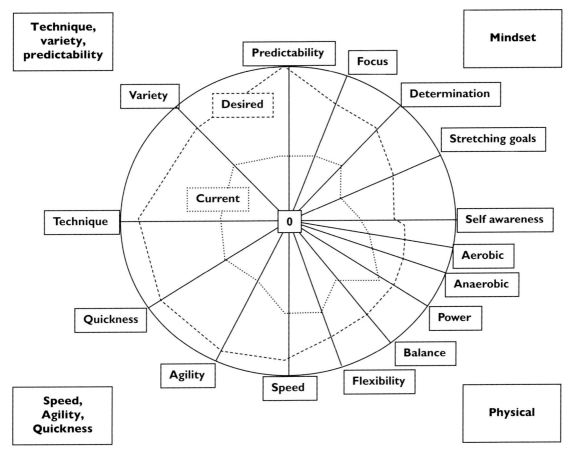

Example of a tvp Wheel of Performance.

The mindset and physical areas are more generic athletic attributes, whereas the SAQ and tvp are very boxing specific.

Percentage of Time Allocated to Attributes during Month 3

Category	Percentage	Notes
Mindset	10%	It is too early to get totally concentrated and engrossed in the fight, but some degree of mindset training is required to motivate through the long journey. This phase of the mindset training is totally dedicated to *meditation and breathing*, allowing the fighter to explore and challenge their mindset. The journey is long and arduous and *determination* will be needed in large quantities.
Physical	20%	Preparing the body for intensive work over a long period requires focus on the key components of fitness. At this stage the focus is on aerobic, anaerobic and flexibility. The flexibility is essential to aid recovery and ensure mobility is always maintained during the programme. The amount of time spent on physical activity should be split equally between *aerobic, anaerobic and stretching*.
SAQ	20%	The role of SAQ is to improve mobility. The training will be very specific to boxing and will focus on developing the basic attributes of movement and power to enable the fighter to punch *harder and move quicker*. Many people try to progress quickly at this stage, but you are looking to re-educate your body and the way it moves: this takes time and needs to be taken slowly, but surely.
tvp	50%	This is the area that will ultimately develop the champion within. At this

stage the focus of the training will be entirely on coaching technique. The timing of training is critical as the body is being stretched in a number of different ways by the other three perspectives, so you need to be wary of tiredness, which will slow down productivity.

In terms of the SAQ Continuum (see Chapter 8), the key areas of focus during this period of training are:

Mechanics of movement: the development of correct movement form for the different aspects of fighting. Foot movement in combat sports provides balance, coordination and transfer of power. Correct foot placement helps the economics of movement and makes the fighter become more efficient.

Innervation: the development of fast feet, agility, coordination and control for fighting and combat sports. This is a transition stage from warm-up to high-intensity foot and hand work that activates the neuro-pathways: in other words you get the nerves to fire the muscles as quickly as possible. The quicker the feet are placed up and down on the floor, the more control the fighter has and more power is generated in punching and kicking.

The key checks for the Technique part of tvp (the ability to deliver the appropriate technique correctly in terms of mechanics) are:
*   Position of non-punching hand
*   Bodyweight transfer when punching
*   Break off from inside position
*   Quality of punching
*   Relaxation and acceleration of punching

Components and their Appropriate Exercises

Component	Exercises general	Exercises specific
Focus		
Determination	Meditation and breathing exercises	
Stretching goals		
Self awareness		
Aerobic	Jogging Rowing Skipping	Speedball Shadow boxing Continuous bag work
Anaerobic	Weight training Target circuits	Pad work Bag work (all varying intensity)
Power		
Balance		
Flexibility	Yoga: stretching and manipulation exercises	
SAQ	General footwork drills using quick foot ladders to engage fast-twitch fibres of muscles	Boxing-based footwork drills using hurdles and quick foot ladders
tvp		Focus pads and bag work Controlled sparring

Sample Weekly Workout During Month 3

	Sun	Mon	Tues	Wed	Thurs	Fri	Sat	Total
Determination		10min		10min		10min		30 (8%)
Aerobics		20min				20min		40 (11%)
Anaerobic			30min		30min			60 (17%)
Flexibility		10min	10min		10min	10min		40 (11%)
SAQ			20min		20min			40 (11%)
tvp™		60min		30min		60min		150 (42%)
TOTAL		100 (28%)	60 (17%)	40 (11%)	60 (17%)	100 (28%)		360min

The focus of the combat sports-specific training for month 3 comprises:

Dynamic flex warm-up: Warm the body up specifically for the punches to follow.

Mechanics: Understand the correct mechanics and the role of the body and feet in delivering the optimal technique in terms of movement and power.

Innervation: This works on the principle that all punches are driven from the feet. The emphasis is on developing agility in technique from the feet first.

As we get further into the training programme the intensity will increase and the balance of sessions will change. This ensures a balanced programme.

Month 4

Having started our training programme, this month is not significantly going to change in terms of balance from last month. We are still some way off having to start focusing on specific preparations for the fight. This month we are going to work on developing the power and explosion in our techniques. In order to avoid boredom and stimulate skills development, the programme will change slightly in terms of our focus on SAQ, as this will assist tremendously in the development of force in our techniques. In addition, we will slightly alter the balance between aerobic and anaerobic activity.

This month's focus is on technique and aerobic capacity with some activity in the other areas of the Wheel of Performance.

Before we start looking at training the development of our punching force we need to fully understand what force is. Going back to our schooldays learning physics, we need to remember that:

$$Force = Mass \times Acceleration$$

This means that force is a function of acceleration and not speed. Speed is the rate at which your fist is moving, whereas acceleration is the rate at which your fist gathers speed. The difference is that your fist needs to get faster as it approaches the target and get even faster as it retracts.

The key elements for the development of the Technique part of tvp (*see* Chapter 5), that is the ability to deliver the appropriate technique correctly in terms of mechanics, which will contribute to the development of power and explosion, are:
* Bodyweight transfer when punching
* Quality of punching
* Relaxation and acceleration of punching

Bodyweight Transfer When Punching

The role of bodyweight transfer when punching is to focus on the following:
* Maximize power with minimal movement
* Preparedness for next technique

The key rules to develop your hitting power are:
* Keep the technique small
* Internalize bodyweight shifting
* Use leverage from all your body

The training template to be used is as follows:
* Tapering techniques to smaller movements
* Providing resistance forcing application of body weight transfer
* Utilize whip and pull effect when delivering the technique
* Body alignment check through applying pressure to a static target

Quality of Punching

The quality of punching is dependent on the following factors:
* Efficiency of effort: minimal effort with maximum impact
* Economy of movement: internalize movements making the delivery quicker
* Effectiveness of movement: giving maximum power

The training template needs to focus on the following:
* Perform slow techniques with resistance and ensure that time is given to contrast phase of the training cycle so that the body can feel the difference between slow and fast
* Use of resistance bands to develop fast-twitch fibres to generate maximum power
* Feet movement and light sparring

The quality of punching can be assessed in terms of the following:
* Speed at which punch is thrown
* Force that generates punch
* Timing of the delivery
* Accuracy of punch
* Judgement of distance
* Amount of relaxation present
* Acceleration of punch
* Retraction

Sample Weekly Workout During Month 4

Times in parentheses show the previous month's allocation

	Sun	Mon	Tues	Wed	Thurs	Fri	Sat	Total
Determination		(10min)	10min	(10min)	10min	(10min)		20 (6%)
Aerobics		10min (20min)	30min	10min	30min	10min (20min)		90 (25%)
Anaerobic			20min (30min)		20min (30min)			40 (11%)
Flexibility		10min	10min		10min	10min		40 (11%)
SAQ		20mins	(20min)	20min	(20min)	20min		60 (17%)
tvp™		60min		30min		60min		150 (42%)
TOTAL		100 (28%)	60 (17%)	60 (17%)	70 (11%)	100 (28%)		360min

Relaxation and Acceleration of Punching

The role of being relaxed is to generate power. The key rules to develop relaxation in technique are:

* Practise the technique both light and heavy
* Practise the technique both soft and hard

The training template is based on the use of resistance bands and dumbbells. The focus of the boxing-specific training for month 4 will be as follows:

Dynamic flex warm-up: Warm the body up specifically for the punches to follow.

Mechanics: Understand the correct mechanics and the role of the body and feet in delivering the optimal technique in terms of movement and power.

Innervation: This works on the principle that all punches are driven from the feet. The emphasis is on developing agility in technique from the feet first.

Month 5

Just to reiterate: we will not start focusing on the specific aspects of the fight strategy until 6 months before. Consequently, the training programme will have minor adjustments in terms of overall balance, but will focus on certain areas. This month we will focus on training variety in our attacks and defences. There will also be more emphasis on developing aspects of movement within the SAQ framework, to coincide with the needs of defending and attacking. In addition we will slightly alter the balance between aerobic and anaerobic activity.

This month's focus is on variety, SAQ and aerobic capacity with some activity in the other areas of the Wheel of Performance.

From a variety perspective we are looking to enhance our arsenal of weapons and responses. This means that our focus is on exploration and testing, with no pressure being imposed for failure.

In terms of the attacking tools there are certain roles and rules that have to be observed. The key roles of the variety phase of training are:

ATTACKING TOOLS	ESSENTIAL FEATURES	CRITICAL SKILL
Traditional jab	Body mechanics	Gathering whip, timing
Up jab	Quick turn of wrist 2" before impact	Timing
Short arm jab	Stopping power	Timing
Speed jab	Continuity	Reflex
Power jab	Complete body tension before impact	Power

Attacking tools.

	Head Jab	Head Hook	Head Uppercut	Body Jab	Body Hook	Body Uppercut
1. Block	X		X	X	X	X
2. Push away	X	X	X	X	X	X
3. Outside parry	X			X		
4. Inside parry	X			X		
5. Dip	X	X				
	X					

Defences.

* Develop a broader range of creative combinations. Experiment and create your combinations.
* Develop an ability to move with any combination between any technique. Your mind is the only barrier.
* Stop the mind from becoming pre-programmed with certain combinations. When you see yourself performing certain combinations – *stop* and re-programme yourself by slowing things down, and performing the combination in a step-by-step fashion.

The key rules to observe are:

* There are no rules! Don't be restricted by prejudice.
* Any combination can work. Only your mind is limiting!
* Any punch can start the combination. Why do most people always start the combination with a jab?
* Any punch can finish the combination.

The accompanying table shows a small selection of attacking tools that we focus on developing. The table also shows the essential features and critical skills that need to be focused on when practising these punches.

Development in the critical skills is essential for these techniques to be pulled off in a competitive situation. A partner, or coach, who can help with providing the right stimuli will ensure the quickest development in a broad variety of techniques.

In addition, there are fourteen different defences, of which the accompanying table shows a few. These defences are practised and developed to deal with the broad variety of punches that a competent fighter should be able to deliver.

At this stage of the training regime, the boxer needs to put themselves into uncomfortable positions. There will be a tendency for the boxer to stick to the defences he knows best, because it is the most automatic reaction. However, the purpose of this stage of training is to develop other responses, which in the longer term will also become automatic, and offer other alternatives.

The focus of the boxing specific training for month 5 will be as follows:

Dynamic flex warm-up: Warm the body up specifically for the variety of punches and defences to follow.

Mechanics: Understand the correct mechanics and the role of the body and feet in delivering the optimal technique in terms of movement and power.

Innervation: This works on the principle that all punches and defences are driven from the feet. The emphasis is on developing agility in technique from the feet first.

Sample Weekly Workout During Month 5

Note that in terms of allocation of time the training has not changed dramatically from last month, but the focus of the training has.

	Sun	Mon	Tues	Wed	Thurs	Fri	Sat	Total
Determination			10min		10min			20 (6%)
Aerobics	10min	30min	10min	30min	10min			90 (25%)
Anaerobic			20min		20min			40 (11%)
Flexibility	10min	10min			10min	10min		40 (11%)
SAQ		20min		20min		20min		60 (17%)
tvp		60min		30min		60min		150 (42%)
TOTAL		100 (28%)	60 (17%)	60 (17%)	70 (11%)	100 (28%)		360min

Sample Weekly Workout During Month 6

Note that the training times have not changed in the last three months, thus ensuring good balance between all elements. This will change dramatically next month.

	Sun	Mon	Tues	Wed	Thurs	Fri	Sat	Total
Determination		10min			10min			20 (6%)
Aerobics	10min	30min		10min	30min	10min		90 (25%)
Anaerobic		20min			20min			40 (11%)
Flexibility	10min	10min			10min	10min		40 (11%)
SAQ		20min		20min		20min		60 (17%)
tvp		60min		30min		60min		150 (42%)
TOTAL		100 (28%)	60 (17%)	60 (17%)	70 (11%)	100 (28%)		360min

Month 6

There are now seven months to go to the fight and this is the last stage of preparation before we start increasing the training level to prepare specifically for the fight. Again the overall balance of our training programme will change very little from previous months, but be aware that next month it will change significantly.

This month we will focus on training to become unpredictable in the way that we fight. We will also focus on SAQ and aerobic capacity with some activity in other areas of the Wheel of Performance.

One of the most visible features of the greatest fighters is their ability to confuse the opponent by being totally unpredictable. However, this ability has to be practised and isolated. Being unpredictable in the same way, repetitively, can itself also make you predictable. Therefore it is important that creativity is used to explore, and stretch, the boundaries of your fighting style.

What makes a fighter unpredictable? What are the dimensions of being unpredictable? Within the tvp framework we have identified five key elements that comprise the skills needed to be unpredictable (see Chapter 5 for more detail). These are:
* Preferred direction of movement
* Footwork patterns
* Movement of head
* Movement patterns and mannerism
* Change of movement speed

The focus of boxing-specific training for month 6 will be as follows:

Dynamic flex warm-up: Warm the body up specifically for movement in all directions and also introduce different speeds of movement.

Mechanics: Understand the correct mechanics and the role of the body and feet in delivering the optimal technique in terms of movement and power.

Innervation: This works on the principle that all punches and defences are driven from the feet. The emphasis is on developing agility in technique from the feet first.

Month 7

The accompanying graph shows how the balance of training needs to change during the twelve-month period. The key timings for changes to training patterns are month 7 and month 10. With six months to go, we are not quite at the stage of tapering the training specifically for this fight, but we are starting to become more focused on elements of competition and personal performance. The focus at this point in the logbook needs to begin to shift to mindset training and get focused on delivering results.

In terms of the Wheel of Performance, this month we will look at how to develop some of the aspects of focus and concentration to improve how we train and perform. Many people tend to leave these aspects of training either to the end of their schedule or don't bother with them altogether. However, the champions treat this stage of training as at least the equal of the other stages, if not more important.

There are many tools used for developing focus. The most common are visualization, mental rehearsing and self mantra, scenario planning and meditation. We are going to look at using autogenic training, a technique used by famous Soviet Olympic athletes, which combines mind training with yoga.

Autogenic Training

Autogenic training involves training and changing your natural responses under physical stress through relaxation

Level of importance

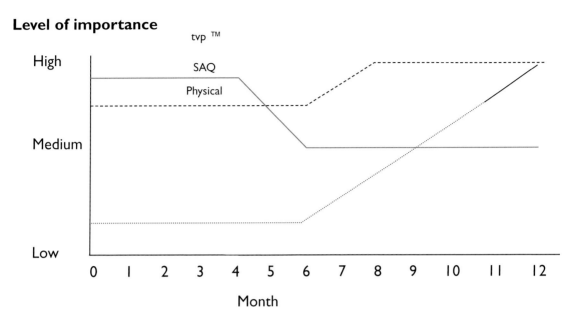

Training focus during 12-month period.

and concentration, that is through training your mind-body system. This form of training demands the responsibility for the training starts to shift from the coach to the fighter. Autogenic training implies development of self-control through techniques such as self-talk and self-mantra, which provide mental reinforcement through the repetition of simple phrases.

The purpose of autogenic training is to develop focus and train attention based primarily on reflex, so changing your natural responses to stressful situations. Additionally, these techniques are used to raise the fighters' mental and physical performance by development of self-discipline and concentration. In competitive situations fighters are inclined to think too much, thus delaying appropriate responses. A fighter who has been trained in autogenic training, or any form of mind training for that matter, will spend time observing an opponents' actions, moves, automatic responses, habits, weaknesses and strengths before deciding to 'let go' to deliver the appropriate trained response.

Before we start discussing the training itself, we need to understand two fundamental assumptions in the training:
* Body and mind are one.
* Words and images can change the performance of an individual.

There are two key stages to the training: physical focus and sport specific.

Physical focus
This step of the training is designed to give the fighter an appreciation of their bodily components and to develop control over the responses that the body provides. The training needs to focus on relevant parts of the body, such as muscles, heart and breathing. This might be, for example, by creating links with your arms, such as 'my arm is heavy', and imagining how it feels. The purpose of this stage is to maximize the effectiveness of the body and its organs.

Sports specific
This step of training is focused on practising specific responses to fight situation. This stage involves studying the fighters' best and worst moments in terms of what you saw, what you were visualizing, what you heard, what you felt and what emotions were going through you during your best and worst moments. The focus of this stage is very much on improving responses in a variety of competitive situations.

The phrases used by the fighter should be simple and positive, reinforcing self-confidence and thus changing thoughts and emotions.

Exercises
Both of these stages should focus on:
Preparatory exercises: deep breathing to relax and move to a stage of tranquillity. Key phrases to be repeated should be in the form 'I am calm, totally calm'.

	Preparatory	Heaviness	Warmth	Calm breathing	Heartbeat
Muscles					
Blood vessels					
Heart					
Breathing					
Head					

Heaviness exercises: experience the sensation of heaviness through all of your body parts. Key phrases should resemble 'my arms are heavy, very heavy'.

Warmth exercises: this develops the sensation of warmth through your body, which aids relaxation and improves blood flow through the arteries and capillaries.

Calm breathing exercise: this part of the process assists respiration with key phrases such as 'my breath is calm and regular'.

Heartbeat exercise: the aim is to feel the quiet beating of your heart using the phrase 'my heartbeat is quiet and strong'.

These are repeated for all body parts, as shown in the checklist.

A typical four week autogenic programme might look as follows:

	Focus	Notes
Week 1	Both arms	
Week 2	Both legs	
Week 3	Whole body	
Week 4	Skills mastery	Repeat for all body regularly

The programme for month 7 focuses on the physical aspects. As we get closer to the fight the focus will shift to more sports-specific autogenic training. Top athletes from many different sports have embraced this form of mindset training on their roads to success. The benefits of autogenic training are the ability to learn new skills more quickly, it aids recovery and creates calm or activated mental state and emotional balance.

Month 8

Continuing our theme from last month, we will focus on the mental preparation needed to prepare for the forthcoming competition.

In terms of the Wheel of Performance the mindset training will concentrate on our determination to achieve our goals. This mental preparation is critical to preparing ourselves for the last three months, where our performance has to step up a level to ensure success.

Determination to succeed is driven by the motivation the fighter has towards achieving a result. Motivation is defined as the direction and intensity of the fighter's efforts towards achieving a goal. This suggests that the fighter needs to be absolutely certain of the desired goal to become champion. In terms of the fight it has to be that the fighter wants to win and needs to visualize himself winning. He needs to smell victory, almost as if he is touching it. The key is for the fighter to establish what situations or outcomes actually attract him.

Sample Weekly Workout During Month 7

Times in parentheses show the previous month's allocation

	Sun	Mon	Tues	Wed	Thurs	Fri	Sat	Total
Determination		30min	(10min)	30min	(10min)	30mins		90 (18%)
Aerobics		10min	30min	10min	30min	10min		90 (18%)
Anaerobic			20min		20min			40 (8%)
Flexibility		10min	20min		20min	10min		60 (12%)
SAQ		20min		20min		20min		60 (12%)
tvp		60min		30min		60min		150 (31%)
TOTAL		130 (27%)	70 (14%)	90 (18%)	70 (14%)	130 (27%)		490min

Determination will drive the intensity of effort the fighter is likely to put into the last three months to achieve the desired results. We see quite regularly fighters who start off very sure of themselves and then start to lose focus, maybe due to fear, as they get closer to the fight. It is amazing how many creative excuses are found as a fight gets closer. The intensity of the fighter refers to how much effort he is prepared to put into the training during the last few weeks of training. The reason why training determination is important is that it works on the arousal, direction and persistence of the fighter during both the training and competition phases.

There are many ways in which determination is developed. There is a mental perspective and also a physical perspective. Determination is demonstrated through the training; a person's attitude to training on their own, shown by the number of solo hours put in, provides a good indication of the level of the fighter's determination to succeed. When a fighter has to be continually pushed, it suggests a lack of determination and is usually a good indicator of time wasting. Once the coach can see determination then more time can be given to the fighter to be the best they can be. A useful test of determination is the use of shadow boxing, which is an ideal vehicle for carrying out different forms of mental training. This subject will be discussed later.

What Motivates a Champion Fighter?

The motivation of fighters is influenced by both situational and personal factors. The key for enhancing motivation in fighters is not to focus attention only on the situation at hand or on personal factors, but to consider the interaction of these factors as these shape the attitude towards the activities at hand. Both recreational fighters and top level fighters have many reasons for being involved in boxing or martial arts. These may be:

* Improving skills
* Getting stronger and fitter
* Having fun
* Being with a friend
* Experiencing an adrenaline rush
* Achieving success

It seems that both recreational and highly competitive fighters value the skill improvement and development of fitness (personal factors). The major differences in motivational factors appear to be in the 'having fun' and 'achieving success' categories. Recreational fighters value highly the joy, pleasure, happiness (having fun), and social experience and affiliation (being with friend), whereas elite fighters are likely to be more motivated to practise and fight by ascetic experiences, such as achieving a personal best and winning

Key Shadow Boxing Drills

Form of shadow boxing	Key areas to emphasize	Notes
1. General: 1 × 3 minutes	Appropriate speed. Visualize your opponent and do not just throw punches out	People tend to go too fast without feeling the techniques and their body movement. The key purpose is link the body and mind as one
2. Visualize specific opponents: 3 × 3 minutes	Visualize the different opponent styles.	The fighter needs to demonstrate an understanding of the characteristics of the different styles and how to move in and out of the ranges of these fighters. Emphasis should also be in observing an understanding knowing which techniques will work against different opponents
3. Meditative shadow boxing: 3 × 3 minutes	Slow, almost tai chi style shadow boxing performed at very slow speed. Emphasis is on the fighter understanding the optimal way of delivering the technique	The fighter has no feel and no understanding of how to deliver different techniques. The slowness of the movement will also magnify any deficiencies in technique
4. Fighting pace shadow boxing – 3 × 4 minutes (Tabata intervals 20s on and 10s rest for 4 mins)	Everything is combined at normal fighting pace, with the coach shouting out different opponent types. This is designed to see the progression and improvement in technique	Be aware there is no change in pace and no modification in style, when needed

Sample Weekly Workout During Month 8

	Sun	Mon	Tues	Wed	Thurs	Fri	Sat	Total
Determination		30min		30min		30min		90 (18%)
Aerobics		10min	30min	10min	30min	10min		90 (18%)
Anaerobic			20min		20min			40 (8%)
Flexibility		10min	20min		20min	10min		60 (12%)
SAQ		20min		20min		20min		60 (12%)
tvp		60min		30min		60min		150 (31%)
TOTAL		130 (27%)	70 (14%)	90 (18%)	70 (14%)	130 (27%)		490min

competitions. Focus is more easily achieved by understanding the motivation of the fighter.

The mental aspects of training are greatly enhanced through more sports-specific means. We tend to use shadow boxing as a form of meditation and mental training. This helps get the fighter into the right mindset, but also helps with the visualization of the fight coming up.

Month 9

The final part of the preparation, before we really up the training programme for the final quarter, will focus on an aspect of mental preparation that is vital in all sports, but especially in boxing.

Elite athletes perceive the world differently. They

Guidelines About Self-talk to Avoid

Rule	Notes
Rule one: avoid thinking that leads to worry or anxiety	Fighters who perform inconsistently focus on self-talk that is centred on being afraid ('I can't do it', 'I haven't trained enough', etc). These statements are excuses and need to be avoided as they erode confidence and create stress
Rule two: avoid thinking about past failures	Don't focus your thoughts on losses in the past as this will create high stress. If you have a negative event from the past, then you must try to take this negative thought out of your mind
Rule three: avoid thinking that ties self-worth to performance	Avoid statements that imply that your self-esteem will be damaged by poor performance. Typical statements are 'If I lose this fight, I am no good' or 'If I don't win, I'll feel worthless'. When the fighter has the attitude that winning is critical for maintaining self-esteem then stakes become too high, creating unnecessary stress
Rule four: avoid reviewing negative odds of your winning	Avoid internal dialogue that includes statements that magnify negative odds. Focus on the odds, however low, of winning

Guidelines About Positive Self-Talk to Include

Rule	Notes
Rule five: monitor your internal dialogue	Monitor what you say to yourself prior to competition. Generally, internal dialogue will follow patterns as statements become habitual. Pay attention by listening to yourself and asking another person such as your coach.
Rule six: use statements that assert your ability to regulate your state	Self-talk can stop the fighter feeling a loss of control due to stress. Statements that help are 'I'm in control of how I feel'.
Rule seven: regard stress as symptoms in a positive way	Rather than saying 'I feel weak', say to yourself 'I feel challenged', 'I feel excited' etc.
Rule eight: convert negative statements into positive ones	Instead of making statements such as 'Don't walk into the punch', change it into a positive statement like 'Keep moving'

perceive events and situations in ways that give them a competitive advantage. These athletes believe in success and their ability to achieve the success. Champion athletes possess a very positive mindset. Champions see advantages where losers see problems. This positive mindset has to be practised at this stage of the training regime due to the fact that this is when doubts begin to set in. Prior to this period the event is long enough for the fighter to convince himself that it is far enough away as not to be a worry. However, four months from the fight stress and negative thoughts begin to enter the fighter's thoughts.

Learning to have positive and winning thoughts is a process that involves replicating the mental habits and thought patterns of the top fighters. The process we are going to describe here is called self-talk. Champion fighters embrace difficulties and challenges in a positive manner rather than treating it in a fearful manner.

Self-talk helps fighters to reinterpret situations so that pressure situations become less stressful. In terms of a fight, the fighter will experience the stress of coming out to an arena packed with fans as well as the negative thoughts associated with the prospect of losing. Each of the preparatory stages of the fight will represent a source of stress that needs to be managed.

Top fighters learn how to convert negative thoughts into winning positive thoughts.

Remember that positive reinforcement is generally essential to ensuring a winning mindset.

The guidelines given here, both concerning self-talk to avoid and positive self-talk to include, are adapted from the writings of the sports psychologist Marie Dalloway (available at http://www.performance-media.com).

Month 10

Approaching the final quarter before we take the big step into the ring, we now have to start thinking about refinement and specific preparation for the opponent we are going to face in the ring.

Our techniques need to get faster and sharper. Our reactions need to become razor sharp and our diet needs to be really focused for the job in hand. A single-mindedness has to take over inside us. Our spare time needs to be spent thinking about our opponent.

In terms of the last 12 weeks our focus will be as follows:

Weeks 12–9	focus on specific competitive fitness
Weeks 8–5	toughness training: focus on preparing for worst case scenario
Weeks 4–1	focus on studying the opponent

Specific Competitive Fitness

The emphasis in training is now on improving the fitness levels that are specifically used within your competitive event. We have all seen Ricky Hatton spending hours training with his coach, hitting his body protector with full power for fifteen rounds at a time, replicating the pressures he is likely to face in the worst case situation. The body needs to prepare for, and be accustomed to, the scenario where the maximum rounds have to be fought at full level.

Running and weight training both play a role in the training programme, but they do not necessarily prepare you for fifteen rounds of boxing. At this stage of the training programme we are not ready to push our body through the destructive pain barrier (a worst case beating up, but continuing . . .). Therefore, we will focus on developing the resistance to muscular fatigue we will face in the event of having to fight for the maximum duration.

Training also needs to focus on getting the body familiar with the stresses to be placed on it in a competitive fight situation. The emphasis needs to be on training for the number of rounds you are going to compete for, plus a little! This also goes for the length of rounds. Our suggestion is to prepare for an event with six two-minute rounds:

Weeks to event	Number of rounds	Duration of rounds
12	6	2 minutes
11	7	2 minutes 30 seconds
10	8	2 minutes 45 seconds
9	9	3 minutes

Three months to the event we should be looking to developing a fitness level that is not only specific to, but also stretching beyond, our event level. The elements to be trained should focus on a combination of equipment training and sparring. We need to remember that the objective of this period of training is to get the body accustomed and ready for the pressures it will face in the event. During a competition there will be considerable mental and physical pressure in terms of:

* Stress due to fighting someone
* Stress due to appearing in front of an audience
* Pressure from being hit and not being in control of your opponent

The one thing we do not want is for us to fail because the body cannot cope with the physical pressures we will face. With the right physical programme good coaches will also try to replicate some of mental pressures that might be faced during an event.

Fighters need to structure the rounds in a way that will also allow them to challenge their traditional thought patterns. For example, some fighters always use the first

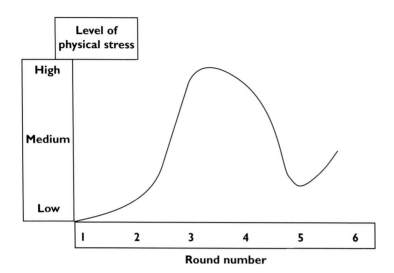

Typical fighter's fight profile for a 6-round fight.

couple of rounds to slowly gauge the preparedness of the opponent. Many opponents come expecting a slow start. Sometimes a fighter like Ricky Hatton succeeds because, being unpredictable, he comes out with all guns blazing. If we have only ever trained with a warm-up mentality, however, we will find it very difficult to get straight into the fight mode.

Be clear about the objective of each round and what role the equipment is playing. Again many training programmes tend to be standard and fairly flat, with little or no variation. When designing the training programme during these weeks, think about your fighter's fight profile. Typically it might look like that shown here for a six-round fight.

The diagram suggests that this fighter will come out slowly, get warmed up, give it his all during the middle of the fight and be relatively tired during the end, but might just push himself in the last round.

We suggest that this fighter's training might focus on developing speed and fitness for the early and late rounds. The key is to vary the training pattern so that, if need be, the fighter can adjust during the fight.

The process we suggest to design the fitness programme during this month's training will be as follows:
1. Plot your fighter's fight profile on a template as shown here. If he is only fighting three rounds, then profile the rounds themselves so you can see any patterns in his style that relate to strength and fitness.

Round	Part of round	Level of technique	Level of speed	Level of endurance	Level of strength
1	Early				
	Middle				
	Late				
2	Early				
	Middle				
	Late				
3	Early				
	Middle				
	Late				
4	Early				
	Middle				
	Late				

Round-Specific Training Exercises

All rounds are 3 minutes with 1 minute rest

Round	Part of round	Equipment training	Floor-ceiling ball	Body sparring	Full sparring
1	Early	Heavy bag: 6-punch combinations			
	Middle			Sparring	
	Late	Heavy bag: 4-punch combinations			
2	Early		Sets of 2/3 punches focus on rhythm, timing and movement		
	Middle		Feint, same combination, switch direction		
	Late		Continuous punching for 1 minute with movement		
3	Early				Sparring
	Middle			Sparring	
	Late				Sparring
4	Early	Shadow boxing: 30s on, 30s off – long range punching			
	Middle	As above with bent arm punches			
	Late	As above with mixed punches			
5	Early	Light bag: movement-based combinations			
	Middle		Sparring		
	Late	Light bag: movement-based combinations			
6	Early	Target circuit (see below)			
	Middle	Target circuit			
	Late	Target circuit			

Target circuit
All with light dumbells for 30 seconds each:
* Dorsal raise   * Press-ups
* V-shaped sit-ups   * Burpee jumps
* Clap push-ups   * Dumbbell punching

2. Identify key pieces of equipment and the training method to be used in the training programme, such as bags, floor-ceiling ball, speed ball, focus pads, semi-sparring, body sparring and full sparring.
3. Design a training programme, such as that shown here for round-specific exercises, around the issues encountered.

Month 11

All of our training to date has been focused on the positive aspects of fighting. We see ourselves winning, we see ourselves fighting to our strengths – but what if . . . ? The time is right now to focus on the worst case situation. As well as maintaining our training on our fitness and recovery, we need to provide extra focus on the worst case scenario.

Firstly, to understand the potential worst case scenarios we need to understand what assumptions we as fighters are making. We need to understand which variables within our assumptions are actually uncertain. We also need to appreciate that our opponent, if he is well coached, will also be preparing equally as well. Our thought processes need to be one step ahead of our opponent.

The first step of the process is to understand the factors on which our training has been based. These

Sample Weekly Workout During Month 10

	Sun	Mon	Tues	Wed	Thurs	Fri	Sat	Total
Determination			30min		30min			60 (19%)
Aerobics (via rounds)		30min		30min		30min		90 (29%)
Anaerobic			20min		20min			40 (13%)
Flexibility		10min	20min		20min	10min		60 (19%)
SAQ		5min		5min		5min		15 (5%)
tvp		15min		15min		15min		45 (15%)
TOTAL		60 (19%)	70 (23%)	50 (16%)	70 (23%)	60 (19%)		310min

factors are most easily identified by using the tvp Wheel of Performance criteria and filling in the assumptions about our own and our opponent's condition:

Factor	Assumption about ourselves	Assumption about opponent
Focus		
Determination		
Stretching goals		
Self-awareness		
Aerobic		
Anaerobic		
Power		
Balance		
Flexibility		
Speed		
Agility		
Quickness		
Technique		
Variety		
Predictability		

In addition to these assumptions, we also need to understand the assumptions behind the fight strategy, based on observing previous fights.

Factor	Assumption about ourselves	Assumption about opponent
Fight strategy		

Discussion with our coach will help us identify all of the factors and assumptions we have made in our training about ourselves and about our opponent.

The next step is to discuss the opposites of our assumptions. This will help us identify the issues that we may have missed. The extreme views provide us with a useful reminder of the points we may have ignored or forgotten. For example, we may make an assumption that

the opponent usually utilizes a specific technique in a fight and we prepare for this. However, what if he decides to use a broader range of techniques? How does this affect your response? How does this challenge your mindset?

As you can see, the focus is moving more and more in our training to the opponent, as we get closer to the fight.

Case Study

Let's just look at a specific example based on *Rocky Balboa* (2006), the last of the Rocky films featuring Sylvester Stallone, as I think this demonstrates a number of points: the analysis is carried out from the perspective of Rocky's opponent, Mason 'The Line' Dixon.

The assessment suggests that Mason Dixon really does not need to prepare too much for this fight. He is the World Champion fighting an old man. This is understandable. However, underdogs are dangerous because they are on edge and will look to find a unique point in their fighting. This was illustrated in the fight by Rocky training very specifically to generate power, since he knew he had no alternative.

In many such cases Mason Dixon's assessment of Rocky might not have been wrong, but this time it was! After carrying out the analysis, he and his coach might have looked at the completed table and asked themselves, 'What if . . . ?'

As you can see, looking at the assumptions from a different angle opens up the possibilities of a new dialogue that would change the preparations for the fight. Remember the fight is not lost in the ring, but in the gym!

Month 12

Before we look at the focus of training one month prior to a fight, let us use the accompanying table to review where the focus has been for the last twelve months.

A month before the fight we need to know our oppo-

As If? Attribute Assumptions Based on *Rocky Balboa*

Factor	Assumption about ourselves (Mason)	Assumption about opponent (Rocky)
Focus	No need to focus too much as the fight is merely an exhibition	Too old. Has a small restaurant so could do with some money. Will not really want to get hit
Determination	Need to do something to get popular, but why should I bother	Why does he really want to get pummelled?
Stretching goals	Just need to turn up and play around with him for a couple of rounds and send him packing	He has already done it all, he is past it and is really just turning up to make up the numbers. He has nothing to prove
Self-awareness	Why does no one love me? I am the best!	Has he lost his marbles coming to a fight like this at his age?
Aerobic	Excellent	Too old
Anaerobic	Excellent	Too old
Power	Excellent. I have knocked out nearly everyone	Used to hit hard, but he is an old man!
Balance	Excellent	Well he was never really that balanced in his prime. It was his sheer willpower!
Flexibility	Excellent	Who cares?
Speed	Excellent	Will be slow due to age?
Agility	Excellent	Will not be mobile?
Quickness	Excellent	Will not be mobile?
Technique	Excellent	Should still be good?
Variety	Excellent	Well, he was always fairly limited in his prime
Predictability	I am very unpredictable	Too predictable. Always was and always will be

nent inside out. The approach from last month goes a long way to improving our understanding of the opponent. This month we need to look at seeing our opponent in action. We need to live and breathe our opponent. A belief that the opponent can be beaten only comes from understanding the strengths of the individual. Ignorance of the opponent's key strengths can only lead to one outcome – defeat.

At this stage of preparations we need to understand the opponent to the point of creating fear. This ensures we are in a state of preparedness for the worst and know we are up for it! We then use the fear to help develop our tactics to cope with the worst case scenario. Champions hang up pictures of the opponents at their worst as a reminder of what they are getting in to. If the opponent is not as good as you thought, no problem – but if he is better than you thought, disaster!

We need to understand our opponent in the ring. The ideal framework to adopt for this analysis is the tvp framework. The following key questions should be considered in the overall assessment of your opponent:

Technique
* Does your opponent get caught as he moves out after delivering an attack?
* Does he get hit when he moves to the left or right?
* How much power does he generate?
* Does he need to lean when reaching with his rear hand?
* Does he fall short with his punches?
* Does he generally defend with his hands?
* Does he get caught after delivering combinations?
* Does he try to punch first?
* Does he move towards his opponent or does he wait?
* Does he hit elbows and forearms a lot?
* Does he follow and catch the opponent?
* Does he know how to cover up?

Variety
* Does he get caught on the ropes?
* Does he lose flow when he moves to the left or right?
* Does he throw a lot of punches to the head?
* Does he get hit in the stomach?
* Is he able to hit when he switches stance?
* Does he get caught with the right hand over his left lead?
* Does he get confused when he changes stance?
* Does he get caught on the ropes and cannot get off them?
* Does he move in one direction all of the time?
* Does he generally throw combinations or single punches?

Rocky's What If? Attribute Assumptions Based on *Rocky Balboa*

Factor	Assumptions about Rocky	What if? test – Rocky
Focus	Too old. Has a small restaurant so could do with some money. Will not really want to get hit	This is his last chance. Has he really lost the fighter in himself? What if he sees this as one more chance of glory? After all he is a winner
Determination	Why does he really want to get pummelled?	He never gives up
Stretching goals	He has already done it all, he is past it and is really just turning up to make up the numbers. He has nothing to prove	Something inside him is burning. His desire based on his last few years could be unexplainable
Self-awareness	Has he lost his marbles coming to a fight like this at his age?	He is clear about his strengths and weaknesses and knows what to focus on
Aerobic	Too old	He trains hard to get fit.
Anaerobic	Too old	He trains hard to get strong
Power	Used to hit hard, but he is an old man!	He has not lost all his power
Balance	Well, he was never really that balanced in his prime. It was his sheer willpower!	This was never that important to him
Flexibility	Who cares?	Does not matter
Speed	Will be slow due to age?	Maybe he can use diversionary tactics to deliver techniques
Agility	Will not be mobile?	How can he cut me off in the ring so that this does not become a factor?
Quickness	Will not be mobile?	As above
Technique	Should still be good?	
Variety	Well, he was always fairly limited in his prime	How critical is this?
Predictability	Too predictable. Always was and always will be	What if have made an incorrect assumption about the above? What are the consequences?

Predictability
* Are his punches blocked easily?
* Does he chase a lot?
* Is he able to change tactics against different opponents?
* Does he try to hold the centre of the ring all of the time at whatever cost?

Answers to these questions form the analysis that then shapes the fight strategy and tactics for the night in order to survive in the ring. The answers to these questions form the cornerstone of the tvp framework.

We will look in depth at one of these possible answers – the art of managing openings. What distinguishes the top fighters from the rest is their ability to create and exploit openings. Inexperienced fighters have a tendency to lead with their hearts rather than leading with their minds. Experienced fighters are masters at being able to create openings and make the opponent go where they want them to. (For the many different approaches to creating openings, see Chapter 11.)

These twelve months are a taster of some of the issues that need to be addressed in preparation for a fight. Best of luck and keep winning and/or learning!

Training Focus for the Past 12 Months

Month	Area of focus	Key points
12	Describe your vision. Where do you want to be?	Create a vision for 12 months' time and longer What are your current performance levels? Agree desired performance levels Agree training plan
11	Specific goal setting	Apply concepts from Wheel of Performance
10	Plan the training	Achieve balance with mind, physical and technical skills
9	Focus on technique and aerobic capacity	Technique comprises: Position of non-punching hand Bodyweight transfer when punching Break off from inside position Quality of punching Relaxation and acceleration of punching
8	Focus on variety, SAQ and aerobic	Understand the correct mechanics and the role of the body and feet in delivering the optimal technique in terms of movement and power Concept of innervation works on the principle that all punches are driven from the feet. The emphasis is on developing agility in technique from the feet first
7	Focus on becoming unpredictable	Key elements of becoming unpredictable are: Preferred direction of movement Footwork patterns Movement of head Movement patterns and mannerism Change of movement speed
6	Shift to mindset training	Creating focus using autogenic training
5	Building determination to succeed	Understanding your motivation to compete
4	Mental preparation for the fight	Self-talk
3	Focus on specific competitive fitness	Getting ready for high stress
2	Preparing for the what ifs!	Assumptions about ourselves and our opponent
1	Preparing for the opponent	See below

CHAPTER 14

FIGHT NIGHT

You have to know you can win. You have to think you can win. You have to feel you can win.
Sugar Ray Leonard

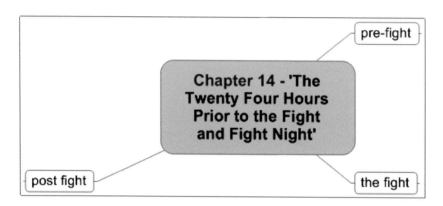

As a conclusion we will look at what has to be done on the day of the competition. There are key activities that need to take place during the final twenty-four hours before the fight.

A thought to remember is that preparation for the fight actually begins three days before and you should ensure that no heavy training takes place during this period. The body needs to be given time to recover if it is to be in optimum condition when the fight begins. Training during this period should be light and focused on ensuring the body is recovering as quickly as possible.

Pre-Fight Preparations

The twenty-four hours before the fight have been split into manageable chunks. The times given here are based on the fight taking place at 20.00.

00.00–08.00

This period needs to be used to ensure the corner team are ready and that all logistics are in place. Everyone needs to be aware of the location of the fight, the entrances to the location and meeting times. There is nothing worse than being ready for the fight and then finding people missing or late, as this can lead to panic.

The corner team should ideally comprise three members – the head coach, number 2 and number 3 – each with carefully delegated roles that will be discussed below. A key consideration for the corner team is cleanliness. All of the corner team should be wearing plastic gloves to ensure bacteria transfer is kept to a minimum.

As part of the preparation the corner team needs to ensure that all the equipment required is ready for use:
* Spray bottle
* Sponge
* Cotton buds
* Gauze pads
* 1000/1 adrenaline solution
* Towel
* Ice pack
* Focus pads
* Stopwatch
* Dressing gown
* Petroleum jelly
* Trainers' tape
* Scissors
* Water bottle

As well as the team, the boxer needs to ensure that they receive adequate rest and sleep. Typically, eight hours' sleep is required to ensure that the boxer is fully refreshed. Too little sleep will leave the boxer tired, while too much sleep can make the boxer lifeless.

Boxers need to be able to switch off and relax to take their mind off the contest.

08.00–16.00

After waking up on the day of the fight the first priority is the management of meals. A good, healthy, balanced breakfast and lunch are vital. The meals should comprise medium to high carbohydrate foods, with protein at a minimal level. Additionally, the boxer needs to ensure they are kept well hydrated by drinking plenty of water during the day. Between meals the boxer should look to gain plenty of rest. Different people have different ways in which they relax. These might involve watching relevant DVDs of the opponent or other motivational DVDs. Many boxers and athletes use visualization and self-talk to maintain focus.

16.00–19.00

Two or three hours before the fight the boxer should eat their main meal, with a similar profile to the earlier meals and coupled with drinking plenty of water. Some boxers also like to indulge in 'feel good' foods. A small amount is fine, but you should not overindulge.

High carbohydrate foods are essential as you want to avoid getting your energy from the muscles as the fight moves to its latter stages.

19.00–Ring Entry

At this stage the fight preparation needs to be more focused and specific. The key activities to be undertaken at this stage are:

Dynamic warm-up: Increase the heart rate, warm the muscles up and begin to control emotions.

Stimulate reactions using focus pads and simulate attacks: The number 2, ideally, should be responsible for taking the boxer through a session on the pads. This should not be too intense, but should be used to get the boxer just ready for the fight. The desired state for the boxer is that he should be switched on (alert and in a ready state), with a heart rate approximately 50 per cent higher than resting.

Massage prior to going into ring: Just before entering the ring the boxer should be relaxed: massage is an ideal way of gaining a relaxed state. It is important to avoid massaging with oils as it makes the skin slippery and can affect performance. This should be the role of the number 2 or 3.

The Fight

The corner team is a vital part of the management of the boxer. During the fight, however, they are not allowed to communicate with the boxer in the ring and shout instructions. Therefore the boxer needs to take responsibility for immediate decisions during the fight.

The role of the head coach in the corner team is to observe the fight, analyse the strengths and weaknesses of both boxers, and be clear about what messages to communicate during the one-minute interval. The objective of the cornermen, outside of general training, is to provide support, give advice and treat a boxer's injuries throughout the course of a fight or bout.

The key activities of the corner team during the minute interval between rounds are:

* Provide clarity in communication. Simple and clear messages should be communicated. The state of the boxer will not be conducive to long, complex messages. In addition, there is little point in providing general feedback.
* Implement the boxer's specific plan. The head coach needs to evaluate the boxer's plan and see what is working and what is not working. Tactical changes need to be implemented. Some of the key warning signs to watch out for are tiredness, laziness and overconfidence.
* Keep the fighter focused on the agreed plan.
* Administer water and apply any first aid measures the boxer may need during the fight.
* Wipe the boxer clean of blood and sweat between boxing rounds. Blood and sweat can inhibit a boxer's vision and could cost him the fight.
* Understand when to throw in the towel. The corner coach must know when the fighter is losing and is in danger of suffering serious injury. This depends on their relationship and knowledge of the fighter's capacity. Do not take risks.

Once the round is over, the boxer should walk slowly back to the corner and should remain in the standing position until his breath is back under control. Only then should the boxer sit down, with his head up and spine erect. The boxer should avoid sitting in a slouched position. Arms should be relaxed and down by the side, so no unnecessary energy is wasted. Sitting down helps to relax the legs and get some recovery before the next round. As the boxer returns to the corner, the number 2 should take the gum shield out of the mouth to facilitate breathing. It is highly unlikely that the boxer is listening while he is regaining control of his breath. Obviously, the fitter the boxer, then the shorter the recovery time.

Team Member Responsibilities

Corner team member	Pre-fight	During fight	Post-fight
Head Coach	Planning, motivation and inspiration	Tactics, motivation, simple communication	Review, recovery plan
Number 2	Warm up	Dry down, hydration, timing of rounds, intervals, dealing with injuries	Warm down
Number 3	Massage	Massage, stools and equipment	

Once the boxer has regained control and is sat down, he should begin to rehydrate himself by sipping water in small, controlled quantities. There are myths that drinking water leads to cramp, but this appears to be untrue. The corner team needs to ensure the water containers are clean.

During this minute the head coach needs to focus on communicating tactics and maintaining the spirit of the boxer.

The role of the number 2 should be to wipe sweat, take care of any injuries and basically assist the boxer with his physical recovery. The role of the number 3 will be to provide any massage to calves and legs, as this speeds the recovery process.

Post-Fight

All boxers should ensure they warm down adequately to supply oxygen to the lactic acid, in order to provide energy.

The approach to be adopted in the post-fight scenario after the warm-down is dependent on the outcome of the fight:

For the winner: The head coach should carry out the post-fight review, take care of celebrations, identify injuries, prescribe medical care and agree the rest plan.

For the loser: Plan the post-fight review for the following day to allow time for reflection. Any injuries should be identified with medical care and a rest plan. In addition, the head coach needs to prepare the plan for confidence building.

Key Injuries

The key injuries that the corner team needs to be able to deal with are:
*   Nose bleeding (more severe bleeding could suggest there is damage to the septum)
*   Fractured nasal bones
*   Abrasions
*   Lacerations
*   Black eyes
*   Fractures and sprains
*   Concussion
*   Rope burns
*   Cuts and bruises
*   Broken teeth and ribs

During the fight the corner team is only qualified to apply first aid. Anything that is more serious will need a qualified medical practitioner.

GOOD LUCK.

RESOURCES

Books

Rakesh Sondhi and Tommy Thompson, *tvp: Comprehensive Boxing Concepts* (BMC Global Services Publishing, 2005).

DVD

Beginning Boxing: Punches, Stances and Movement (Summersdale, 2007).

Websites

www.martialboxing.com
www.bmcglobalservices.com
These sites cover the activities of the Elite Performance Academy, Nottingham, and tvp[tm] Boxing.

Monthly coaching sessions are held for coaches and personnel are available for workshops and seminars.

Coaching qualifications at Assistant and Full Coach level are offered by attendance at workshops or online.

www.businessballs.com
Self/personal development methods, including the Visual-Auditory-Kinesthetic (VAK) learning styles test.

www.performance-media.com
Peak performance information and self-talk analysis.

http://usaboxing.org
Download link for *2008–2009 USA Boxing Rulebook.*

INDEX

RELATED TITLES FROM CROWOOD

Boxing – Training, Skills and
Techniques
Gary Blower
ISBN 978 1 86126 902 7
112pp, 150 illustrations

The Essence of Jeet Kune Do
Dave Carnell
ISBN 978 1 84797 220 0
160pp, 400 illustrations

Jeet Kune Do
Dave Carnell
ISBN 978 1 84797 003 9
160pp, 360 illustrations

Kickboxing
Justyn Billingham
ISBN 978 1 84797 037 4
192pp, 550 illustrations

Kickboxing Sparring
Justyn Billingham
ISBN 978 1 84797 130 2
224pp, 600 illustrations

Kickboxing Training Drills
Justyn Billingham
ISBN 978 1 84797 287 3
192pp, 500 illustrations

In case of difficulty ordering, contact the Sales Office:

The Crowood Press Ltd, Ramsbury, Wiltshire, SN8 2HR, UK   Tel: 44 (0) 1672 520320
enquiries@crowood.com

www.crowood.com